STRAWBERRY
MARSHMALLOW

ICHIGO MASHIMARO

W9-CEO-403

Strawberry Marshmallow Vol 1
Created by Barasui

Translation - Emi Onishi
English Adaptation - Nathan Johnson
Retouch and Lettering - Tomas Montalvo-Lagos
Production Artist - Erika Terriquez
Graphic Designer - James Lee

Editor - Elizabeth Hurchalla
Digital Imaging Manager - Chris Buford
Production Manager - Elisabeth Brizzi
Managing Editor - Lindsey Johnston
VP of Production - Ron Klamert
Editor-in-Chief - Rob Tokar
Publisher - Mike Kiley
President and C.O.O. - John Parker
C.E.O. and Chief Creative Officer - Stuart Levy

A  Manga

TOKYOPOP Inc.
5900 Wilshire Blvd. Suite 2000
Los Angeles, CA 90036

E-mail: info@TOKYOPOP.com
Come visit us online at www.TOKYOPOP.com

ISBN: 978-1-59816-494-7

First TOKYOPOP printing: July 2006
10 9 8 7 6 5 4 3 2
Printed in the USA

STRAWBERRY MARSHMALLOW

ICHIGO MASHIMARO

VOL. 1

BY Barasui

HAMBURG // LONDON // LOS ANGELES // TOKYO

STRAWBERRY MARSHMALLOW

ICHIGO MASHIMARO

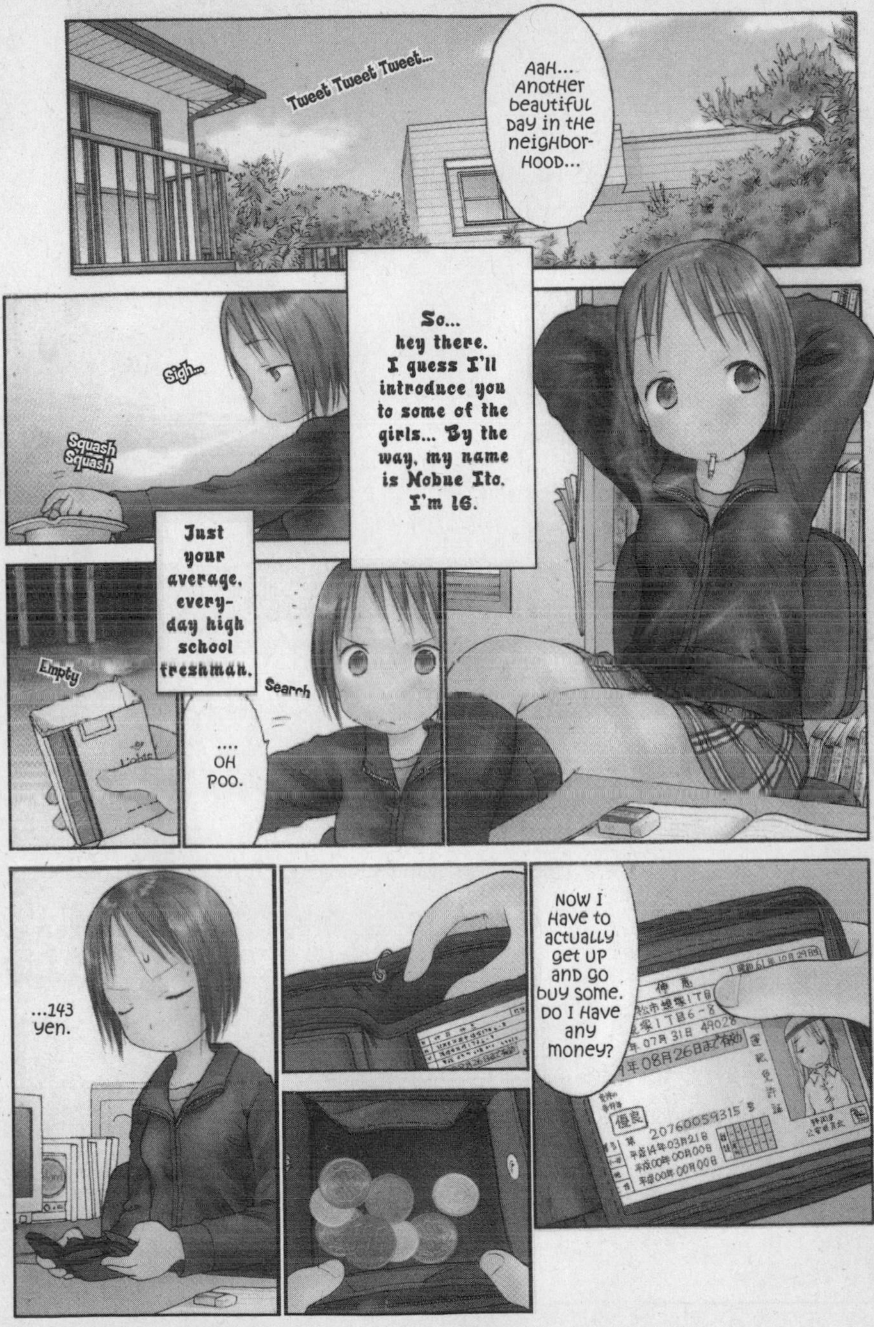
AAH... ANOTHER BEAUTIFUL DAY IN THE NEIGHBOR-HOOD...
Tweet Tweet Tweet...
So... hey there. I guess I'll introduce you to some of the girls... By the way, my name is Nobue Ito. I'm 16.
Sigh...
Squash Squash
Just your average, every-day high school freshman.
Search
.... OH POO.
Empty
NOW I HAVE TO ACTUALLY GET UP AND GO BUY SOME. DO I HAVE ANY MONEY?
...143 yen.

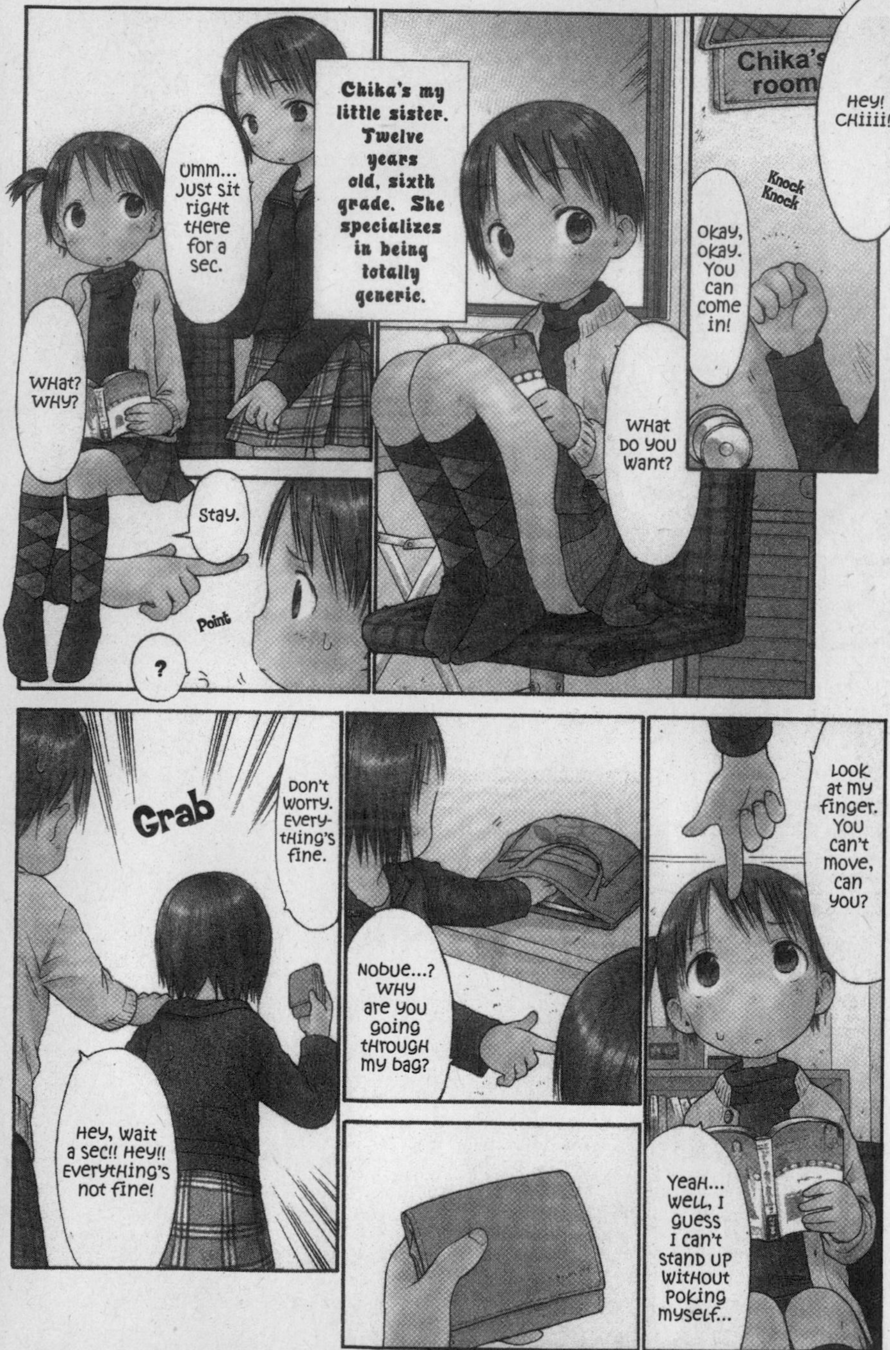
Chika's room
Hey! Chiiiii!!
Knock Knock
Okay, okay. You can come in!
Chika's my little sister. Twelve years old, sixth grade. She specializes in being totally generic.
What do you want?
Umm... Just sit right there for a sec.
What? Why?
Stay.
Point
?
Look at my finger. You can't move, can you?
Yeah... well, I guess I can't stand up without poking myself...
Nobue...? Why are you going through my bag?
Don't worry. Every-thing's fine.
Grab
Hey, wait a sec!! Hey!! Everything's not fine!

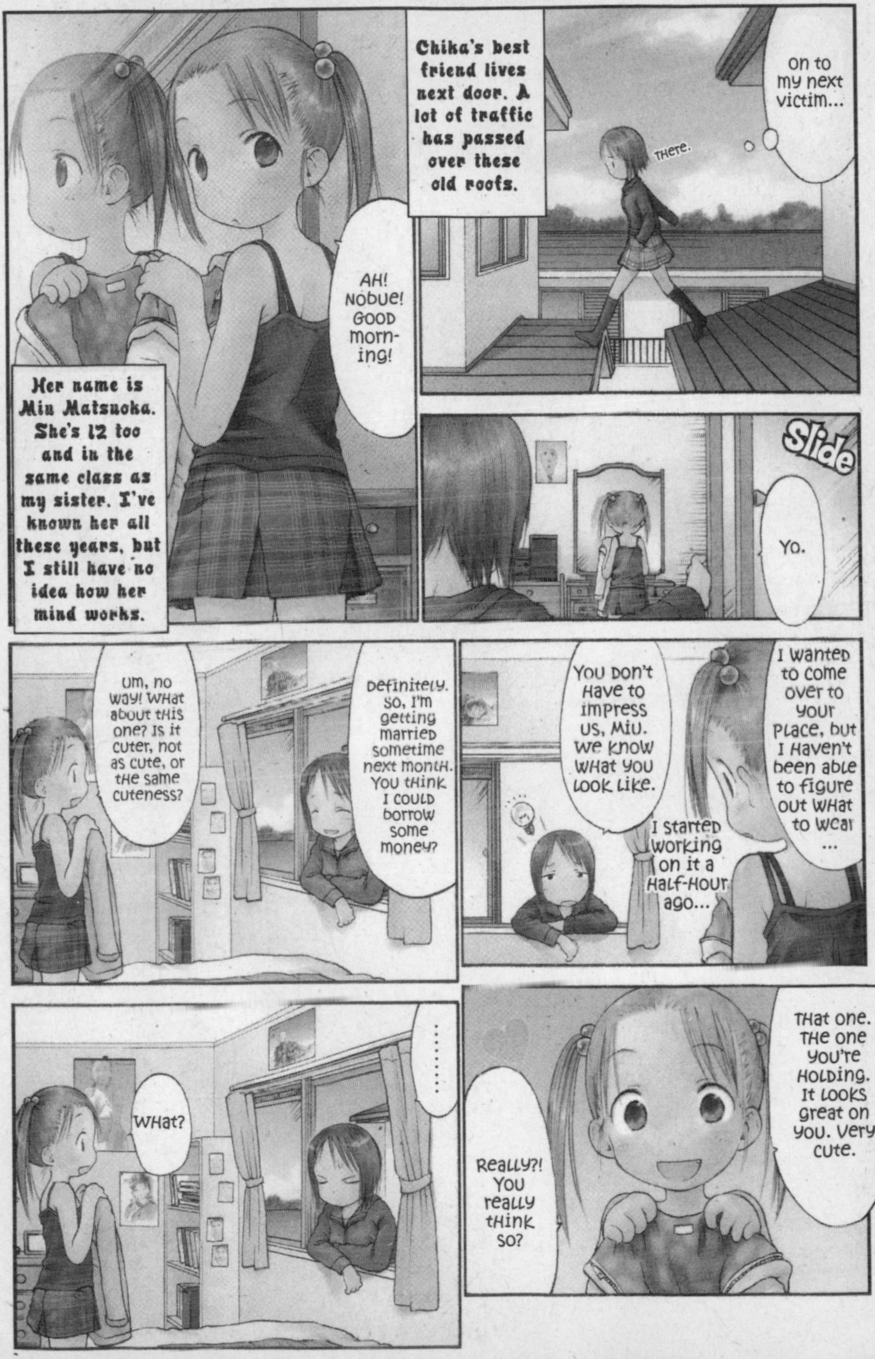
Chika's best friend lives next door. A lot of traffic has passed over these old roofs.
On to my next victim...
There.
Slide
Yo.
AH! NOBUE! GOOD Morning!
Her name is Miu Matsuoka. She's 12 too and in the same class as my sister. I've known her all these years, but I still have no idea how her mind works.
I wanted to come over to your place, but I haven't been able to figure out what to wear ...
You don't have to impress us, Miu. We know what you look like.
I started working on it a half-hour ago...
Definitely. So, I'm getting married sometime next month. You think I could borrow some money?
Um, no way! What about this one? Is it cuter, not as cute, or the same cuteness?
That one. The one you're holding. It looks great on you. Very cute.
Really?! You really think so?
....
What?

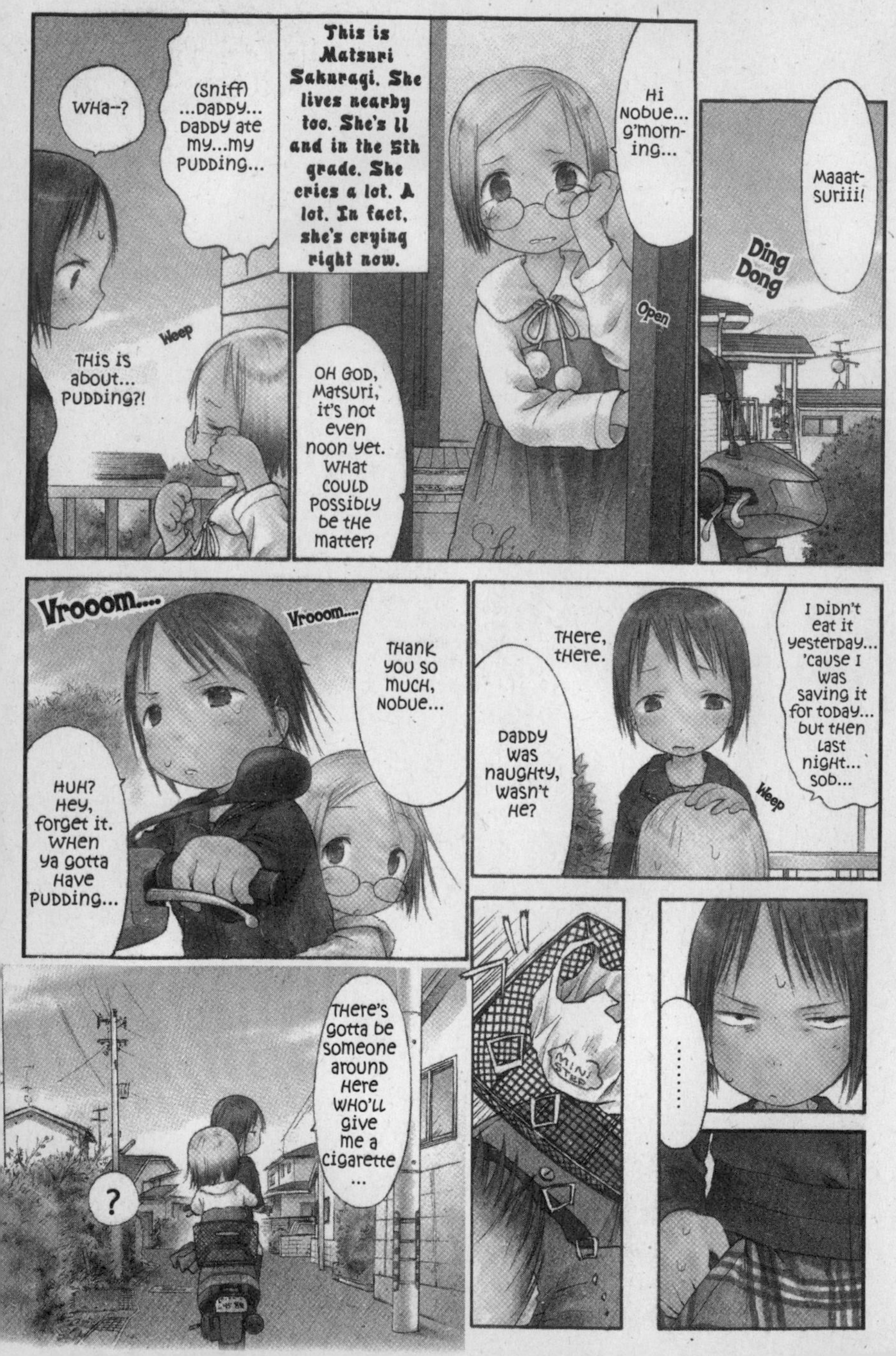
Maaat-suriii!
Ding Dong
Hi Nobue... g'morn-ing...
Open
This is Matsuri Sakuragi. She lives nearby too. She's 11 and in the 5th grade. She cries a lot. A lot. In fact, she's crying right now.
Oh God, Matsuri, it's not even noon yet. What could possibly be the matter?
(Sniff) ...Daddy... Daddy ate my...my pudding...
Wha--?
Weep
This is about... pudding?!
I didn't eat it yesterday... 'cause I was saving it for today... but then last night... sob...
There, there.
Weep
Daddy was naughty, wasn't he?
Thank you so much, Nobue...
Vrooom....
Vrooom....
Huh? Hey, forget it. When ya gotta have pudding...
......
MINI STOP
There's gotta be someone around here who'll give me a cigarette ...
?

The Strawberry Marshmallow
Volume 1
Cartoon by Barasui

B a r a s u i

The Strawberry Marshmallow
Volume1
Cartoon by Barasui

MATSURI

CONTENTS

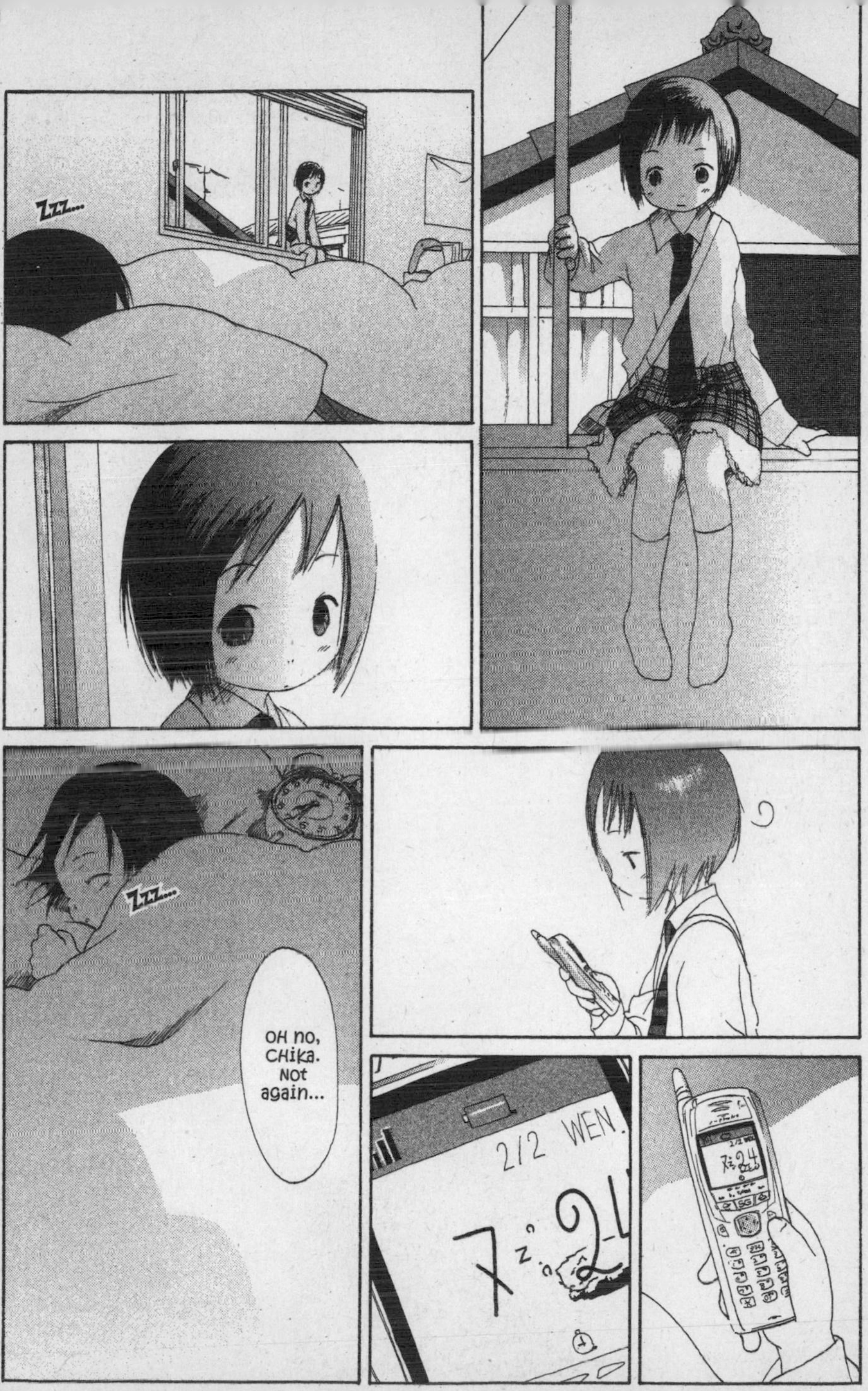
Zzz...
2/2 WEN.
7:24
Zzz...
OH no, CHIKA. Not again...

Episode.1

IZU ANGUISH

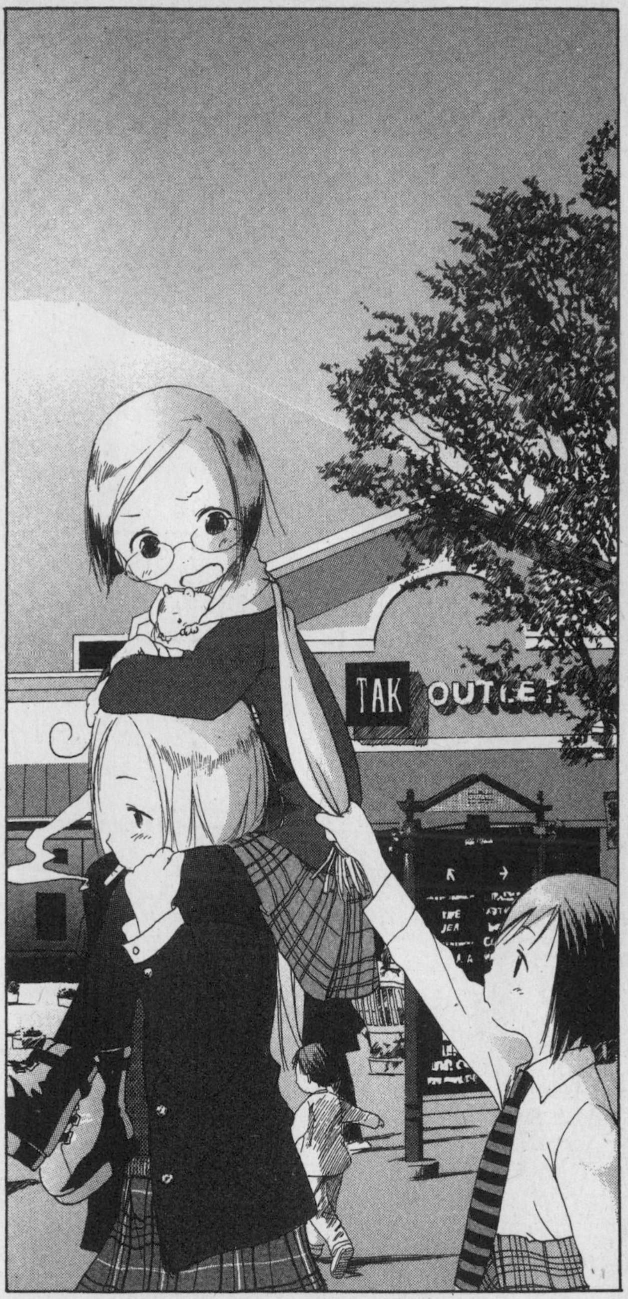
TAK OUTLET

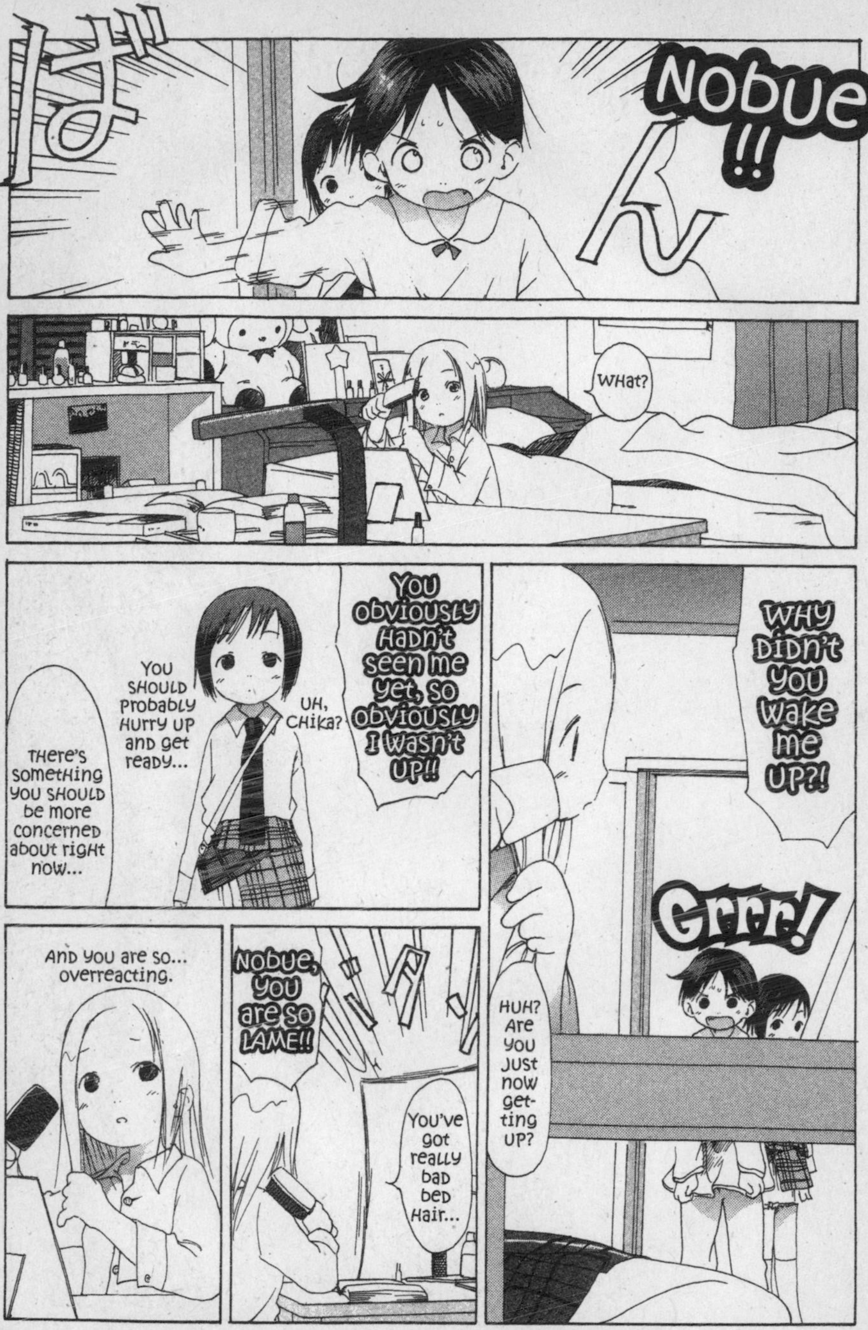
Nobue !!
ばん
WHAT?
WHY DIDN'T YOU WAKE ME UP?!
Grrr!
HUH? Are you just now get-ting up?
You obviously hadn't seen me yet, so obviously I wasn't up!!
UH, CHIKA?
You should probably hurry up and get ready...
There's something you should be more concerned about right now...
Nobue, you are so LAME!!
You've got really bad bed hair...
And you are so... overreacting.

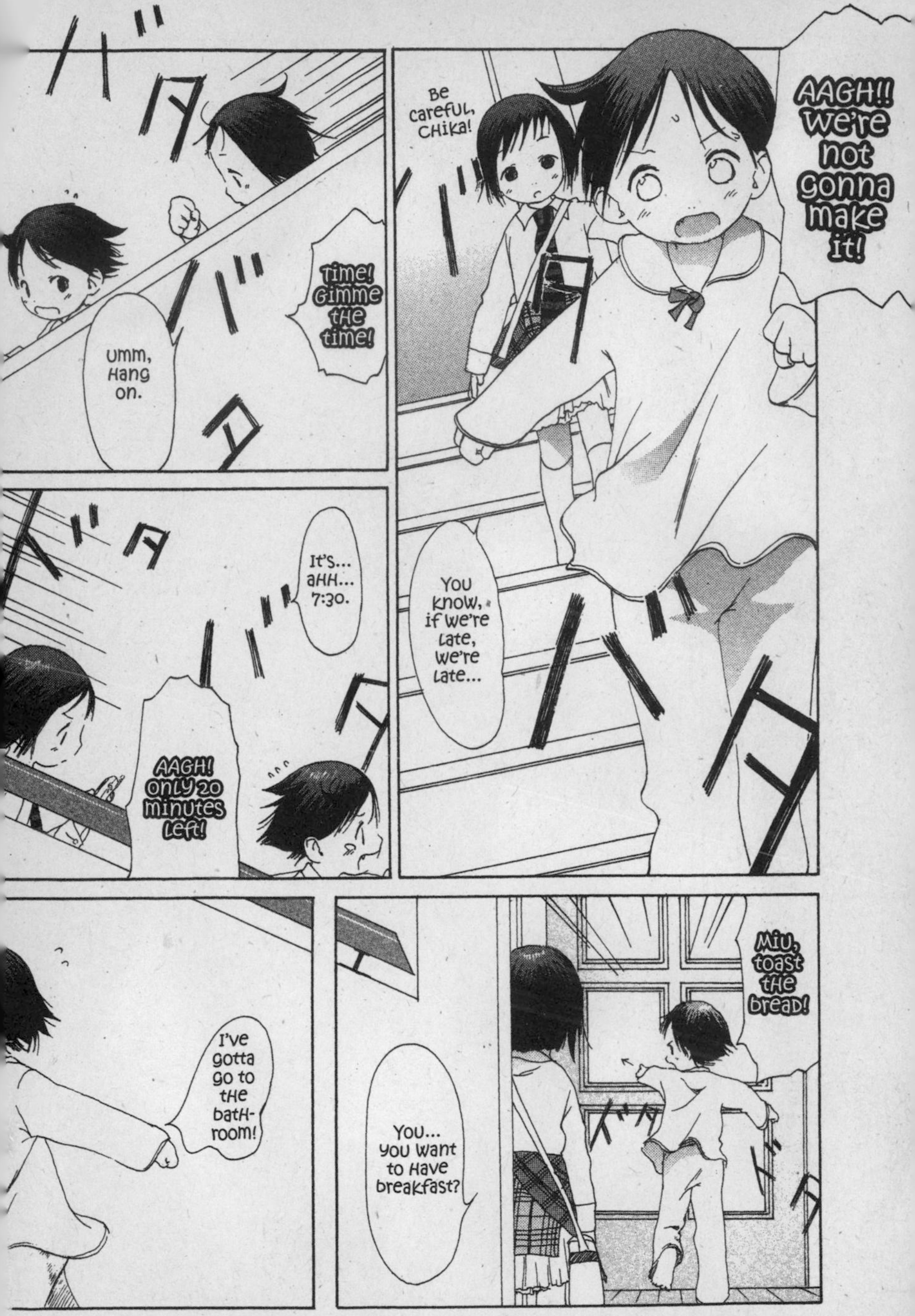
AAGH!! We're not gonna make it!
Be careful, Chika!
You know, if we're late, we're late...
Time! Gimme the time!
Umm, hang on.
It's... ahh... 7:30.
AAGH! Only 20 minutes left!
Miu, toast the bread!
You... you want to have breakfast?
I've gotta go to the bathroom!

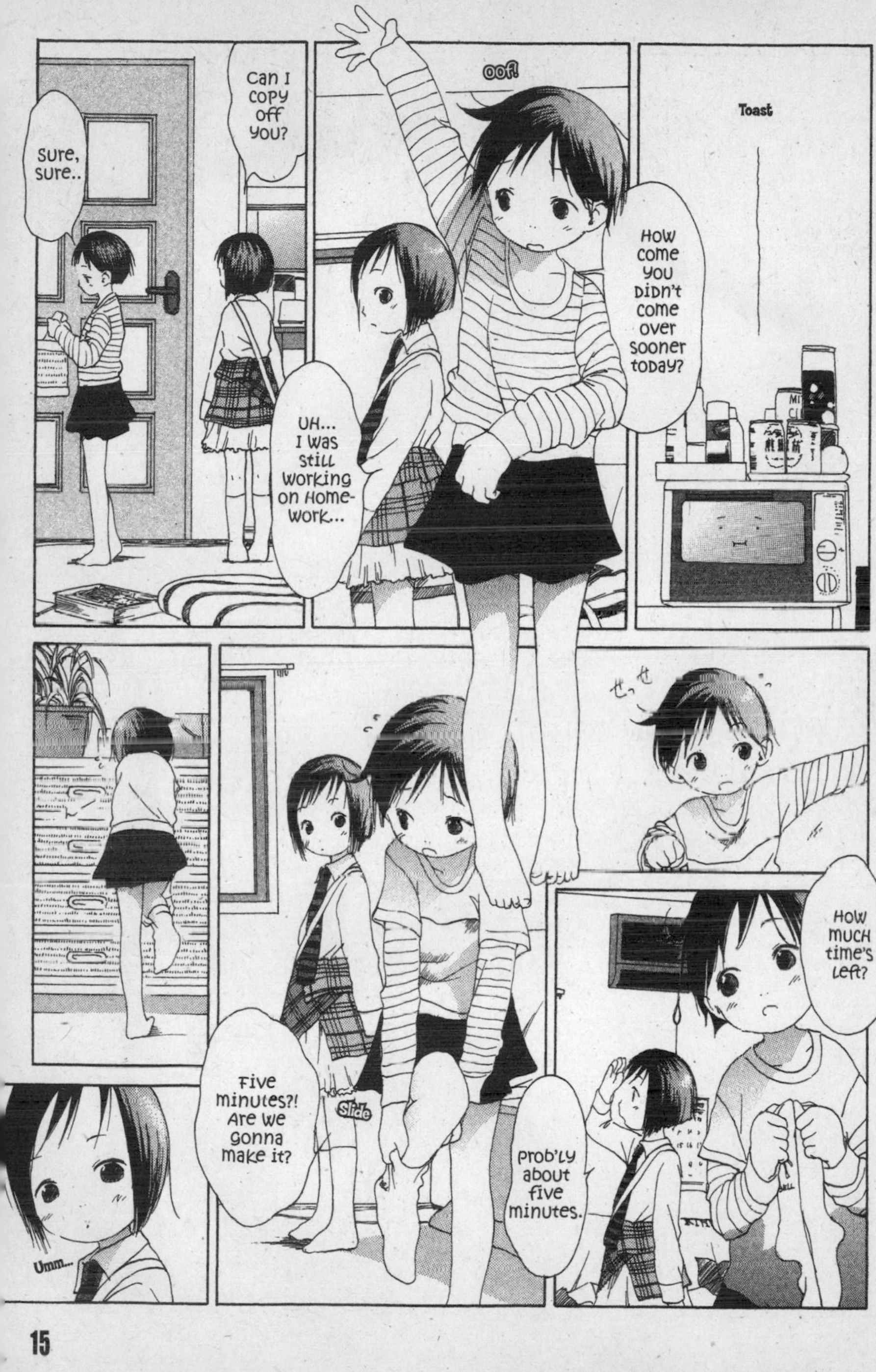
Toast
oof!
How come you didn't come over sooner today?
Uh... I was still working on Home-work...
Can I copy off you?
Sure, sure..
せっせ
How much time's left?
Prob'ly about five minutes.
Five minutes?! Are we gonna make it?
Slide
Umm...

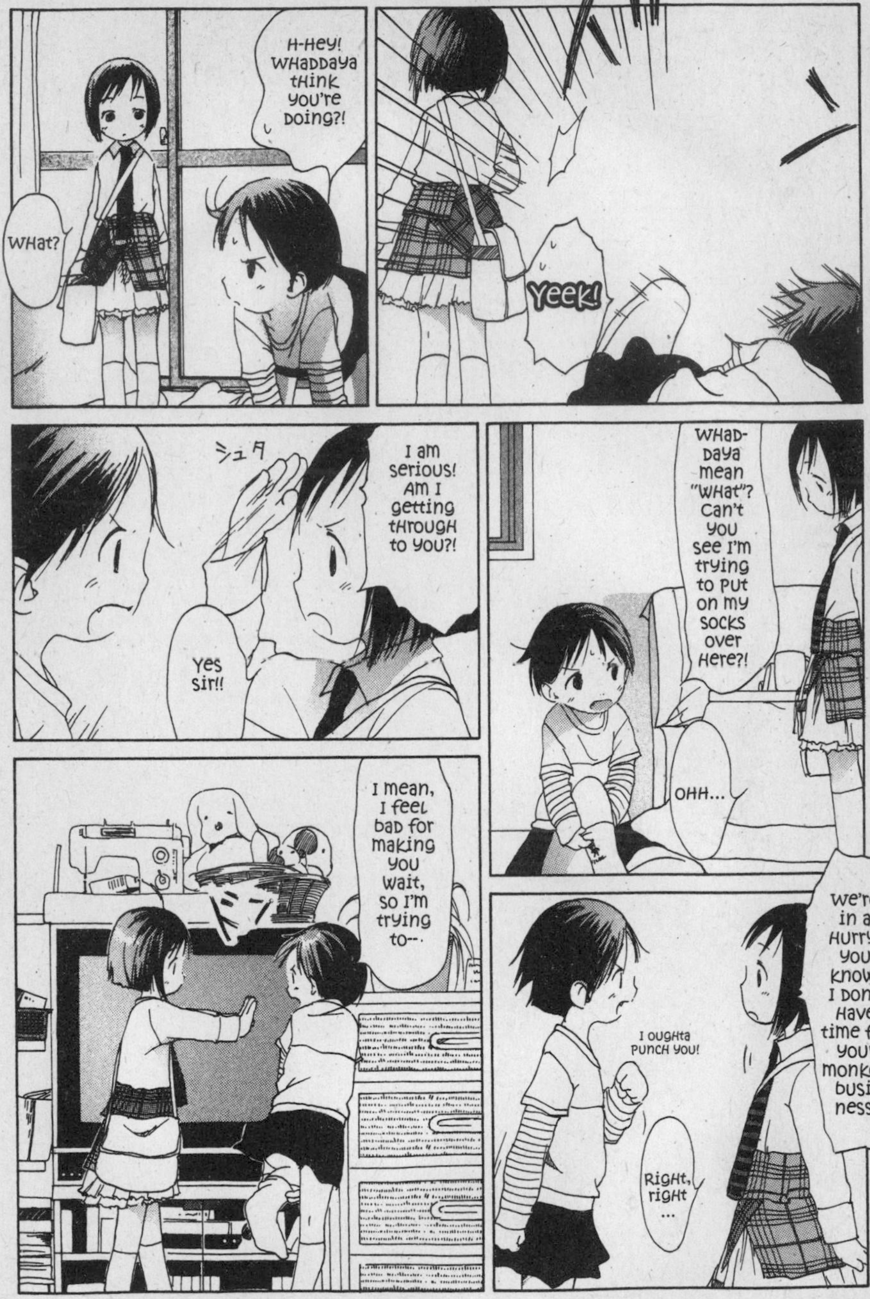
Yeek!
H-Hey! Whaddaya think you're doing?!
What?
Whad-daya mean "what"? Can't you see I'm trying to put on my socks over here?!
Ohh...
I am serious! Am I getting through to you?!
シュタ
Yes sir!!
I mean, I feel bad for making you wait, so I'm trying to--
We're in a hurry, you know! I don't have time for your monkey busi-ness!
I oughta punch you!
Right, right ...

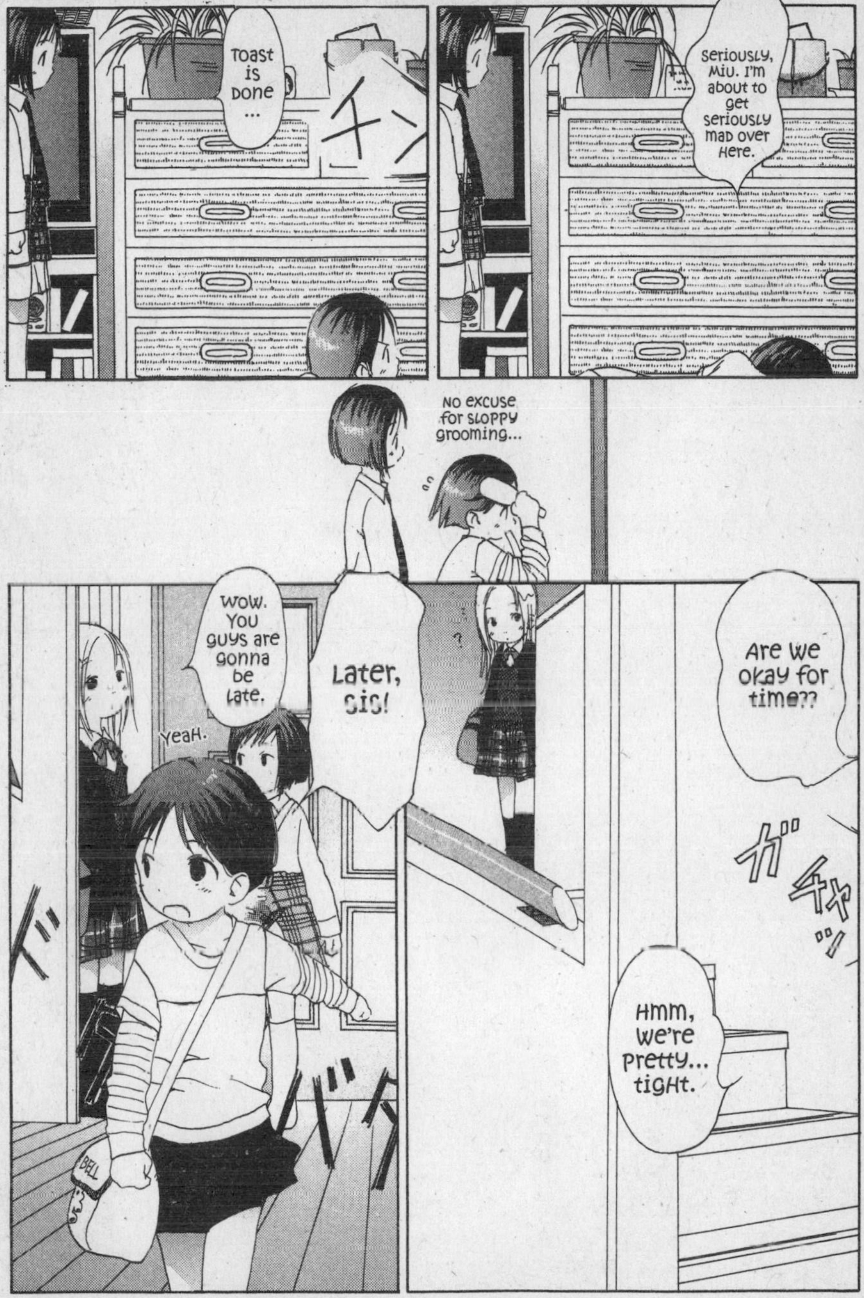
Seriously, Miu. I'm about to get seriously mad over here.
Toast is done...
チン
No excuse for sloppy grooming...
Are we okay for time??
ガチャッ
Hmm, we're pretty... tight.
Later, sis!
Wow. You guys are gonna be late.
Yeah.

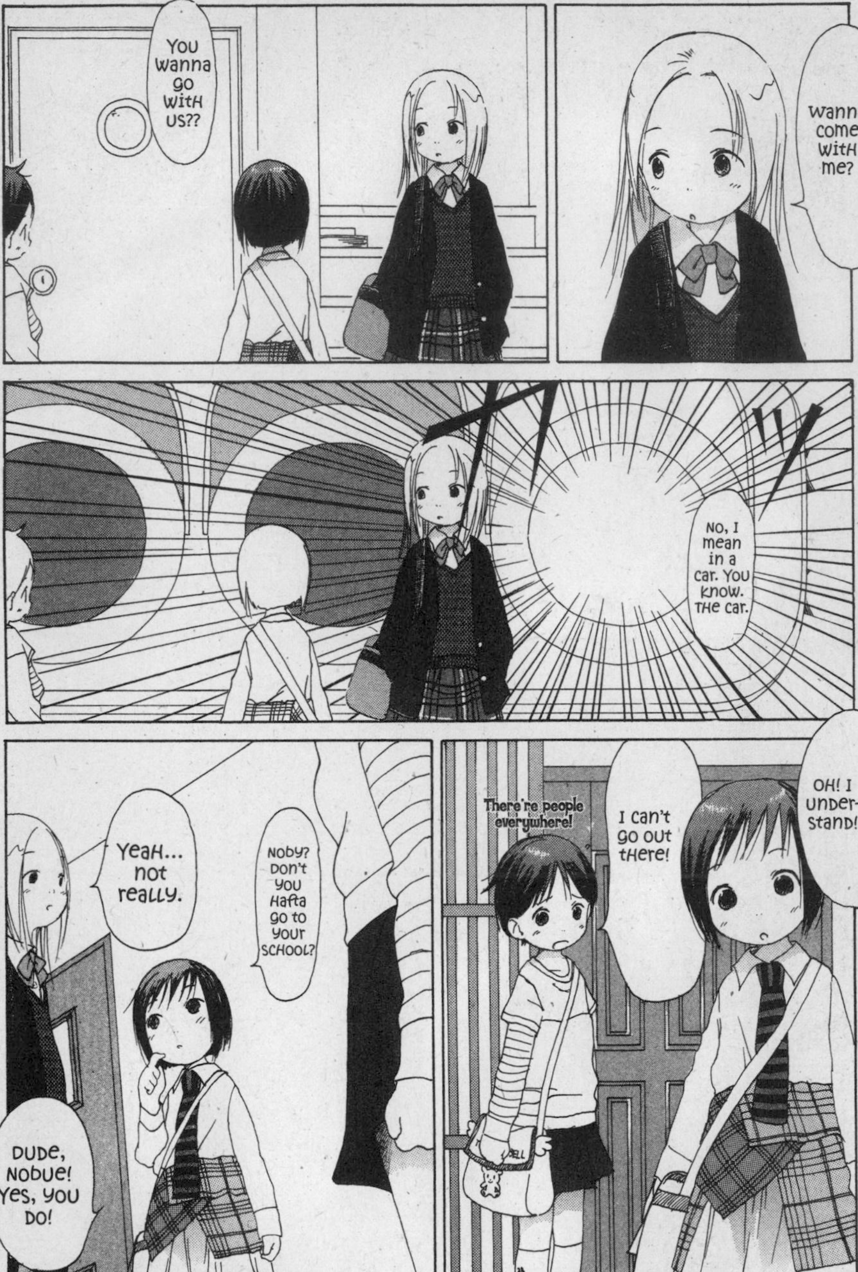
Wanna come with me?
You wanna go with us??
No, I mean in a car. You know. The car.
Oh! I under-stand!
I can't go out there!
There're people everywhere!
Noby? Don't you hafta go to your school?
Yeah... not really.
Dude, Nobue! Yes, you do!

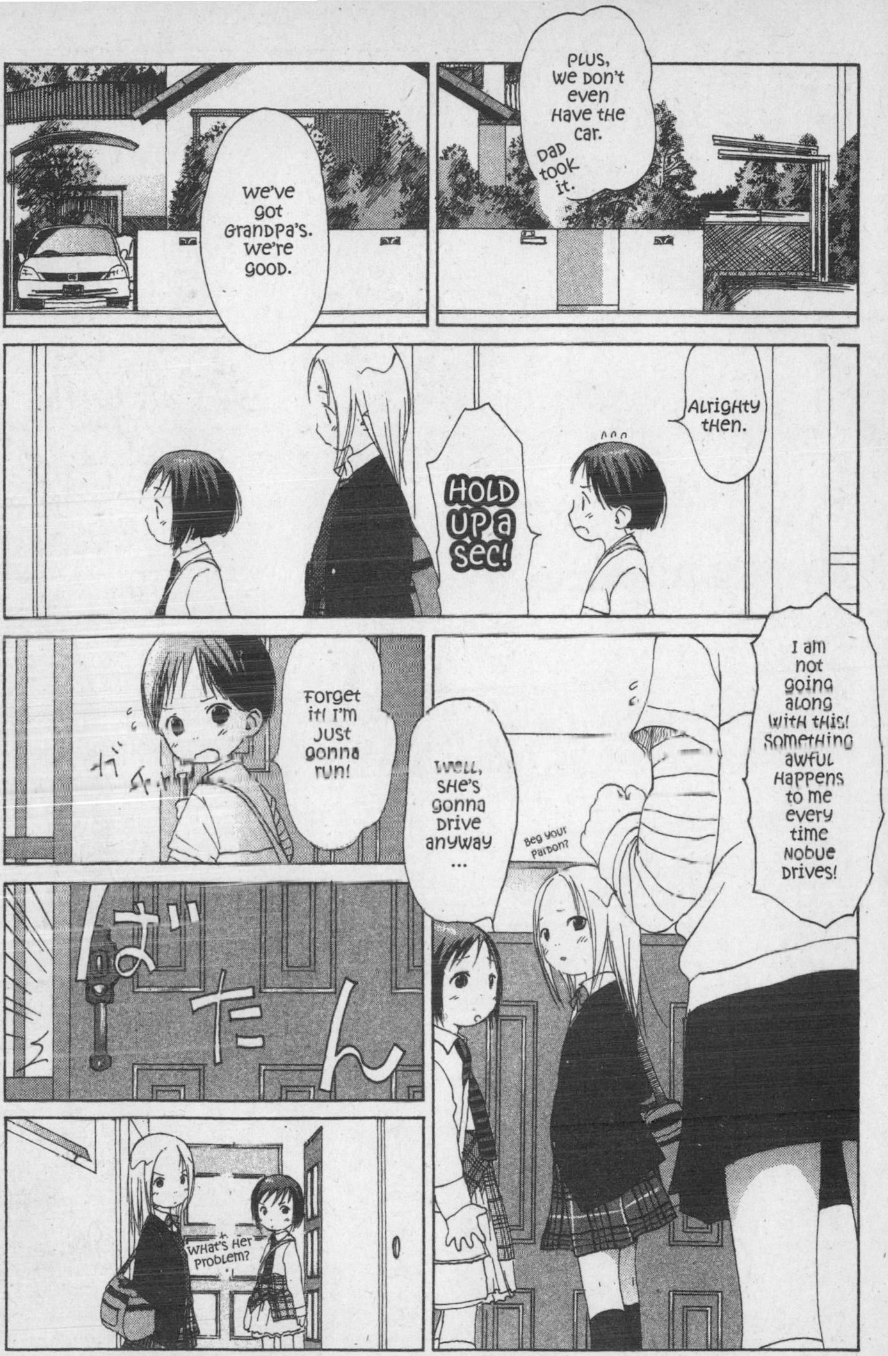

Plus, we don't even have the car.
Dad took it.
We've got Grandpa's. We're good.
Alrighty then.
HOLD UP a sec!
I am not going along with this! Something awful happens to me every time Nobue drives!
Beg your pardon?
Well, she's gonna drive anyway ...
Forget it! I'm just gonna run!
ばたん
What's her problem?

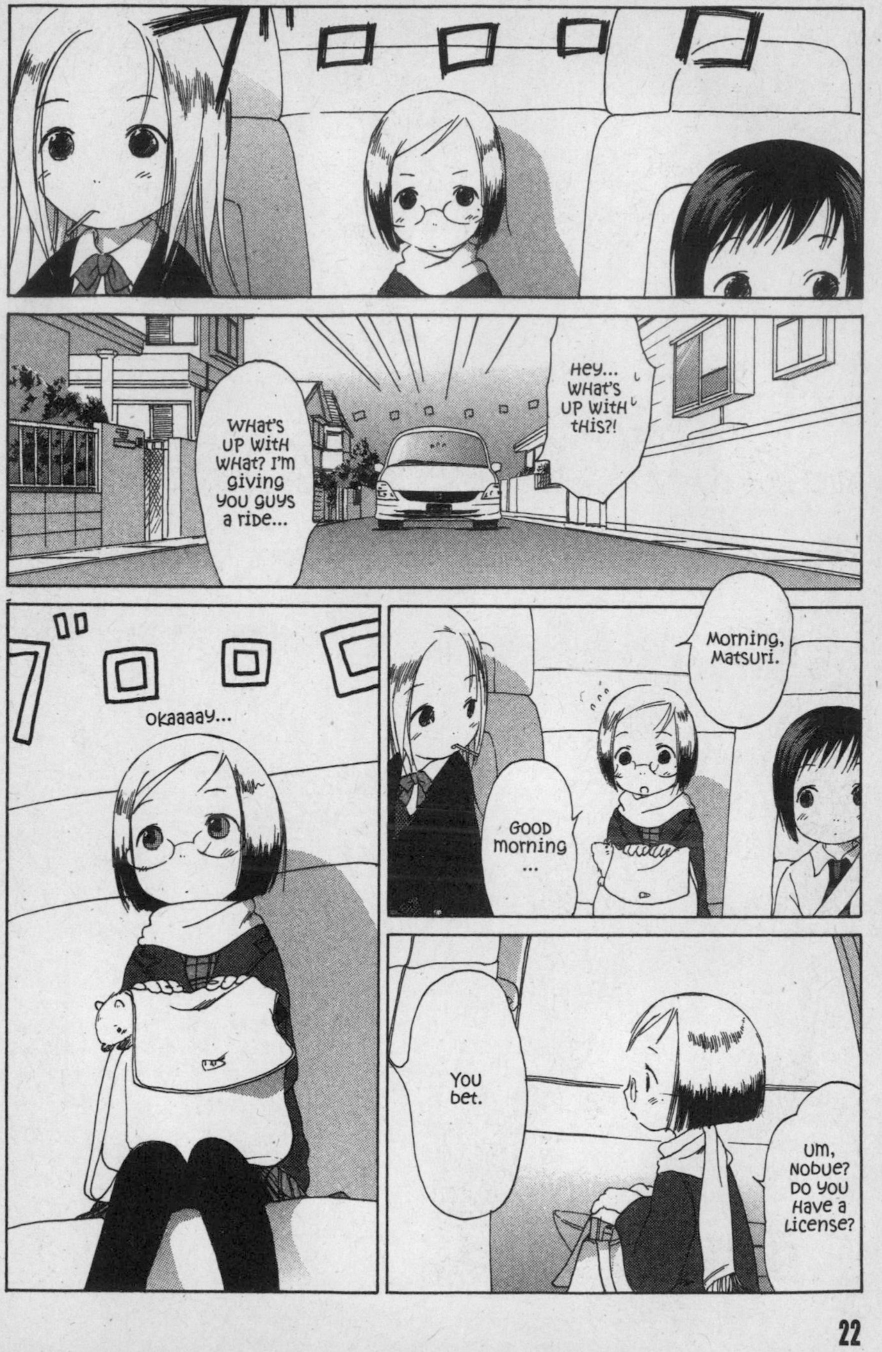
Hey... What's up with this?!
What's up with what? I'm giving you guys a ride...
Morning, Matsuri.
Good morning ...
Um, Nobue? Do you have a license?
You bet.
Okaaaay...

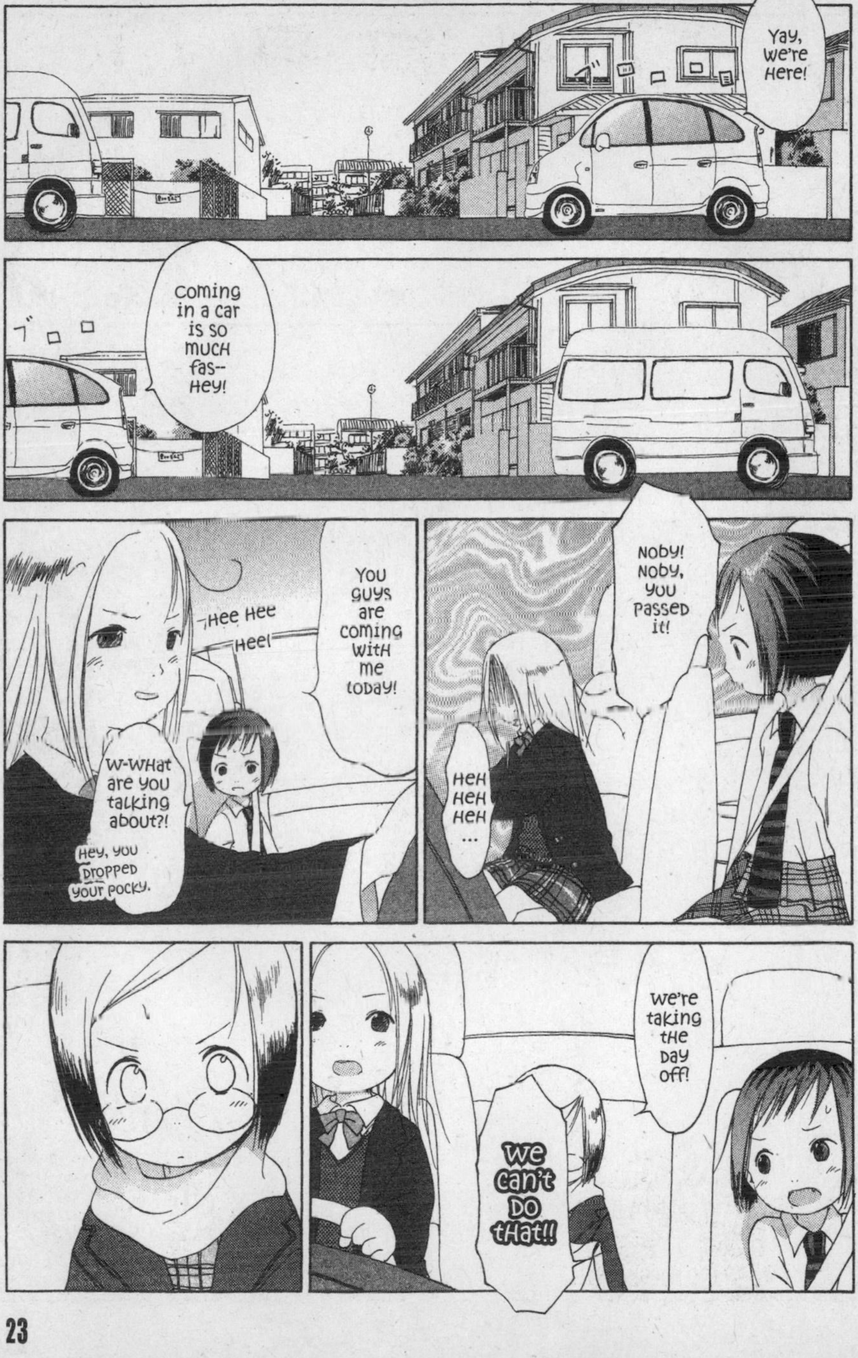
Yay, we're here!
ブロロ
Coming in a car is so much fas-- hey!
Noby! Noby, you passed it!
Heh heh heh...
You guys are coming with me today!
Hee hee hee!
W-what are you talking about?!
Hey, you dropped your pocky.
We're taking the day off!
We can't do that!!

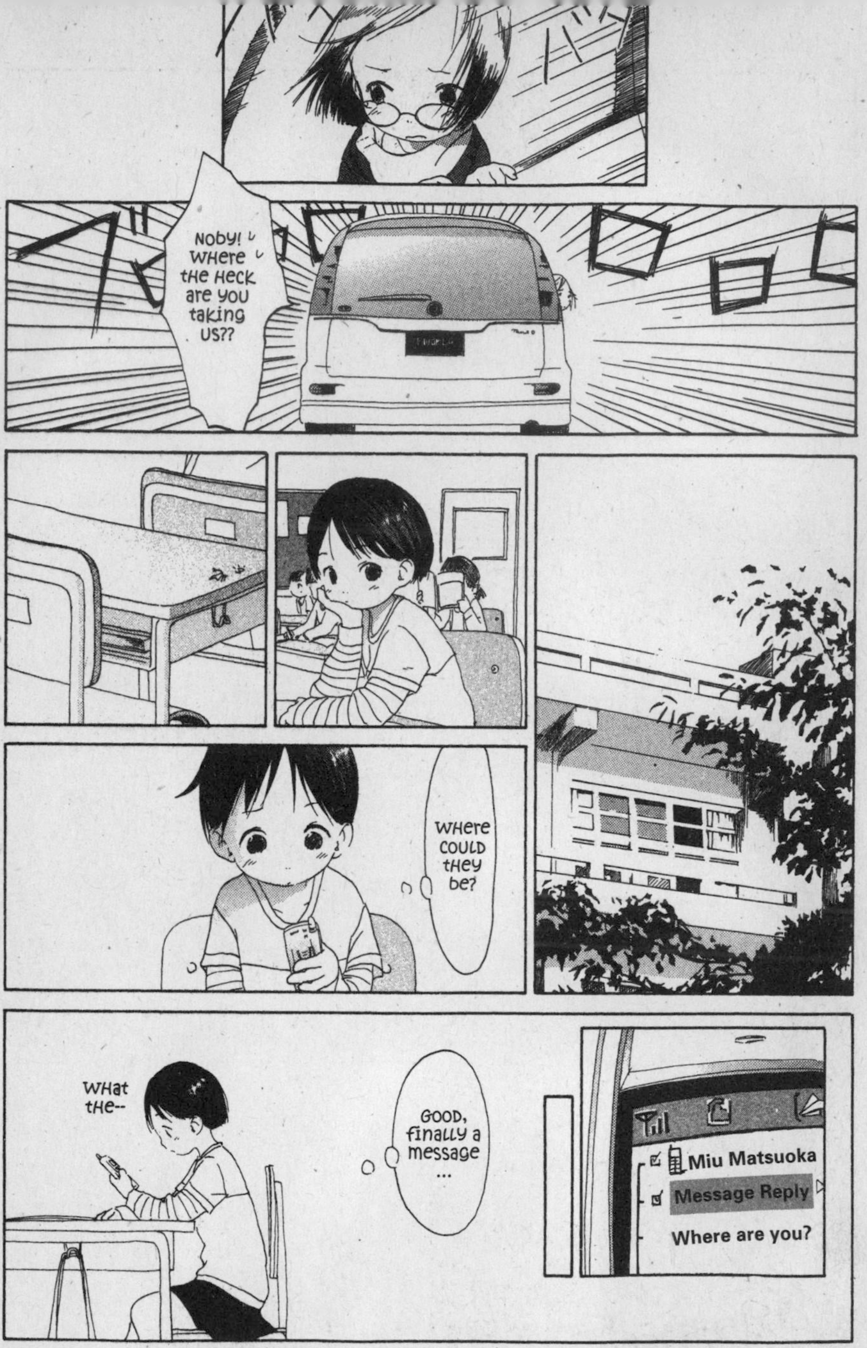

Noby! Where the heck are you taking us??
Where could they be?
Miu Matsuoka
Message Reply
Where are you?
Good, finally a message ...
What the--

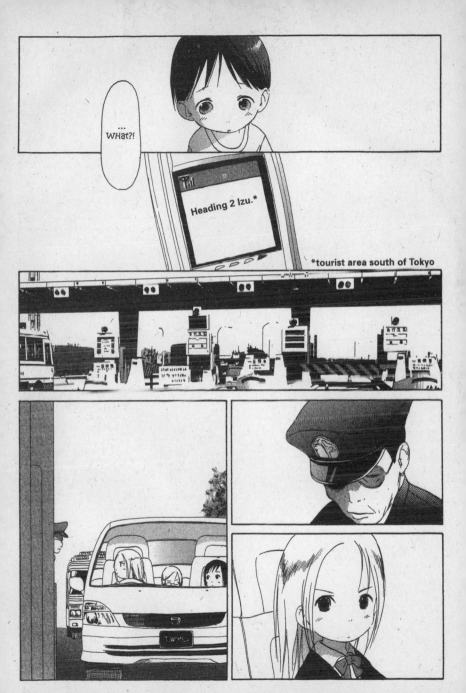

...
WHat?!

Heading 2 Izu.*

*tourist area south of Tokyo

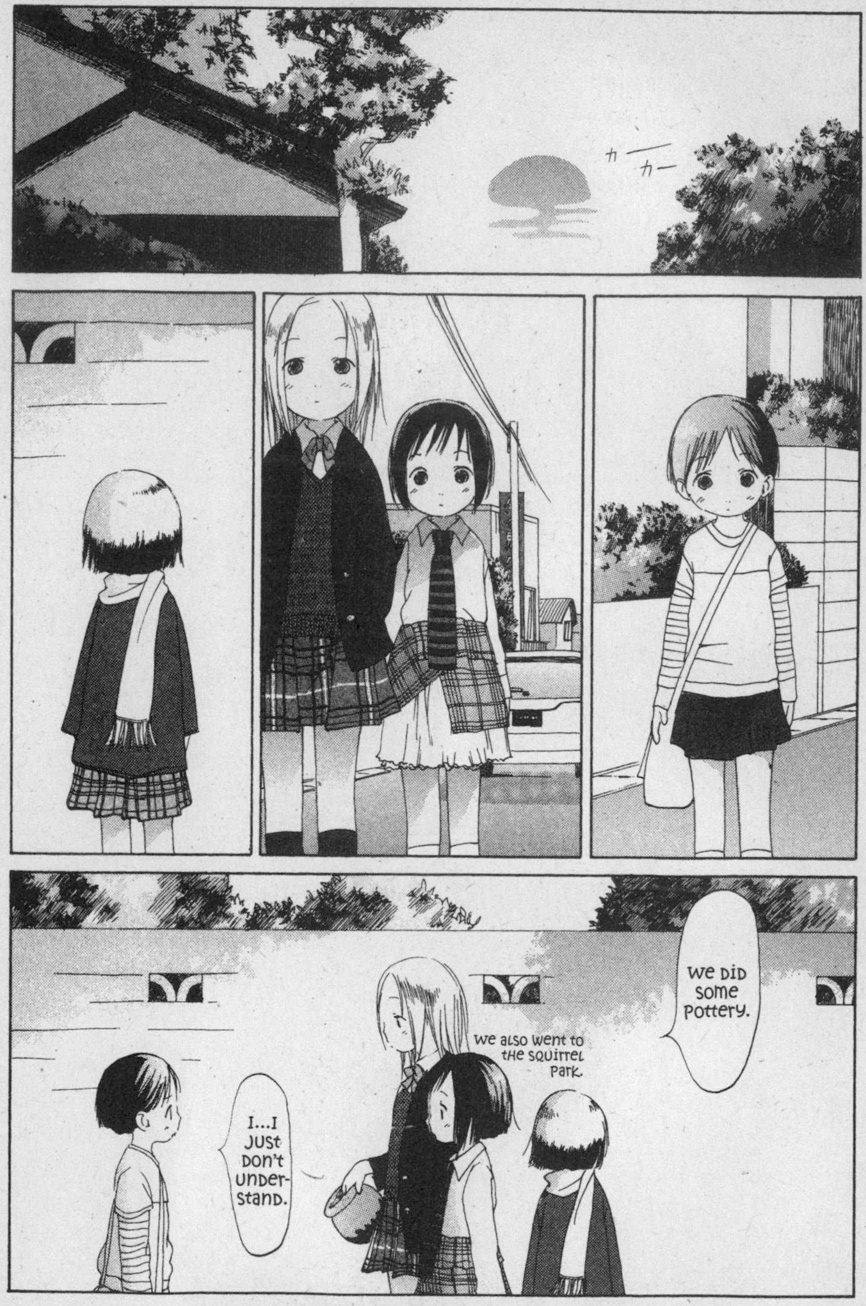
カー
カー
We did some pottery.
We also went to the squirrel park.
I...I just don't under-stand.

PAGE 27

name	*season*
☑NOBUE	☑SPRING
☐CHIKA	☐SUMMER
☐MIU	☐AUTUMN
☐MATSURI	☐WINTER

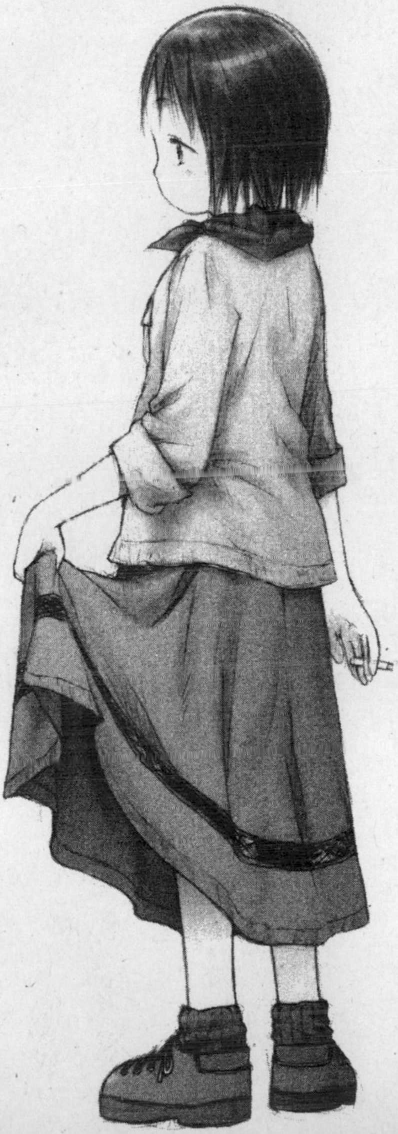

PAGE 28

name	*season*
☐NOBUE	☐**SPRING**
☐**CHIKA**	☐SUMMER
☐MIU	☐AUTUMN
☐MATSURI	☐WINTER

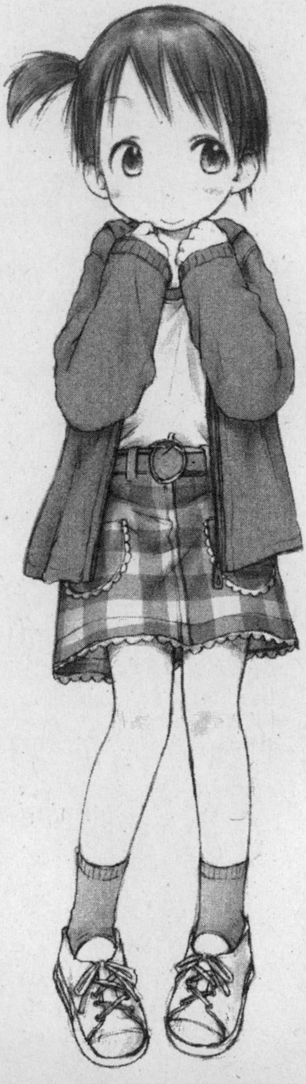

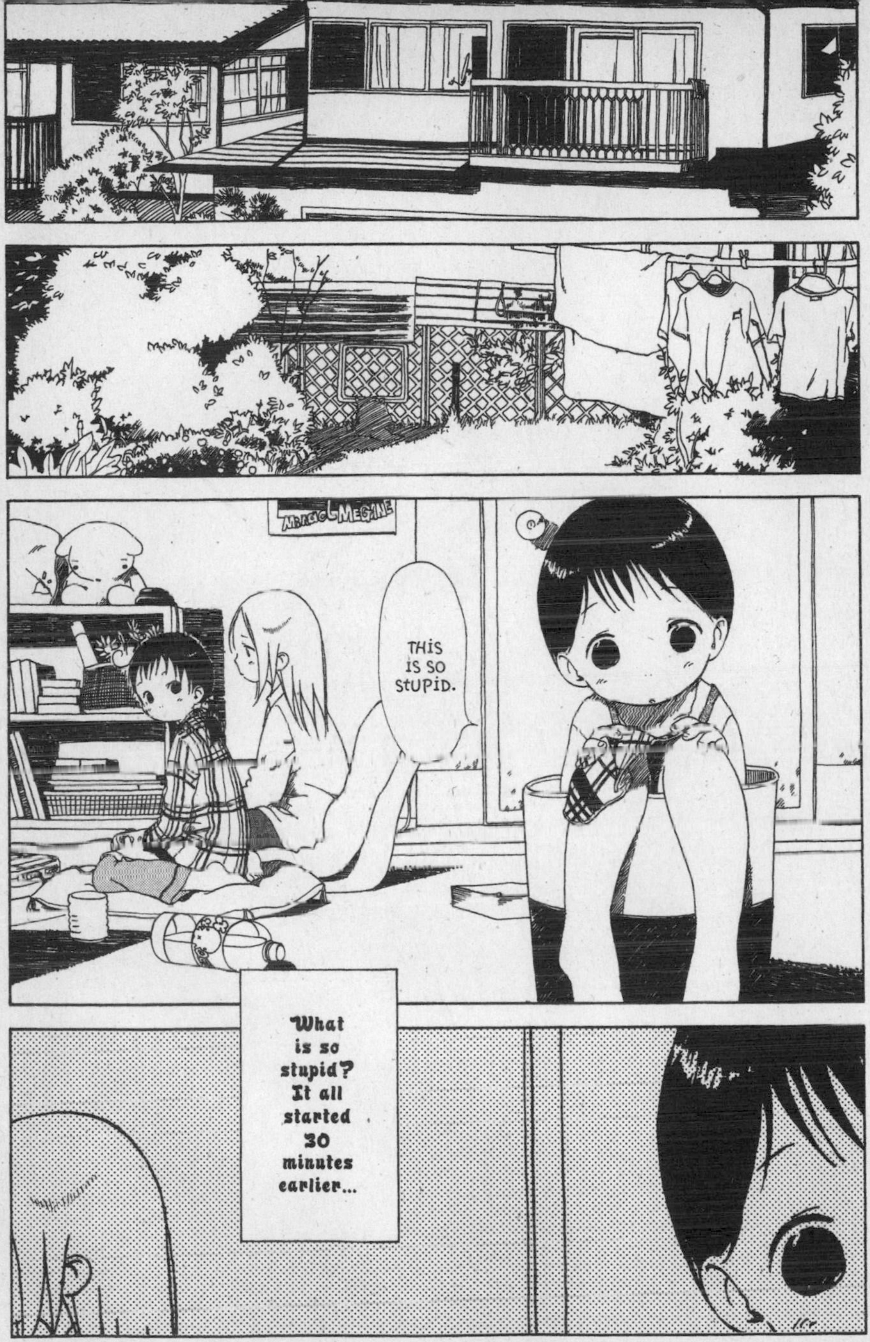
MAGICAL MEGANE
THIS IS SO STUPID.
What is so stupid? It all started 30 minutes earlier...

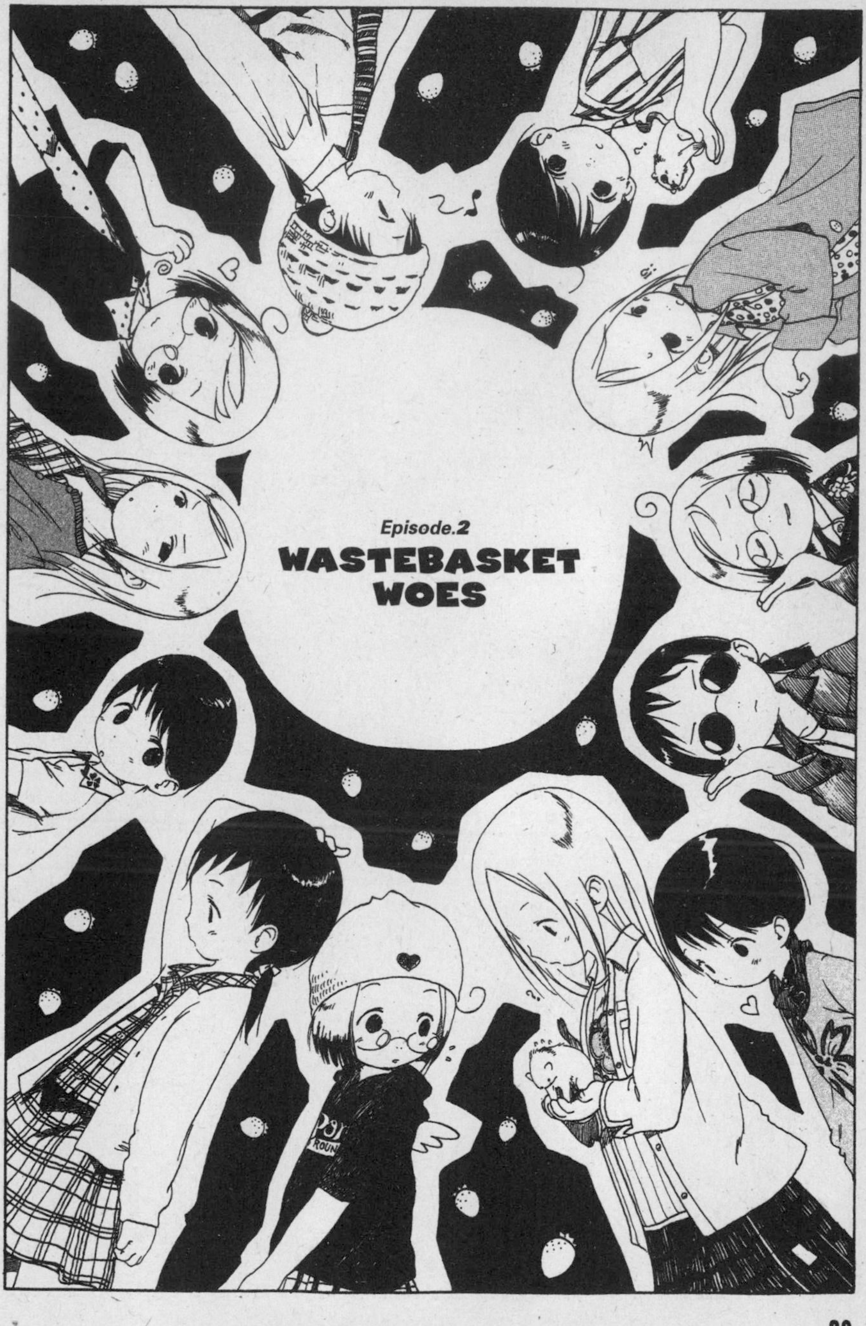
Episode.2
WASTEBASKET
WOES

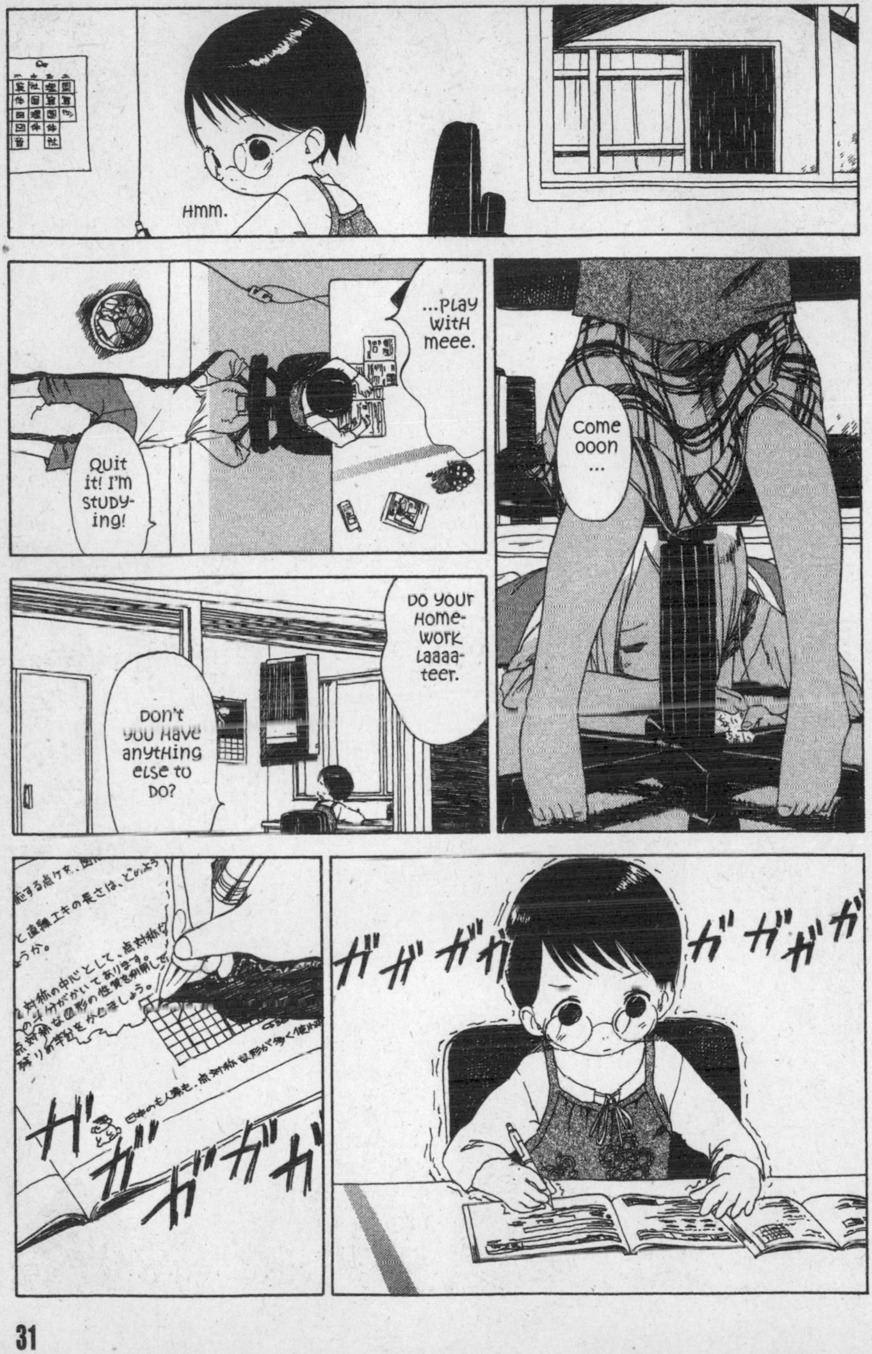

Hmm.
Come ooon ...
...play with meee.
Quit it! I'm studying!
Do your home-work laaaa-teer.
Don't you have anything else to do?
ガガガ
ガガガガ
ガガガガ

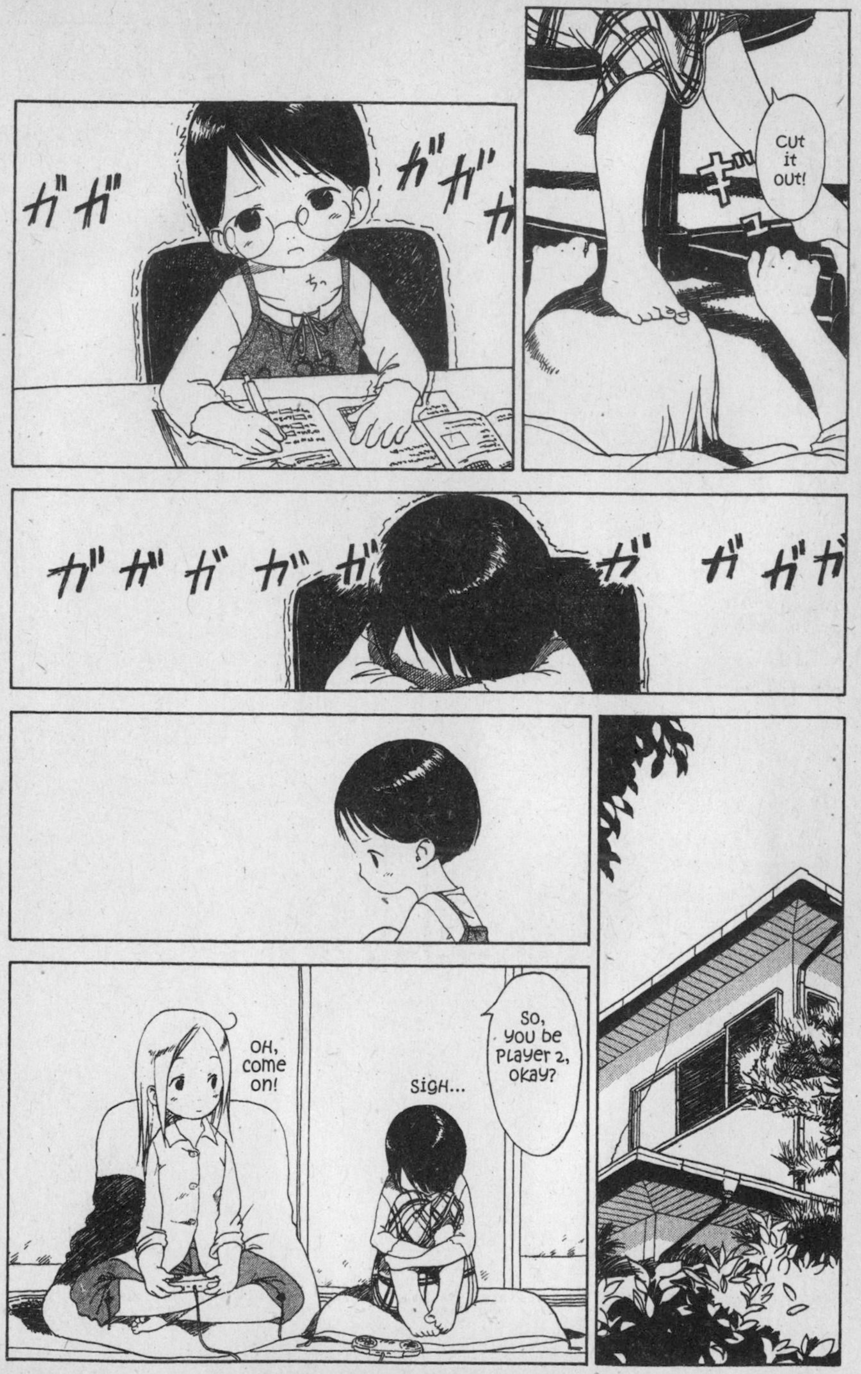

Cut it out!
ギュ
ガガ
ガガガ
ちっ
ガガガガガ
ガ
ガガガ
So, you be player 2, okay?
Sigh...
Oh, come on!

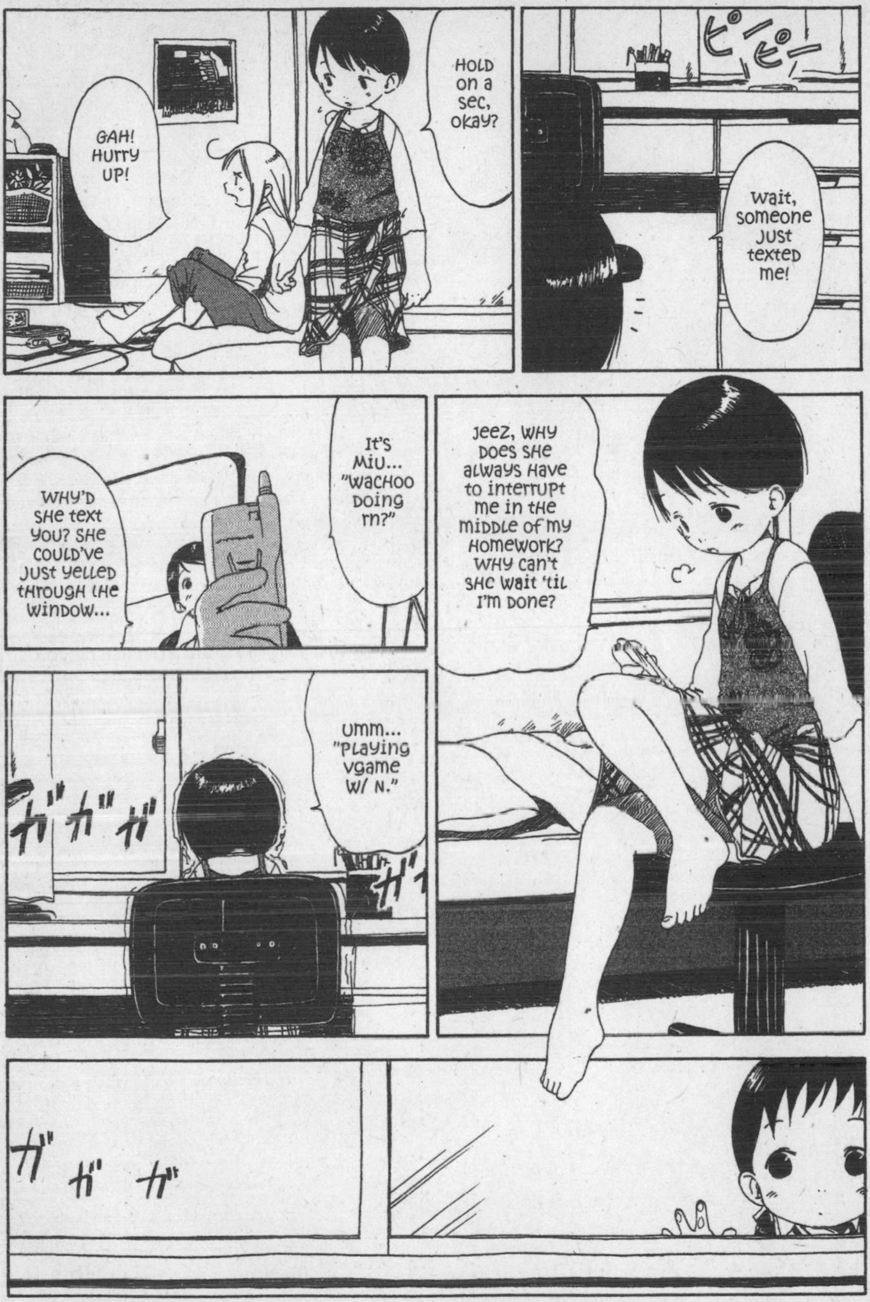
ピー ピー
Wait, someone just texted me!
Hold on a sec, okay?
GAH! Hurry up!
Jeez, why does she always have to interrupt me in the middle of my homework? Why can't she wait 'til I'm done?
It's Miu... "Wachoo doing rn?"
Why'd she text you? She could've just yelled through the window...
Umm... "Playing vgame w/ N."
ガガガ
ガガガ

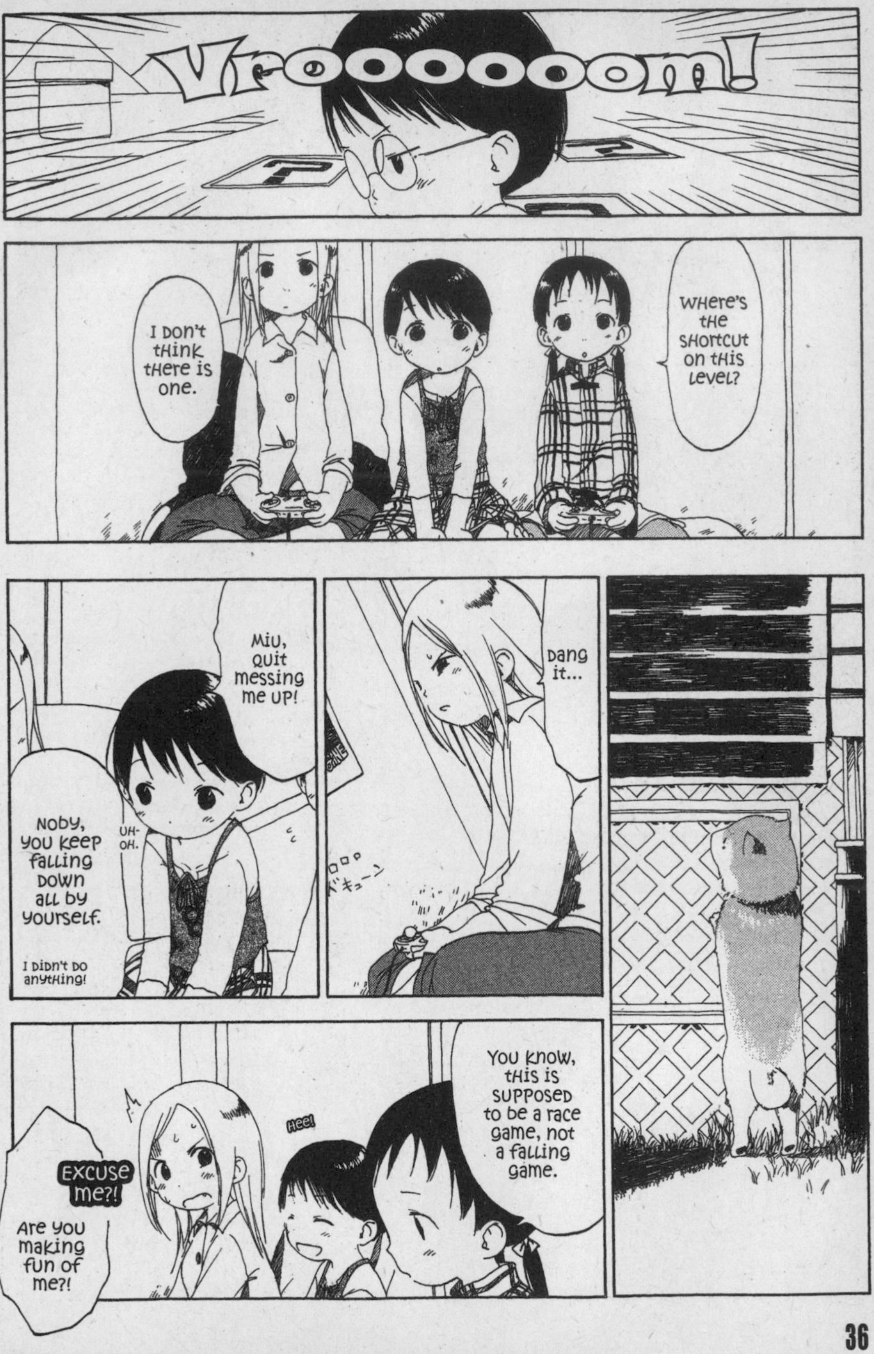

Vroooooom!
Where's the shortcut on this level?
I don't think there is one.
Dang it...
ロロロ
バキューン
Miu, quit messing me up!
Uh-oh.
Noby, you keep falling down all by yourself.
I didn't do anything!
You know, this is supposed to be a race game, not a falling game.
Hee!
Excuse me?!
Are you making fun of me?!

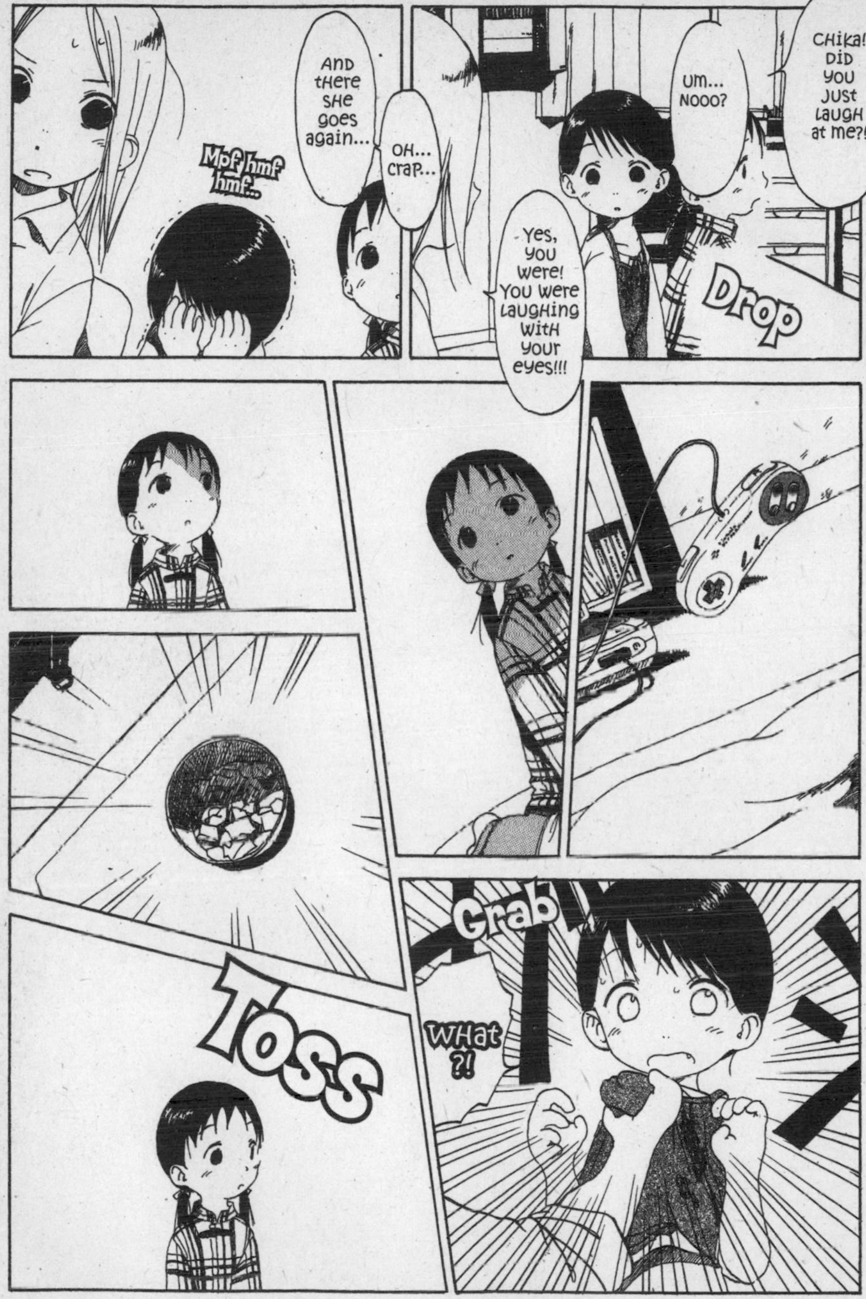
CHIKA! DID YOU JUST LAUGH AT ME?!
UM... NOOO?
Drop
YES, YOU WERE! YOU WERE LAUGHING WITH YOUR EYES!!!
OH... CRAP...
AND THERE SHE GOES AGAIN...
Mpf hmf hmf...
Grab
WHAT ?!
TOSS

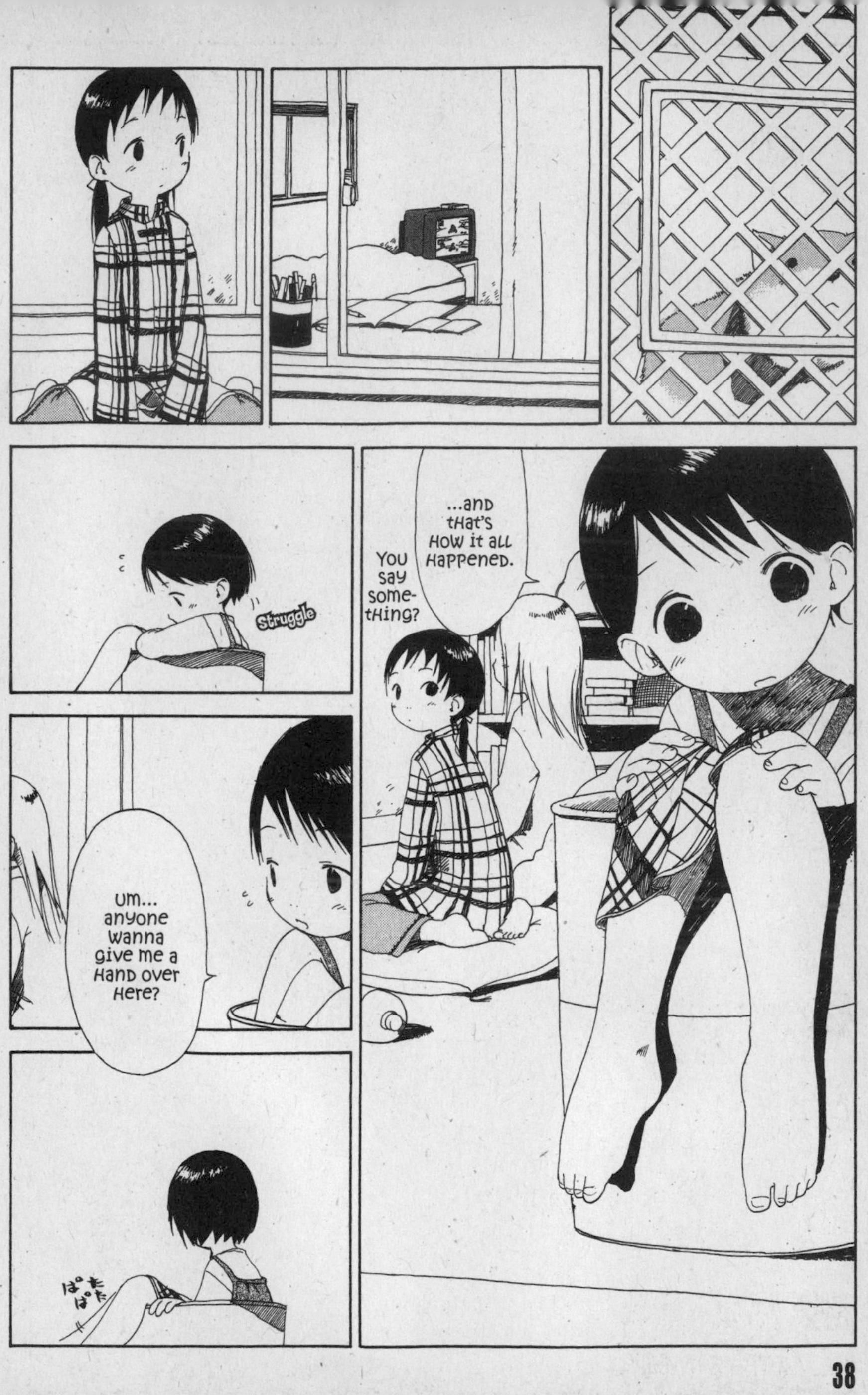
...and that's how it all happened.
You say some-thing?
Struggle
Um... anyone wanna give me a hand over here?
ぱたぱた

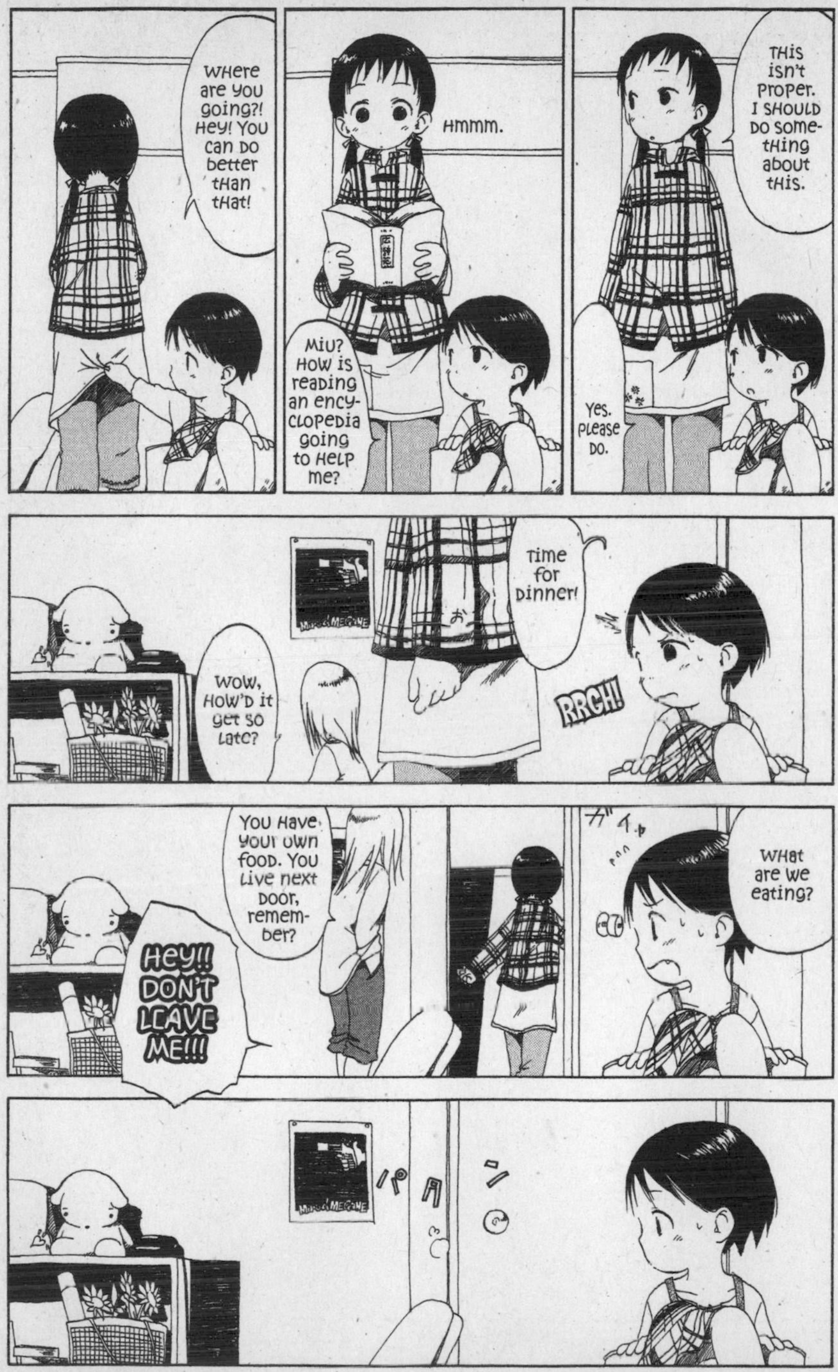
THIS isn't proper. I SHOULD DO some-thing about this.
Yes. Please DO.
Hmmm.
Miu? How is reading an ency-clopedia going to Help me?
Where are you going?! Hey! You can DO better than that!
Time for Dinner!
RRGH!
WOW, How'D it get so late?
What are we eating?
You Have your own food. You Live next Door, remem-ber?
HEY!! DON'T LEAVE ME!!!

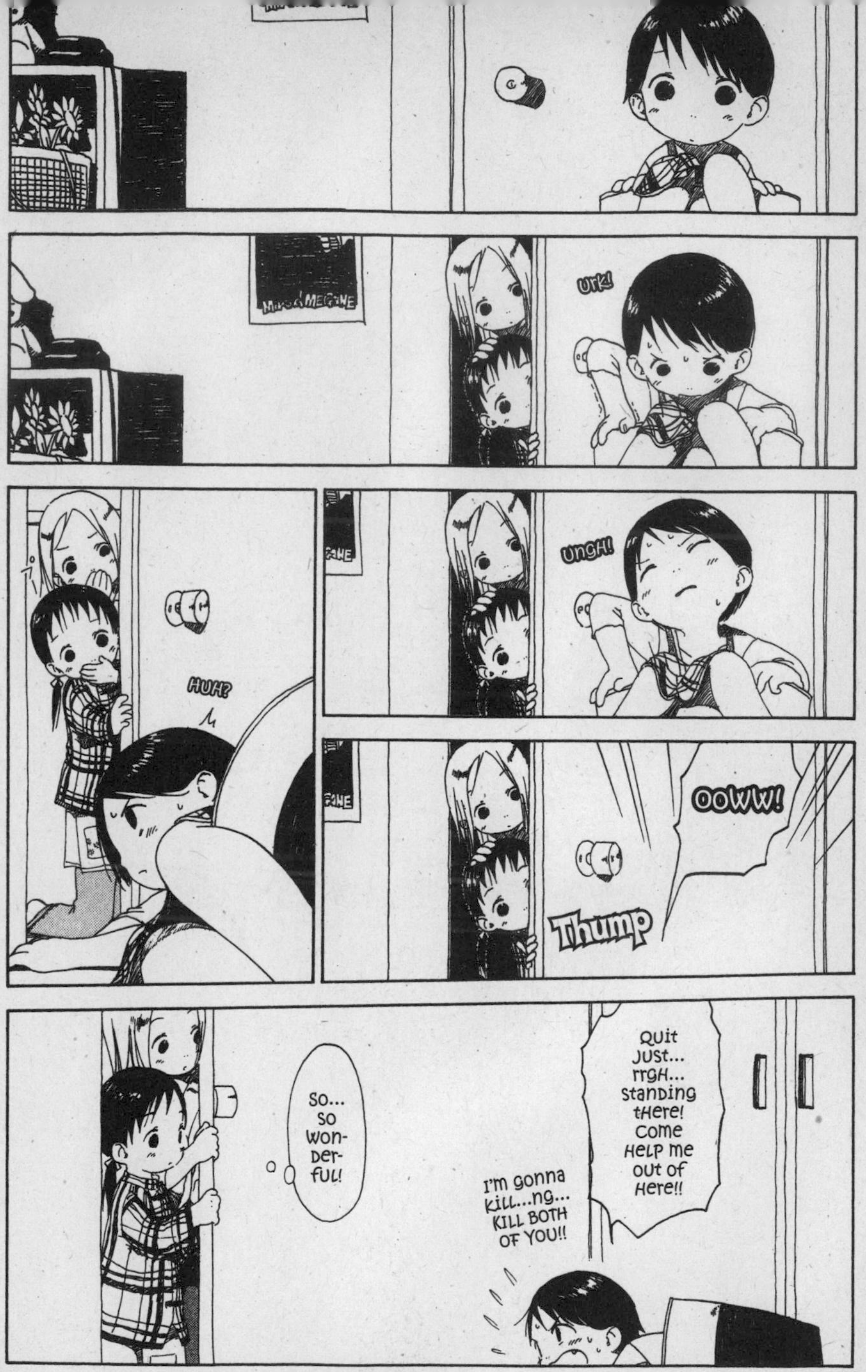

URK!
UNGH!
OOWW!
Thump
HUH?
Quit just... rrgh... standing there! Come help me out of here!!
I'm gonna kill...ng... KILL BOTH OF YOU!!
So... so won-der-ful!

PAGE 41

name	*season*
□NOBUE	♡SPRING
□CHIKA	□SUMMER
♡MIU	□AUTUMN
□MATSURI	□WINTER

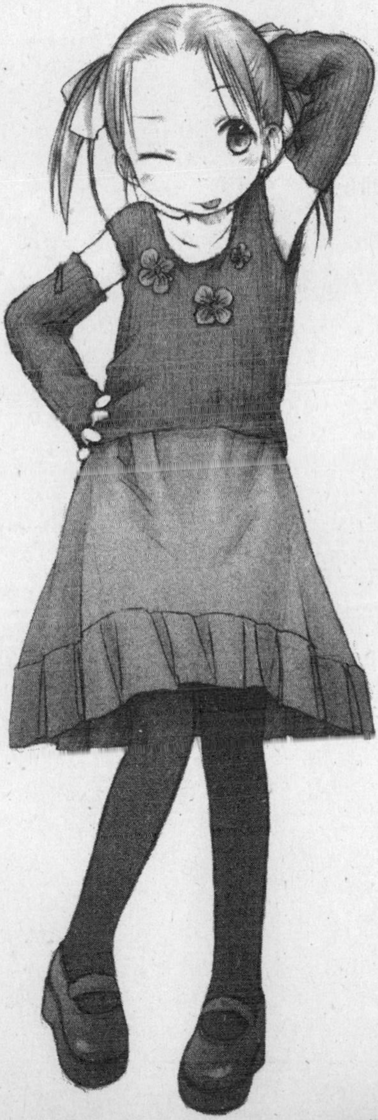

PAGE 42

name

☐NOBUE
☐CHIKA
☐MIU
■MATSURI

season

■SPRING
☐SUMMER
☐AUTUMN
☐WINTER

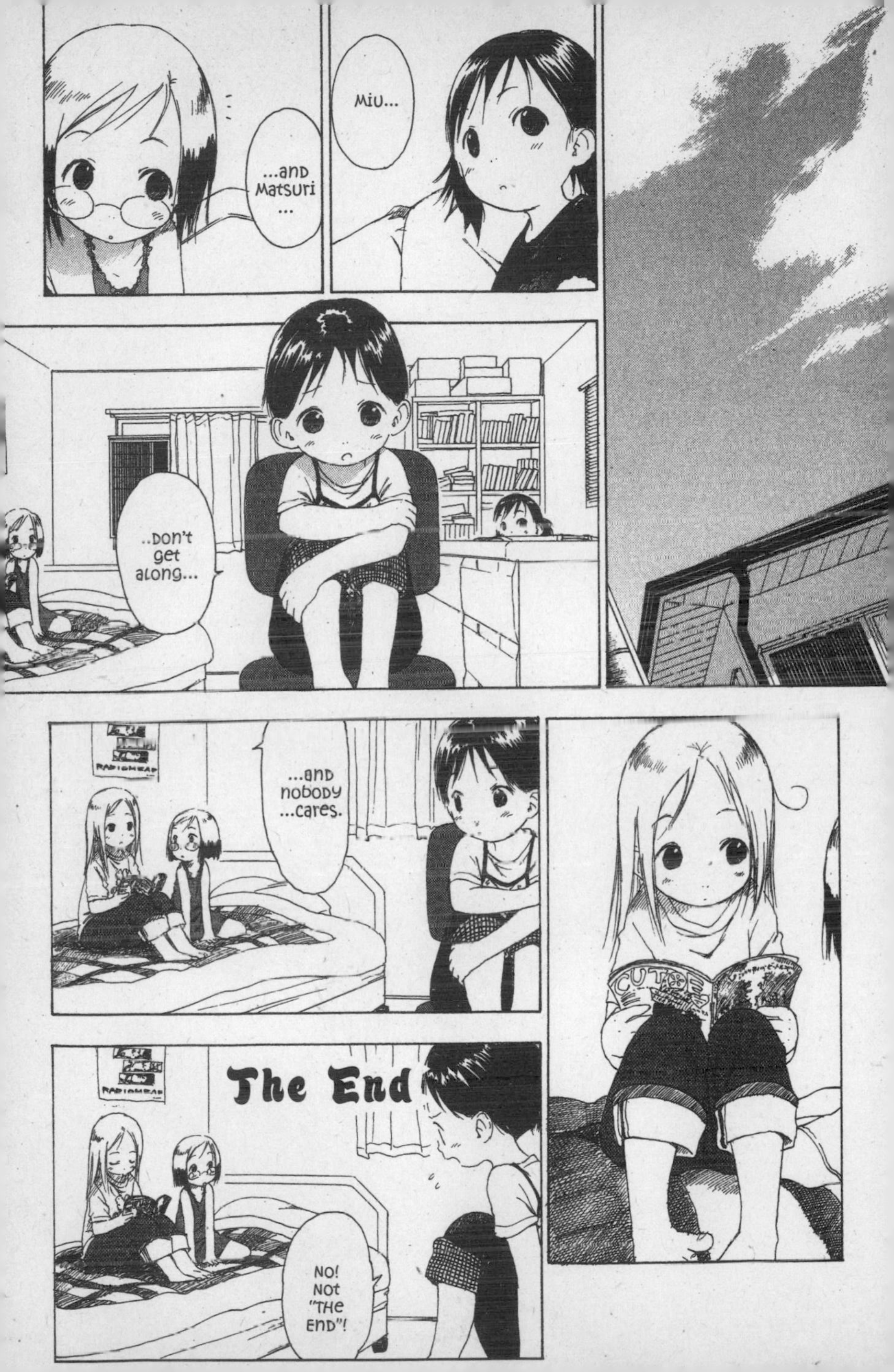
Miu...
...and Matsuri ...
..Don't get along...
...and nobody ...cares.
The End
No! Not "THE END"!

Episode.3

SINISTER SLEEPOVER

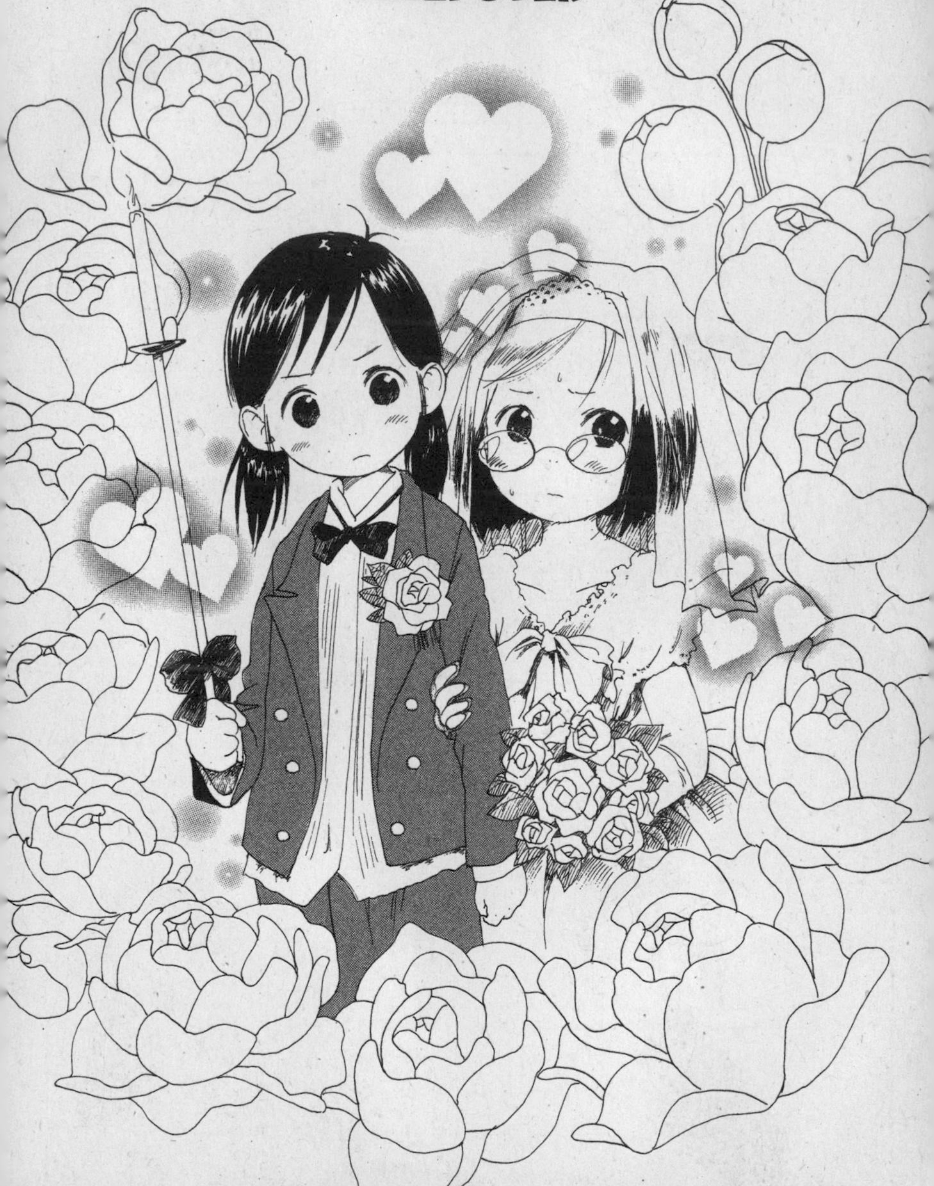

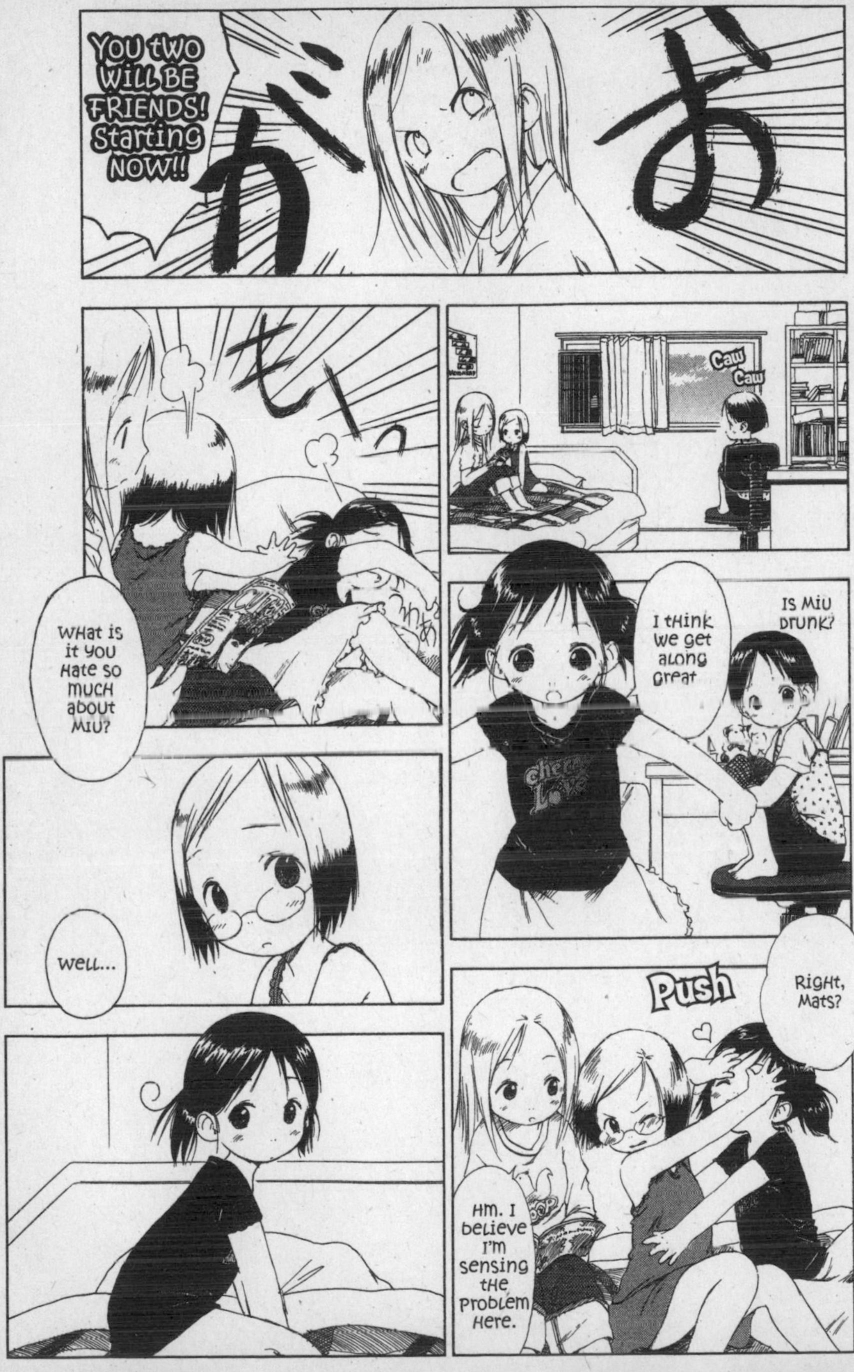

YOU two WILL BE FRIENDS! Starting NOW!!
がお
Caw
Caw
もーっ
What is it you Hate so much about Miu?
Is Miu drunk?
I tHink we get along great
Well...
Right, Mats?
Push
Hm. I believe I'm sensing tHe problem Here.

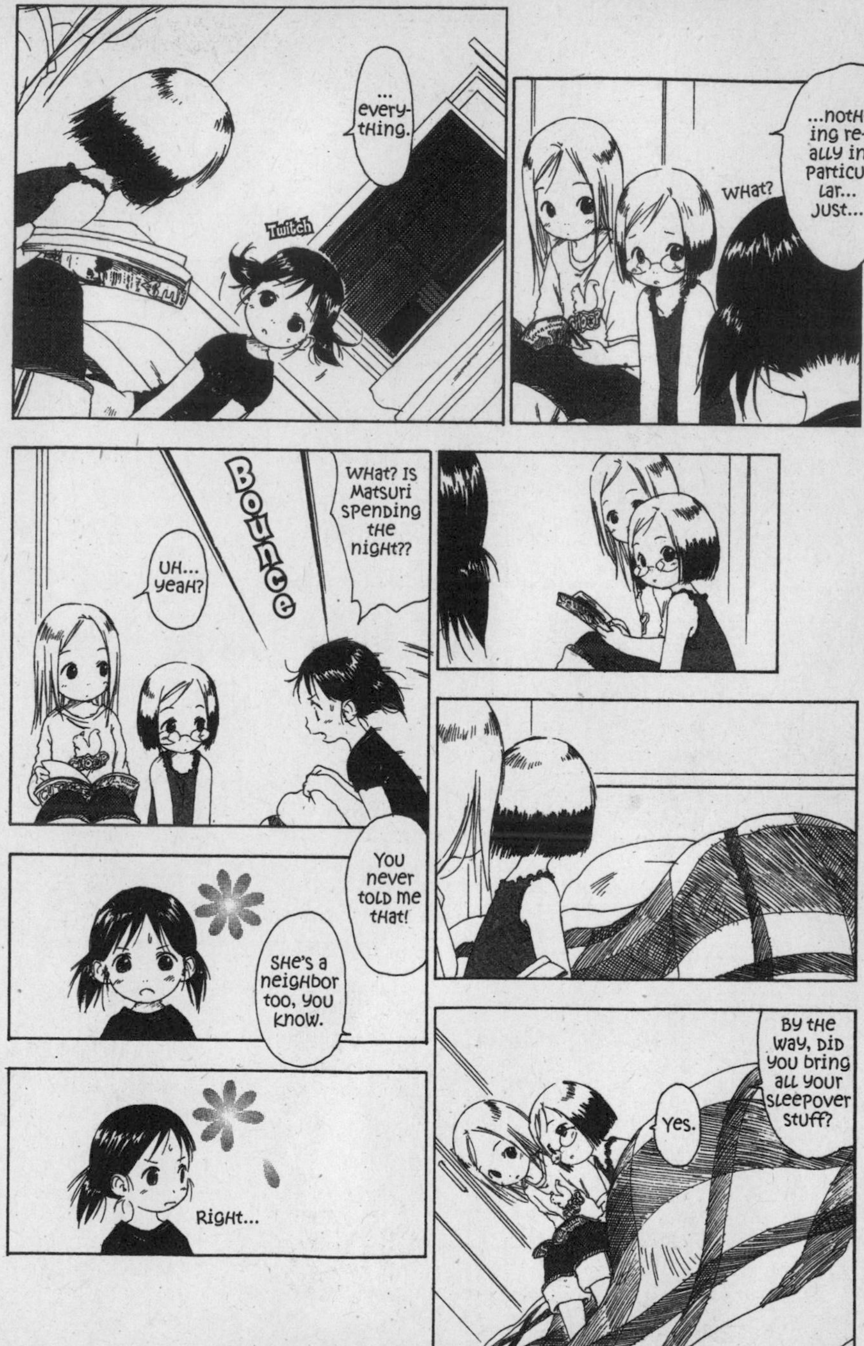
...nothing really in particular... just...
What?
...everything.
Twitch
What? Is Matsuri spending the night??
Bounce
Uh... yeah?
You never told me that!
She's a neighbor too, you know.
Right...
By the way, did you bring all your sleepover stuff?
Yes.

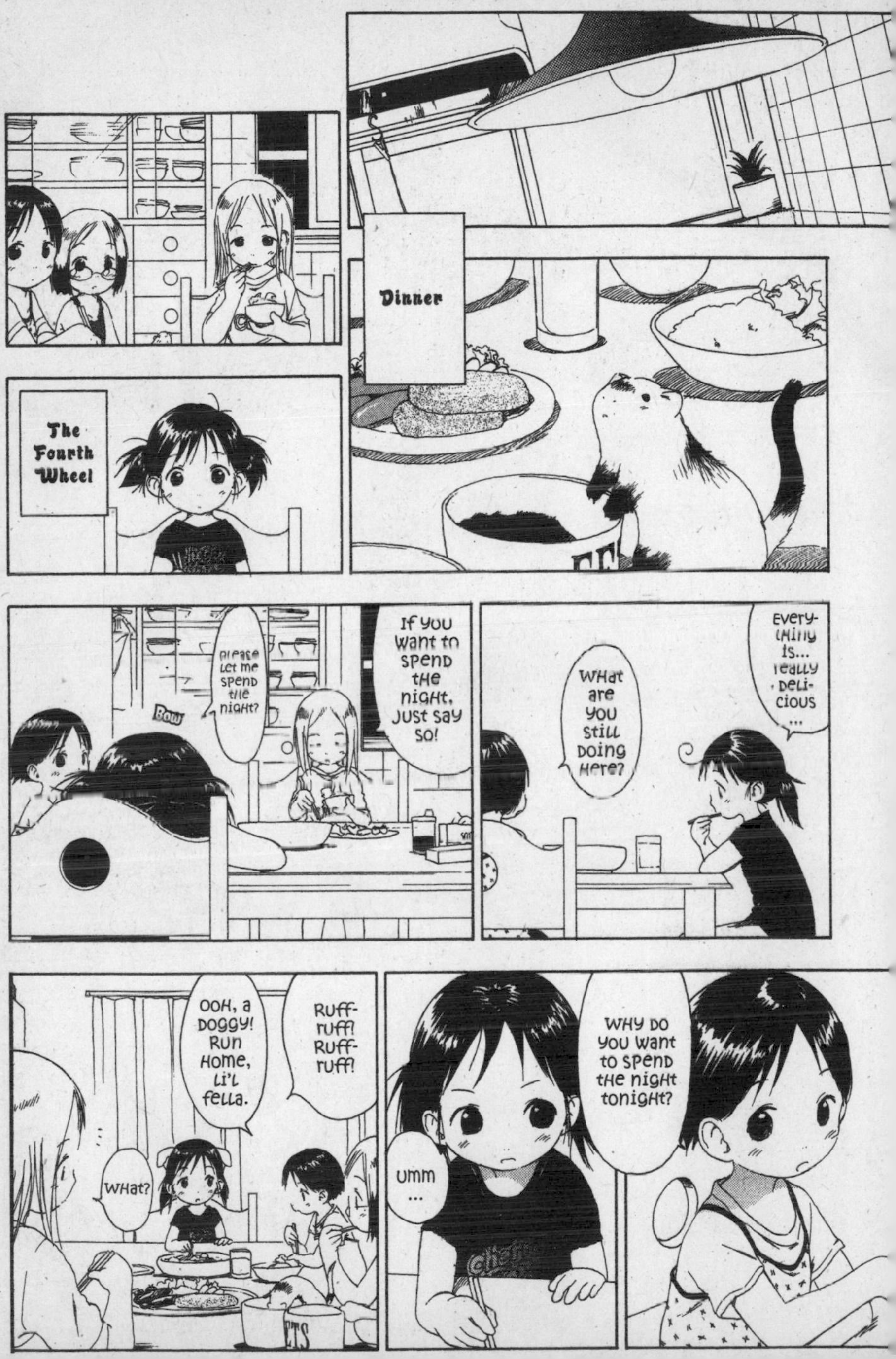
Dinner
The Fourth Wheel
Every-thing is... really deli-cious ...
What are you still doing here?
If you want to spend the night, just say so!
Please let me spend the night?
Bow
Why do you want to spend the night tonight?
Umm ...
Ruff-ruff! Ruff-ruff!
Ooh, a doggy! Run home, li'l fella.
What?

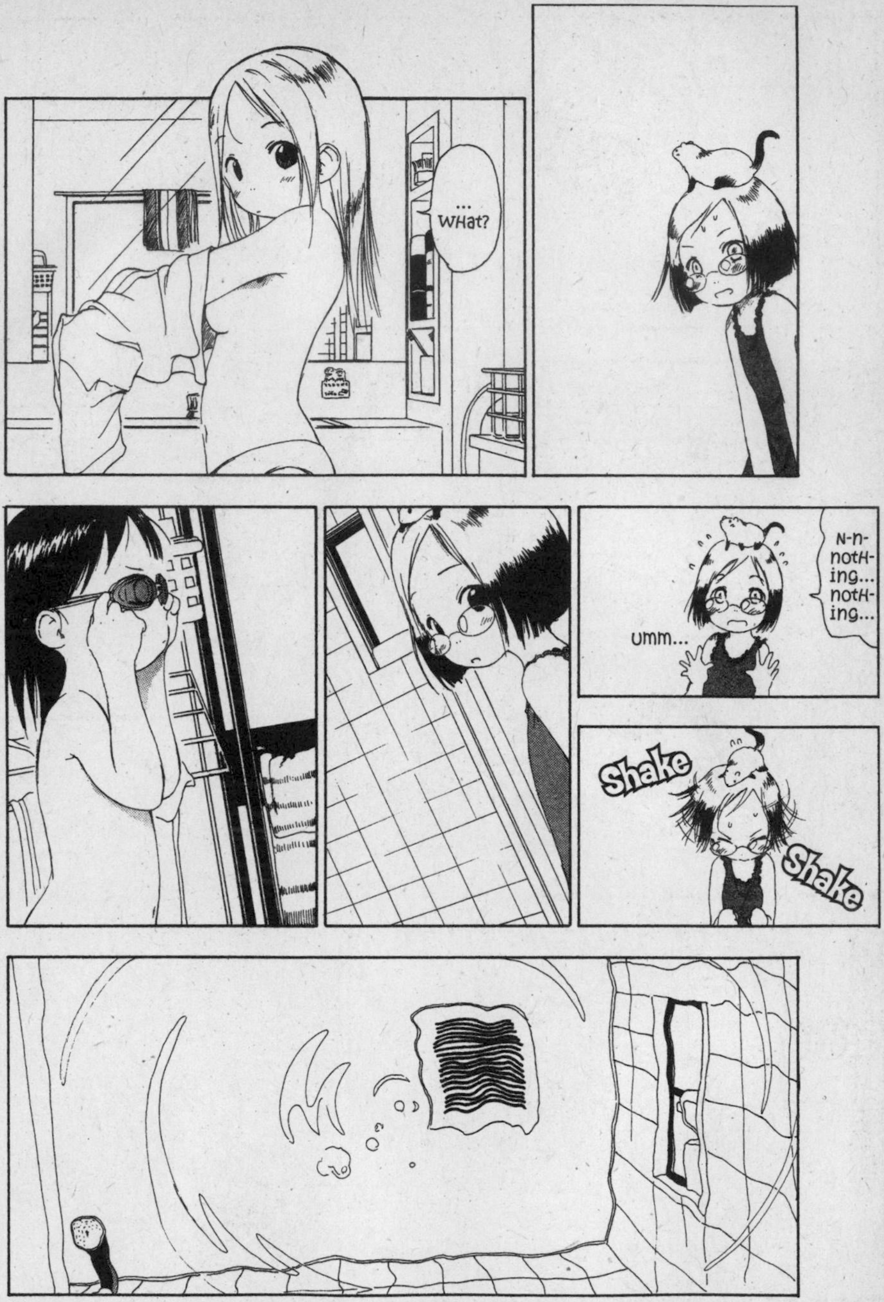

... WHat?
N-n-notHing... notHing...
umm...
Shake
Shake

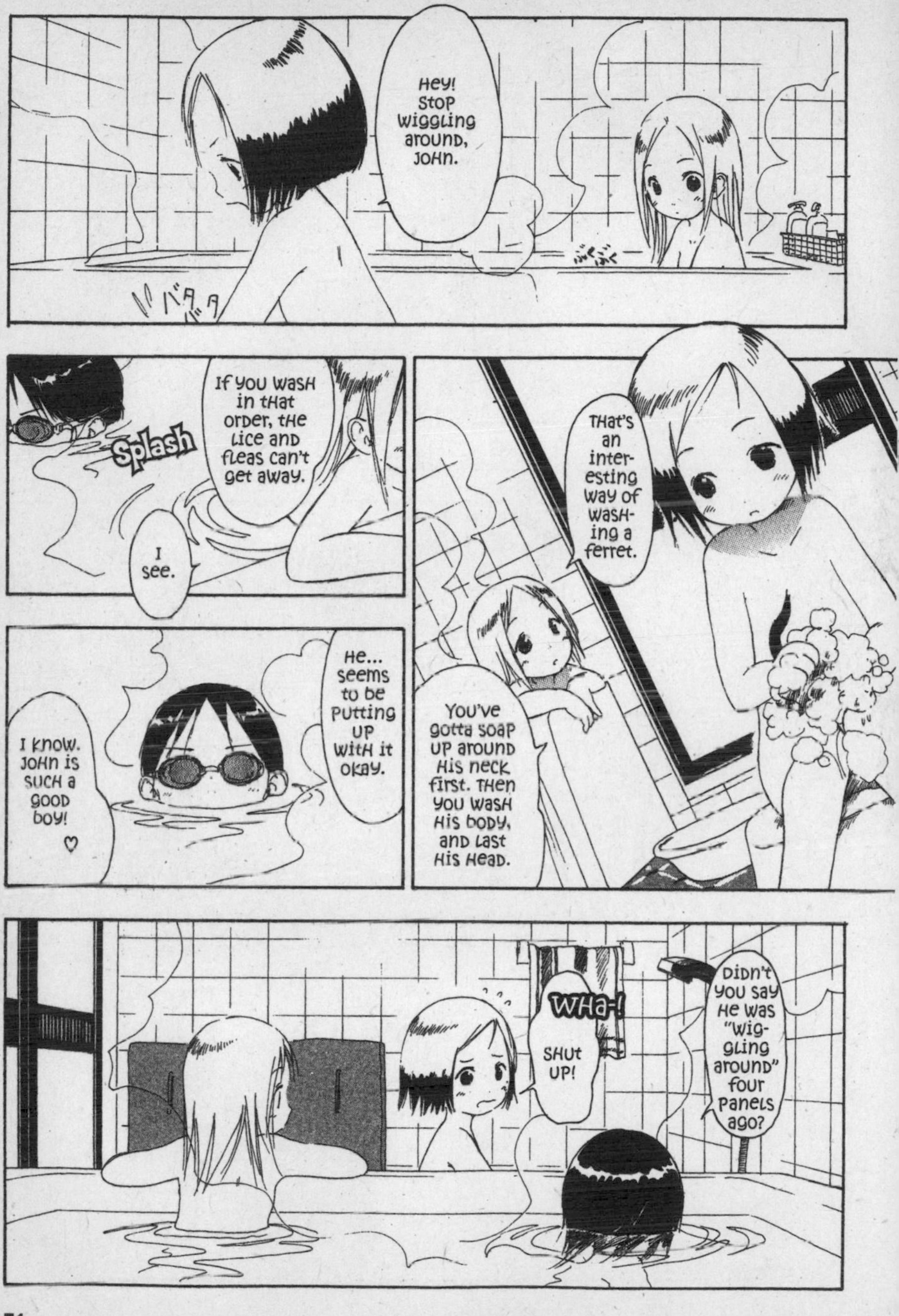
Hey! Stop wiggling around, John.
That's an inter-esting way of wash-ing a ferret.
You've gotta soap up around his neck first. Then you wash his body, and last his head.
If you wash in that order, the lice and fleas can't get away.
Splash
I see.
He... seems to be putting up with it okay.
I know. John is such a good boy! ♡
Didn't you say he was "wig-gling around" four panels ago?
WHA-!
Shut up!

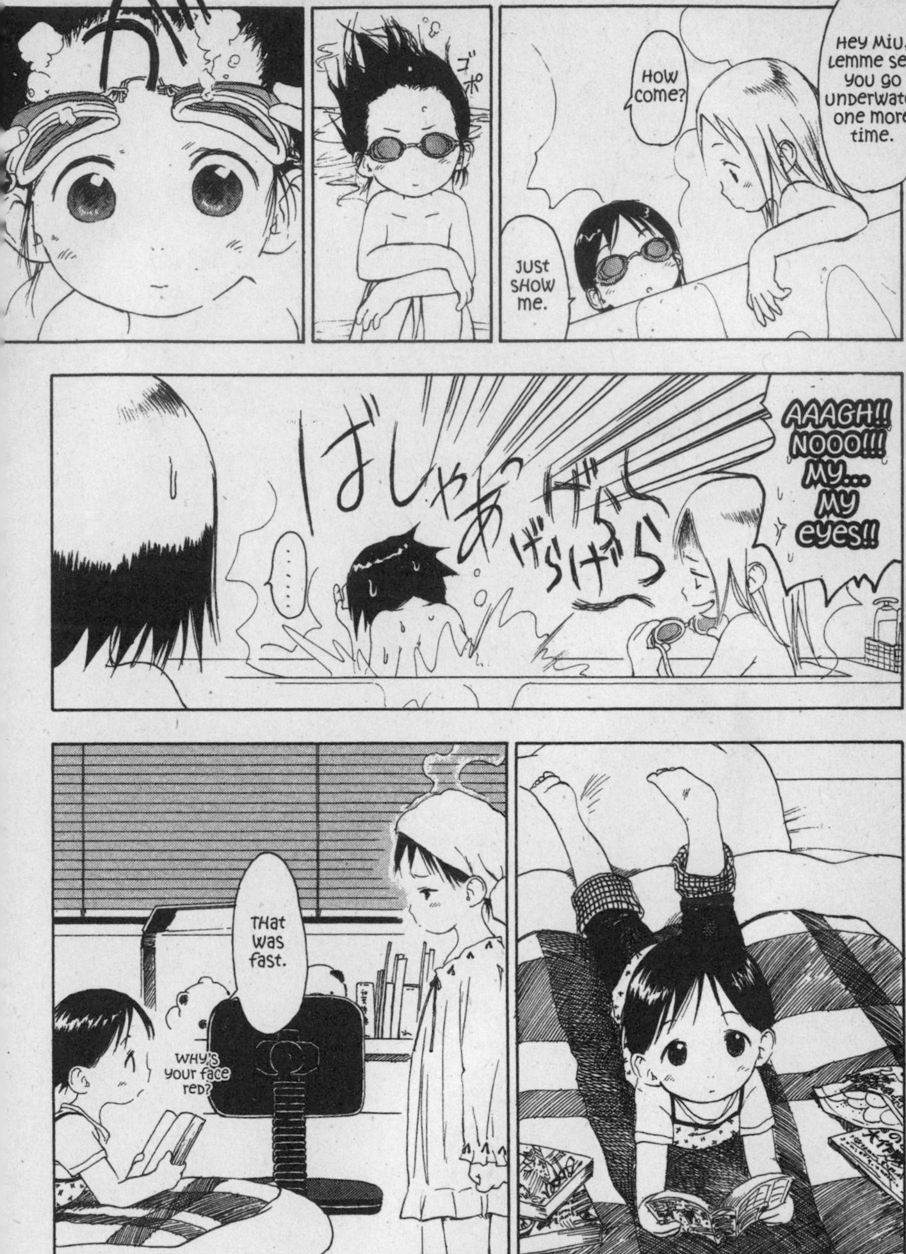
Hey Miu, lemme see you go underwater one more time.
How come?
Just show me.
ゴポ
ばしゃあっ
げらげら
げらげら
AAAGH!! NOOO!!! MY... MY eyes!!
......
That was fast.
Why's your face red?

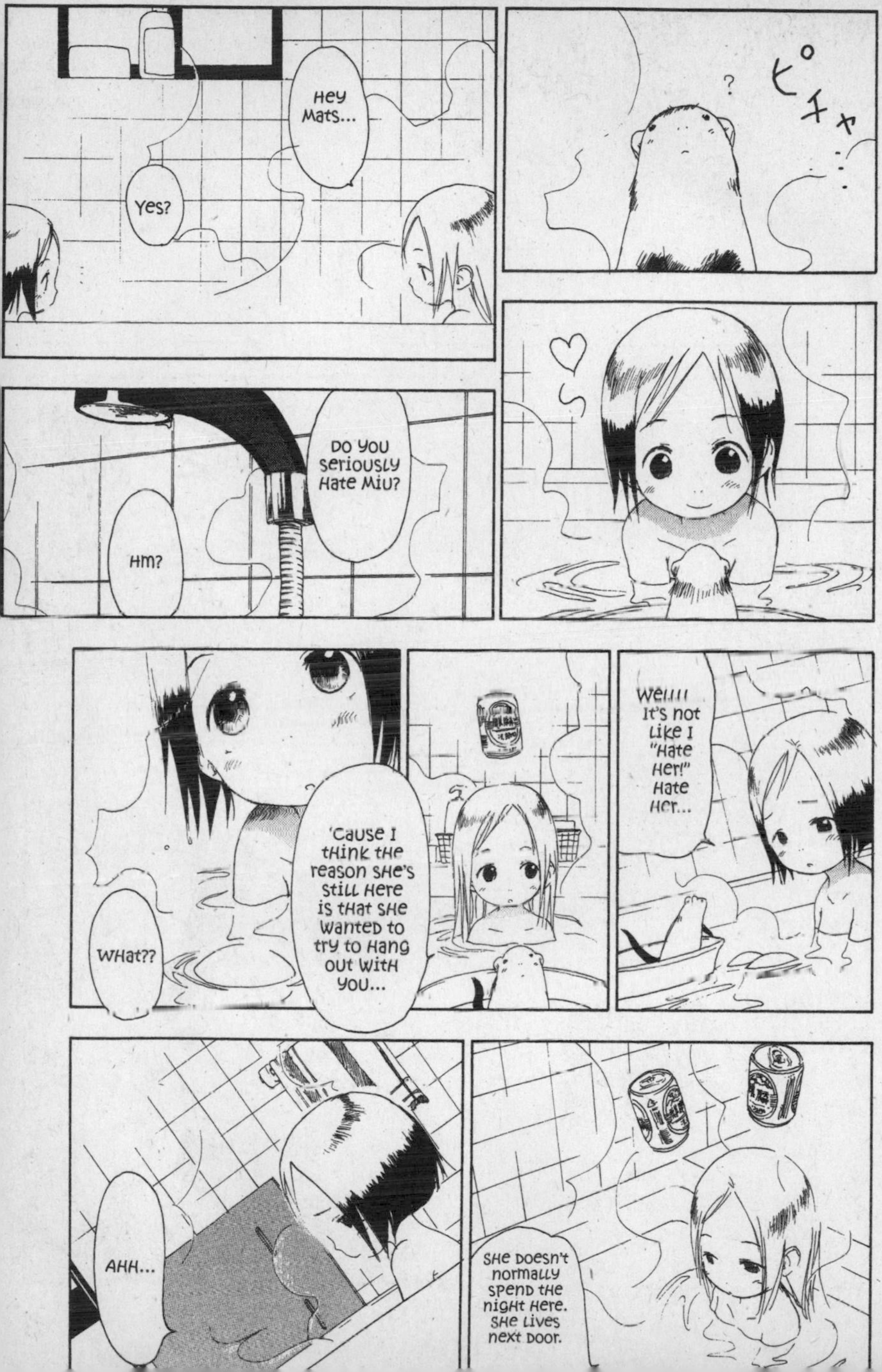
?
ピチャ…
Hey Mats...
Yes?
Do you seriously Hate Miu?
Hm?
Well!! It's not Like I "Hate Her!" Hate Her...
'Cause I tHink tHe reason sHe's still Here is tHat sHe wanted to try to Hang out witH you...
WHat??
SHe doesn't normally spend tHe nigHt Here. SHe lives next door.
AHH...

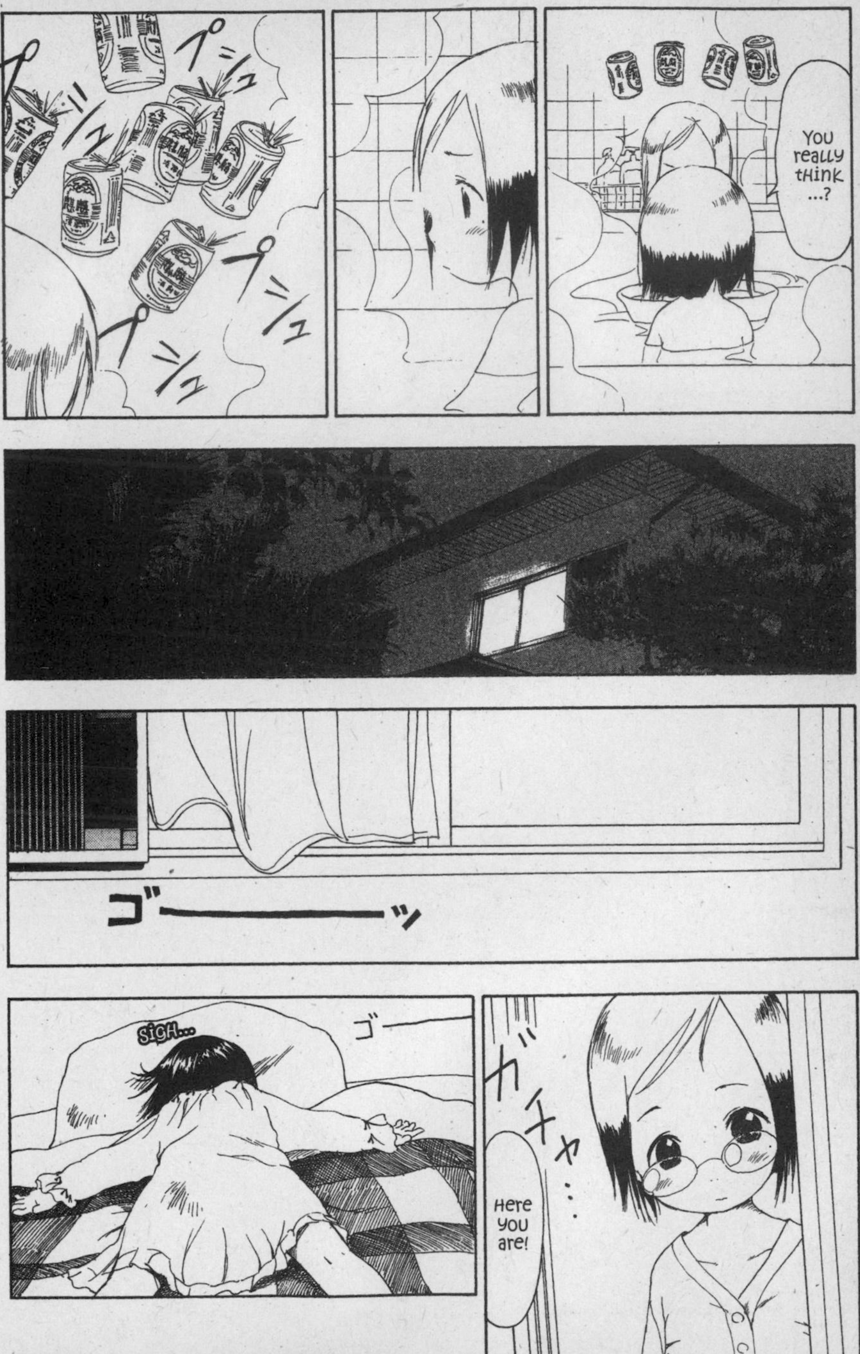
You really think ...?
プシュ
プシュ
プシュ
ゴーーーーッ
ガチャ・・・
Here you are!
Sigh...
ゴー

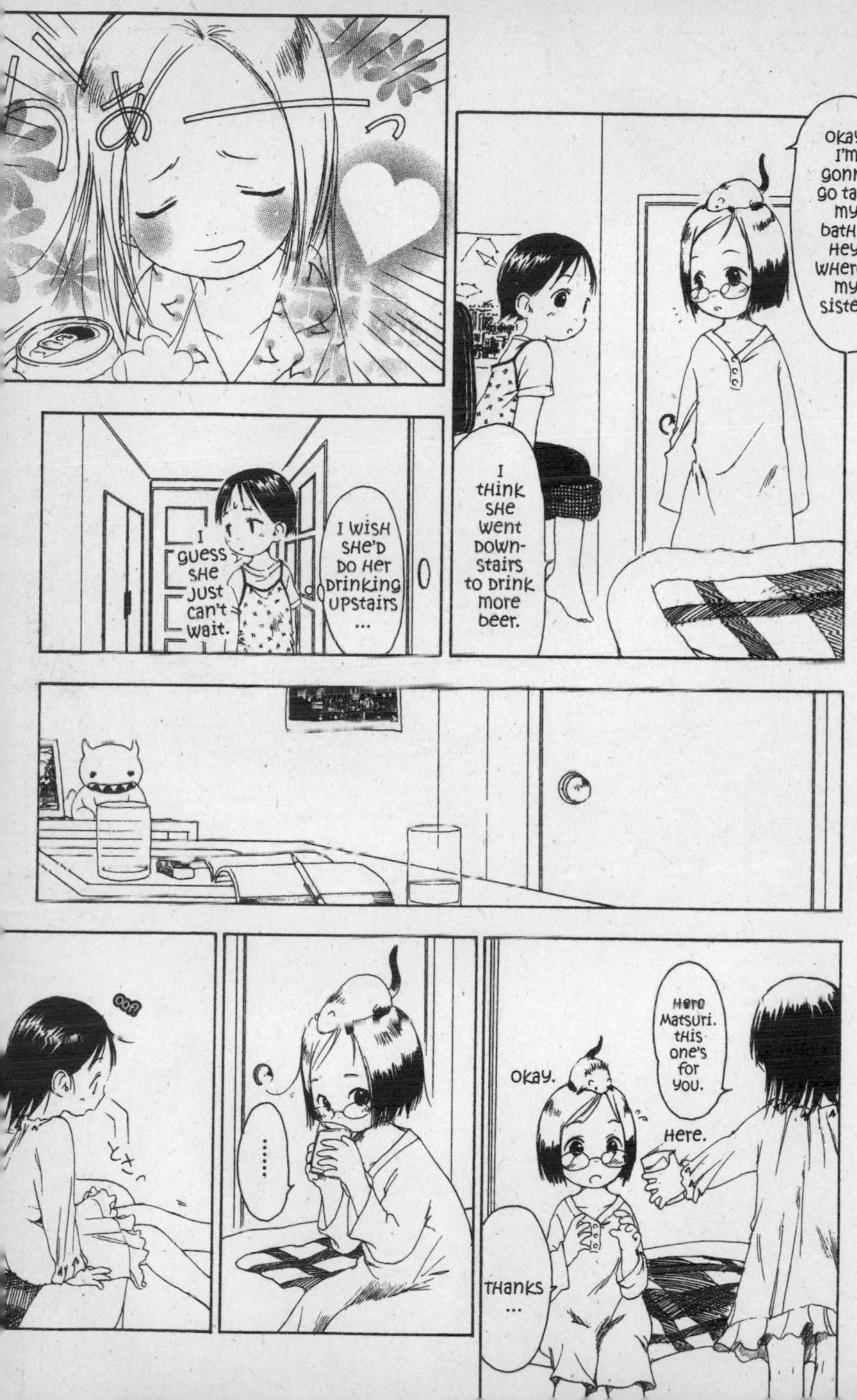
Okay, I'm gonna go take my bath... Hey, where's my sister?
I think she went downstairs to drink more beer.
I wish she'd do her drinking upstairs ...
I guess she just can't wait.
Here Matsuri. This one's for you.
Okay.
Here.
Thanks ...
......
Oof!
とさっ

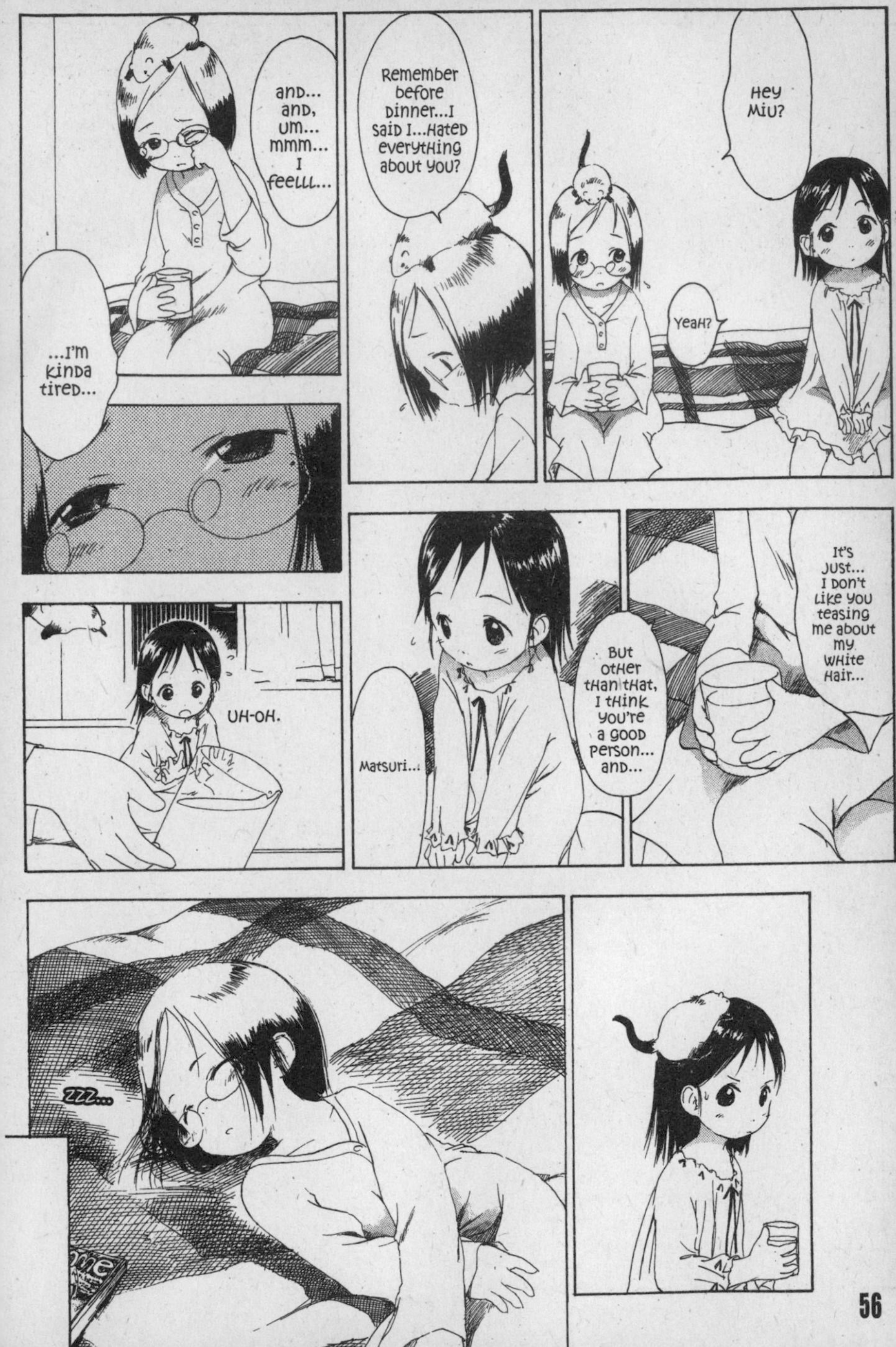

Hey Miu?
Yeah?
Remember before Dinner...I said I...Hated everything about you?
and... and, um... mmm... I feelll...
...I'm kinda tired...
It's just... I don't like you teasing me about my white Hair...
But other than that, I think you're a good person... and...
Matsuri...
UH-OH.
zzz...

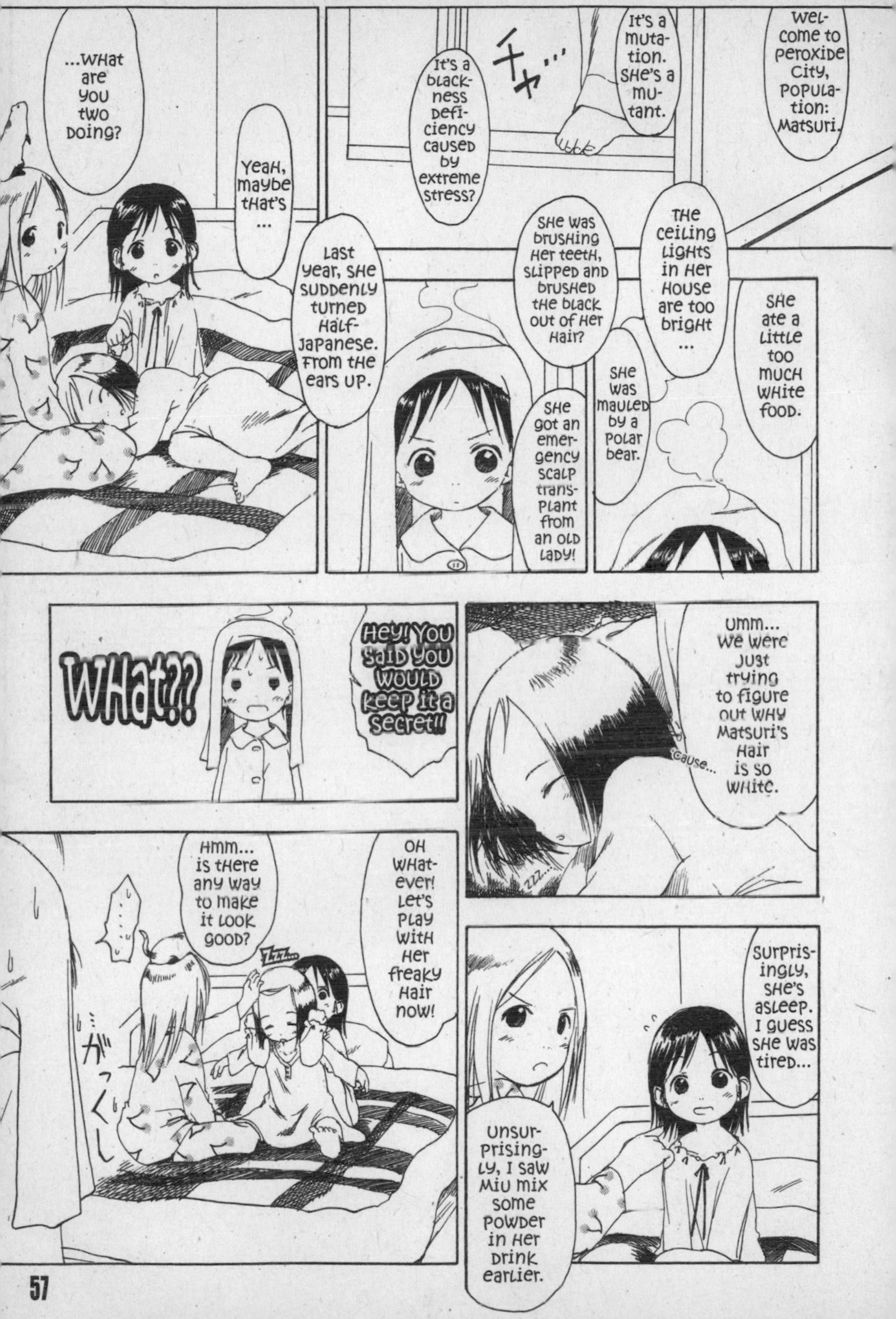
Welcome to peroxide city, population: Matsuri.
It's a mutation. She's a mutant.
チャ…
It's a blackness deficiency caused by extreme stress?
She ate a little too much white food.
The ceiling lights in her house are too bright…
She was mauled by a polar bear.
She was brushing her teeth, slipped and brushed the black out of her hair?
She got an emergency scalp transplant from an old lady!
Last year, she suddenly turned half-Japanese. From the ears up.
Yeah, maybe that's…
…What are you two doing?
Umm… we were just trying to figure out why Matsuri's hair is so white.
'cause…
zzz…
Hey! You said you would keep it a secret!!
WHAT??
Surprisingly, she's asleep. I guess she was tired…
Unsurprisingly, I saw Miu mix some powder in her drink earlier.
Oh whatever! Let's play with her freaky hair now!
Hmm… is there any way to make it look good?
Zzzz…
…
がっくし

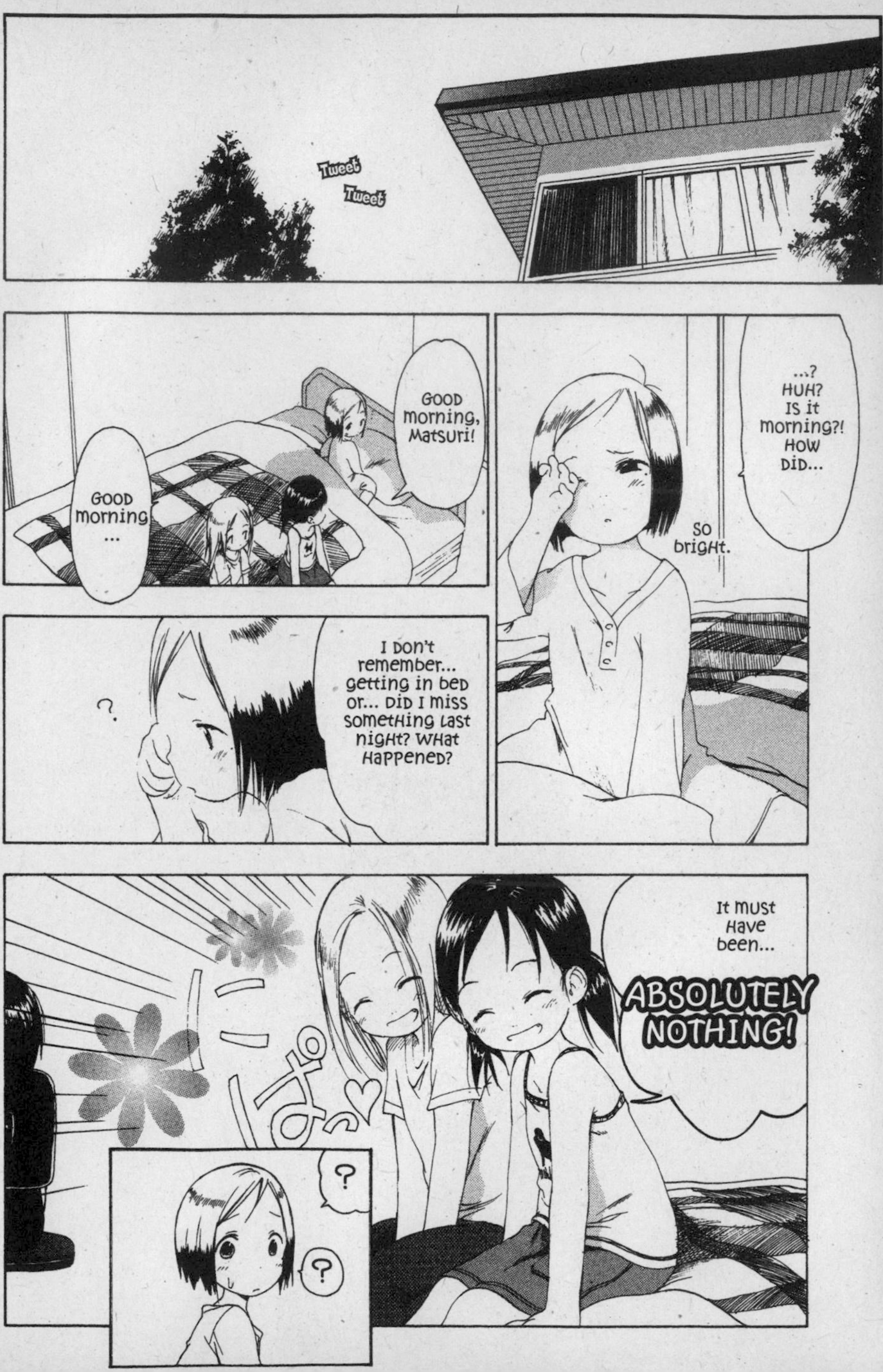
Tweet
Tweet
...? HUH? IS it morning?! HOW DID...
SO bright.
GOOD morning, Matsuri!
GOOD morning ...
I DON't remember... getting in beD or... DID I miss something last night? WHAT HappeneD?
?
It must Have been...
ABSOLUTELY NOTHING!
?
?

PAGES 57

name	season
☑NOBUE	☐SPRING
☐CHIKA	☑SUMMER
☐MIU	☐AUTUMN
☐MATSURI	☐WINTER

PAGE 58

name	*season*
☐NOBUE	☐SPRING
☐CHIKA	☐SUMMER
☐MIU	☐AUTUMN
☐MATSURI	☐WINTER

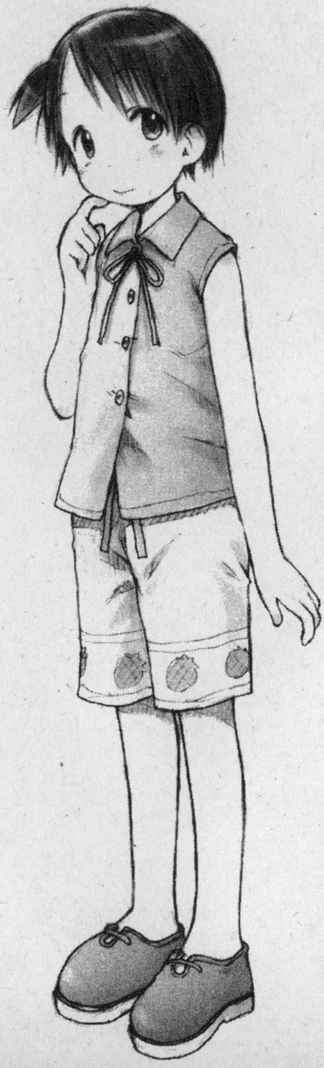

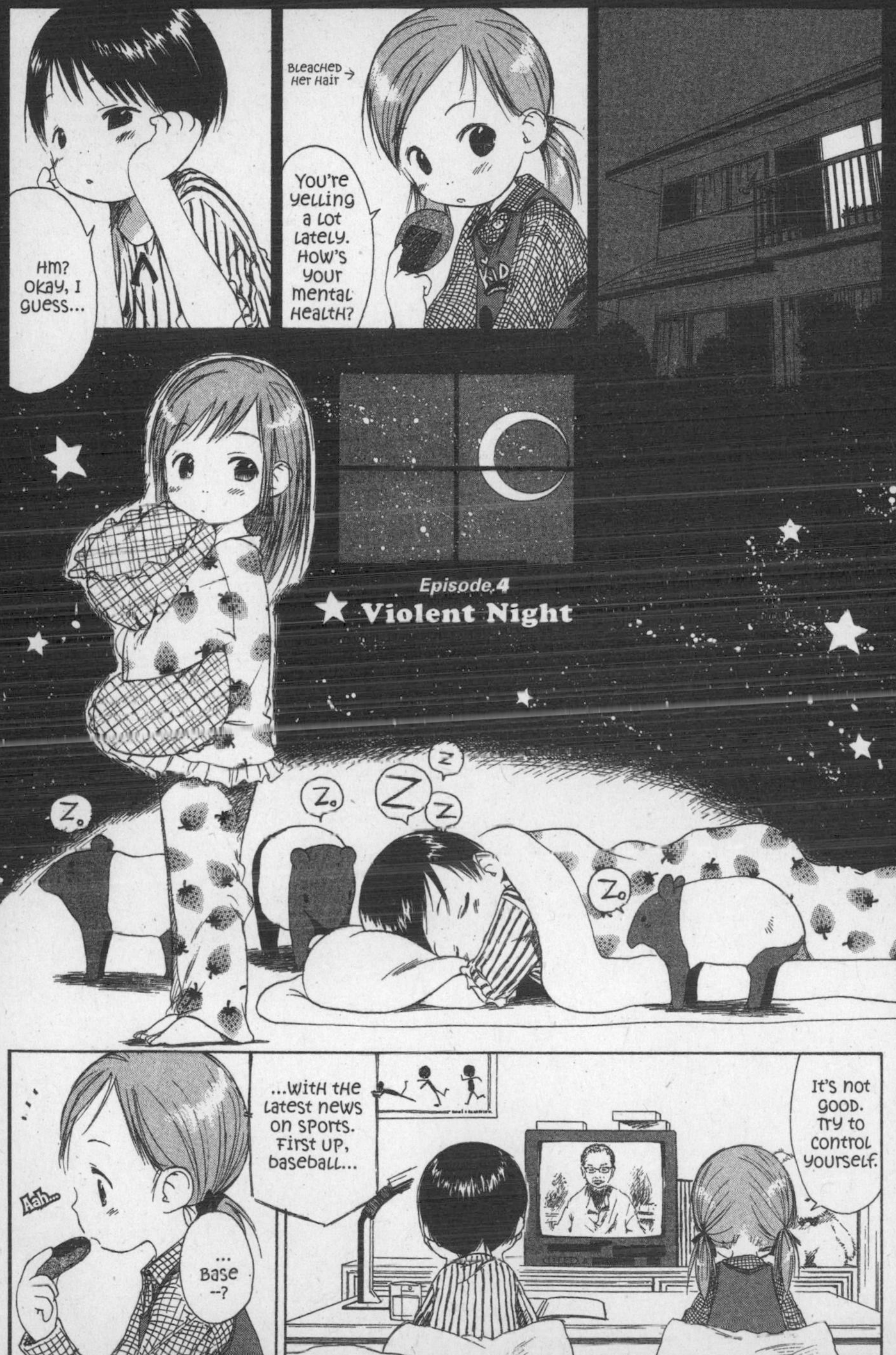
Bleached her hair →
You're yelling a lot lately. How's your mental health?
Hm? Okay, I guess...
Episode.4
★ Violent Night
It's not good. Try to control yourself.
...With the latest news on sports. First up, baseball...
...Base--?
Aah...

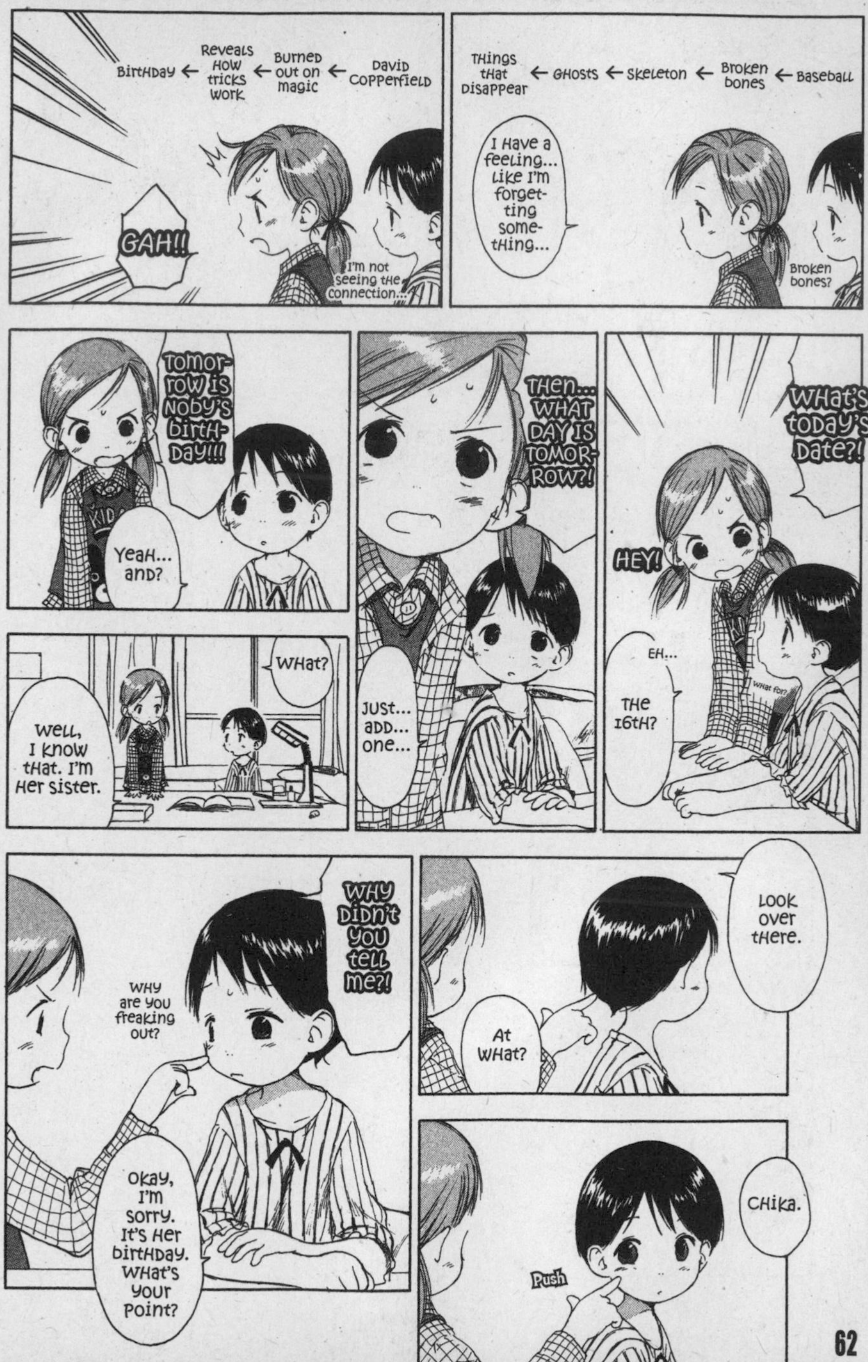

Baseball
Broken bones
Skeleton
Ghosts
Things that disappear
I have a feeling... like I'm forget-ting some-thing...
Broken bones?
David Copperfield
Burned out on magic
Reveals how tricks work
Birthday
GAH!!
I'm not seeing the connection...
What's today's date?!
HEY!
Eh... The 16th?
What for?
Then... what day is tomor-row?!
Just... add... one...
Tomor-row is Noby's birth-day!!!
Yeah... and?
What?
Well, I know that. I'm her sister.
Look over there.
At what?
Chika.
Push
Why didn't you tell me?!
Why are you freaking out?
Okay, I'm sorry. It's her birthday. What's your point?

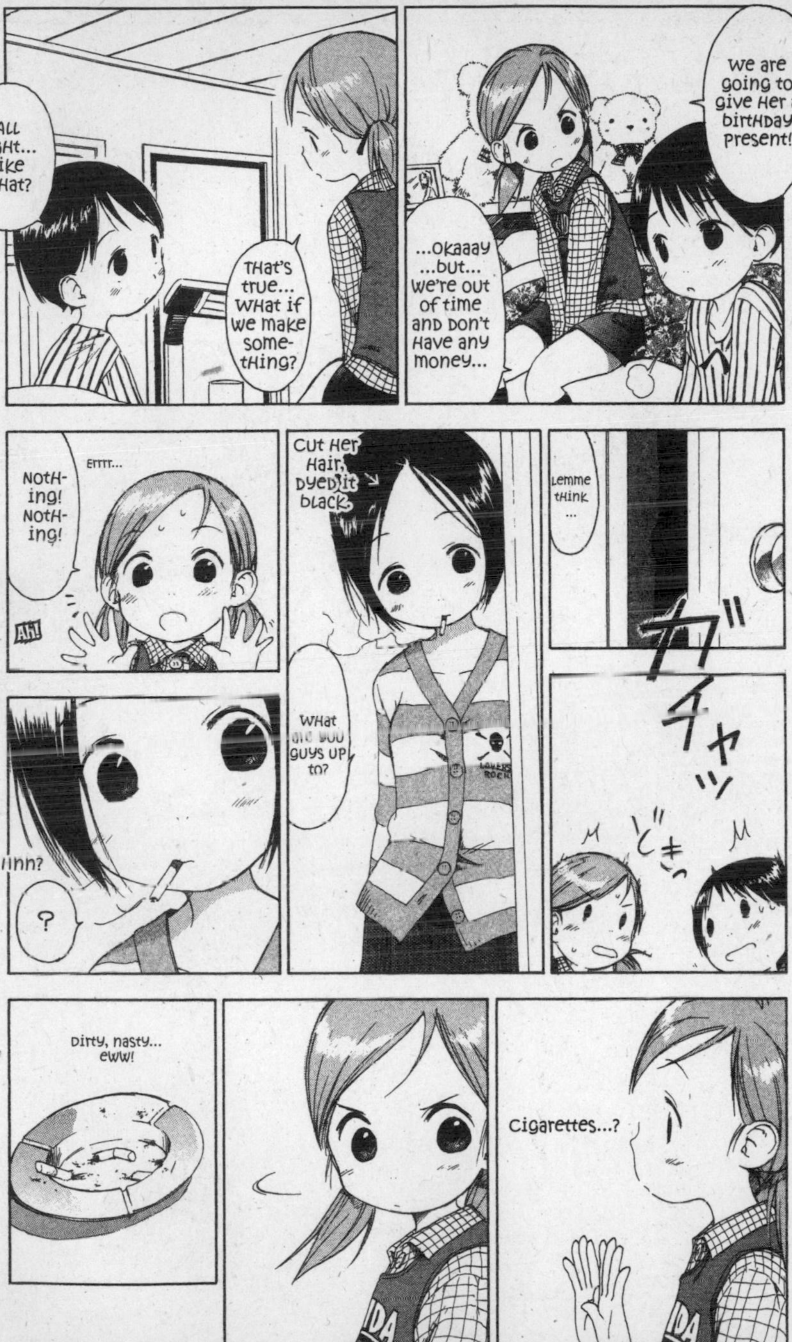
We are going to give her a birthday present!
...Okaaay ...but... we're out of time and don't have any money...
That's true... What if we make some-thing?
All right... like what?
Lemme think ...
ガチャッ
どきっ
Cut her hair, dyed it black
What did you guys up to?
Errrr...
Noth-ing! Noth-ing!
Ah!
Mnn?
?
Cigarettes...?
Dirty, nasty... eww!

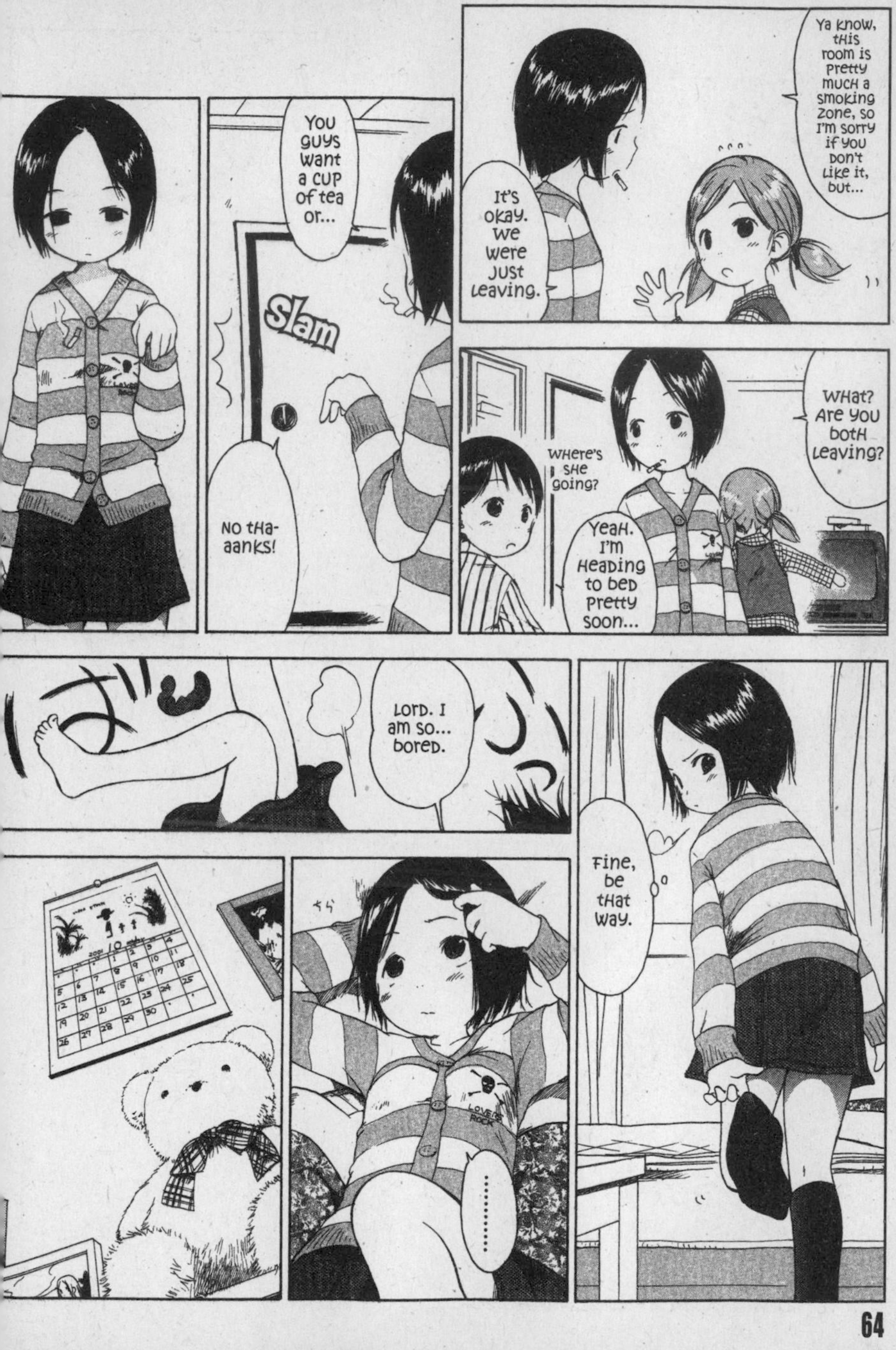
Ya know, this room is pretty much a smoking zone, so I'm sorry if you don't like it, but...
It's okay. We were just leaving.
What? Are you both leaving?
Where's she going?
Yeah. I'm heading to bed pretty soon...
You guys want a cup of tea or...
Slam
No thaanks!
Fine, be that way.
Lord. I am so... bored.
……

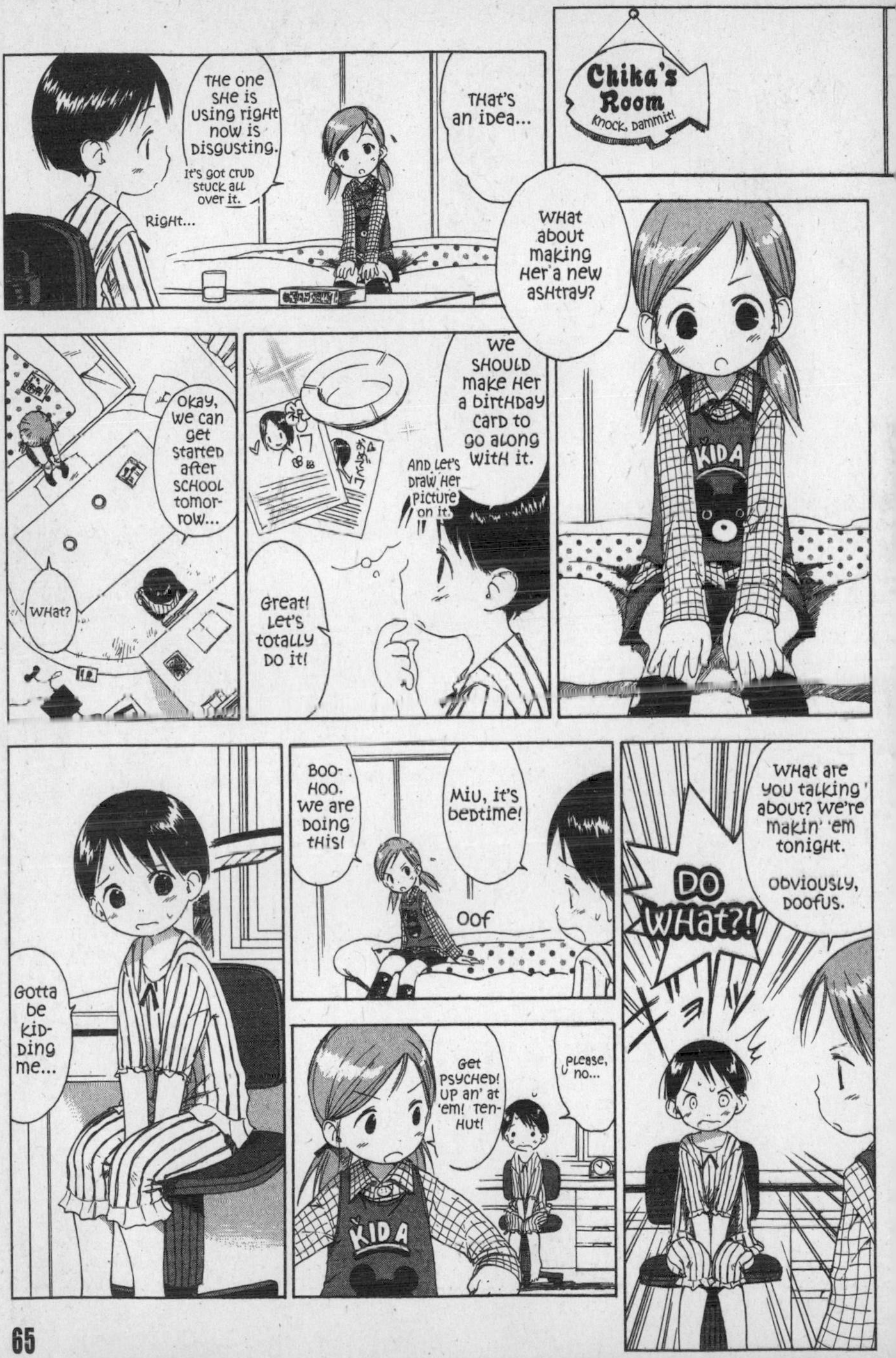

Chika's Room
Knock, dammit!
What about making her a new ashtray?
That's an idea...
The one she is using right now is disgusting.
It's got crud stuck all over it.
Right...
We should make her a birthday card to go along with it.
And let's draw her picture on it.
Great! Let's totally do it!
Okay, we can get started after school tomor-row...
What?
What are you talking about? We're makin' 'em tonight.
Obviously, doofus.
DO WHAT?!
Miu, it's bedtime!
Boo-hoo. We are doing this!
Oof
Please, no...
Get psyched! Up an' at 'em! Ten-hut!
Gotta be kid-ding me...

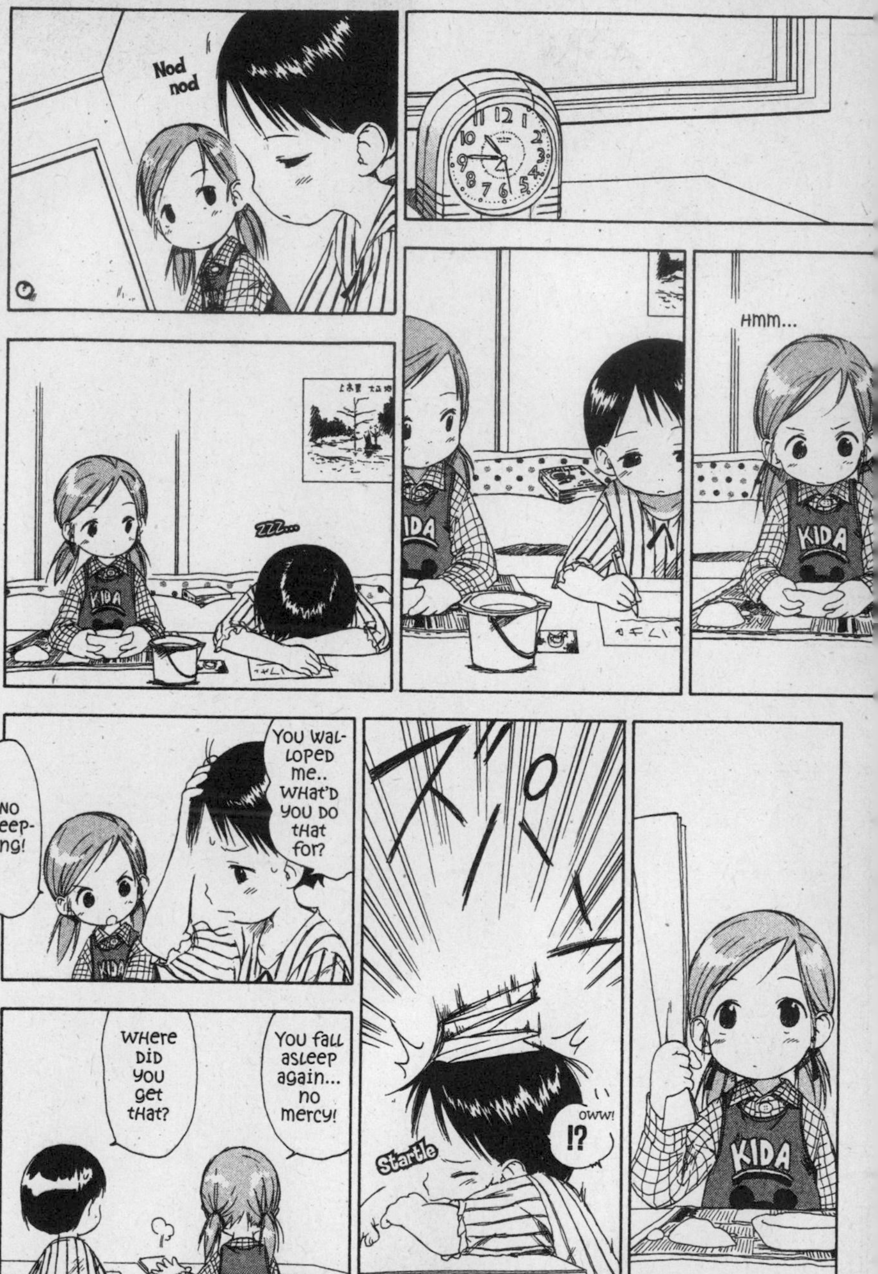
Nod nod
Hmm...
ZZZ...
!?
OWW!
Startle
You wal-loped me.. What'd you do that for?
No sleep-ing!
You fall asleep again... no mercy!
Where did you get that?

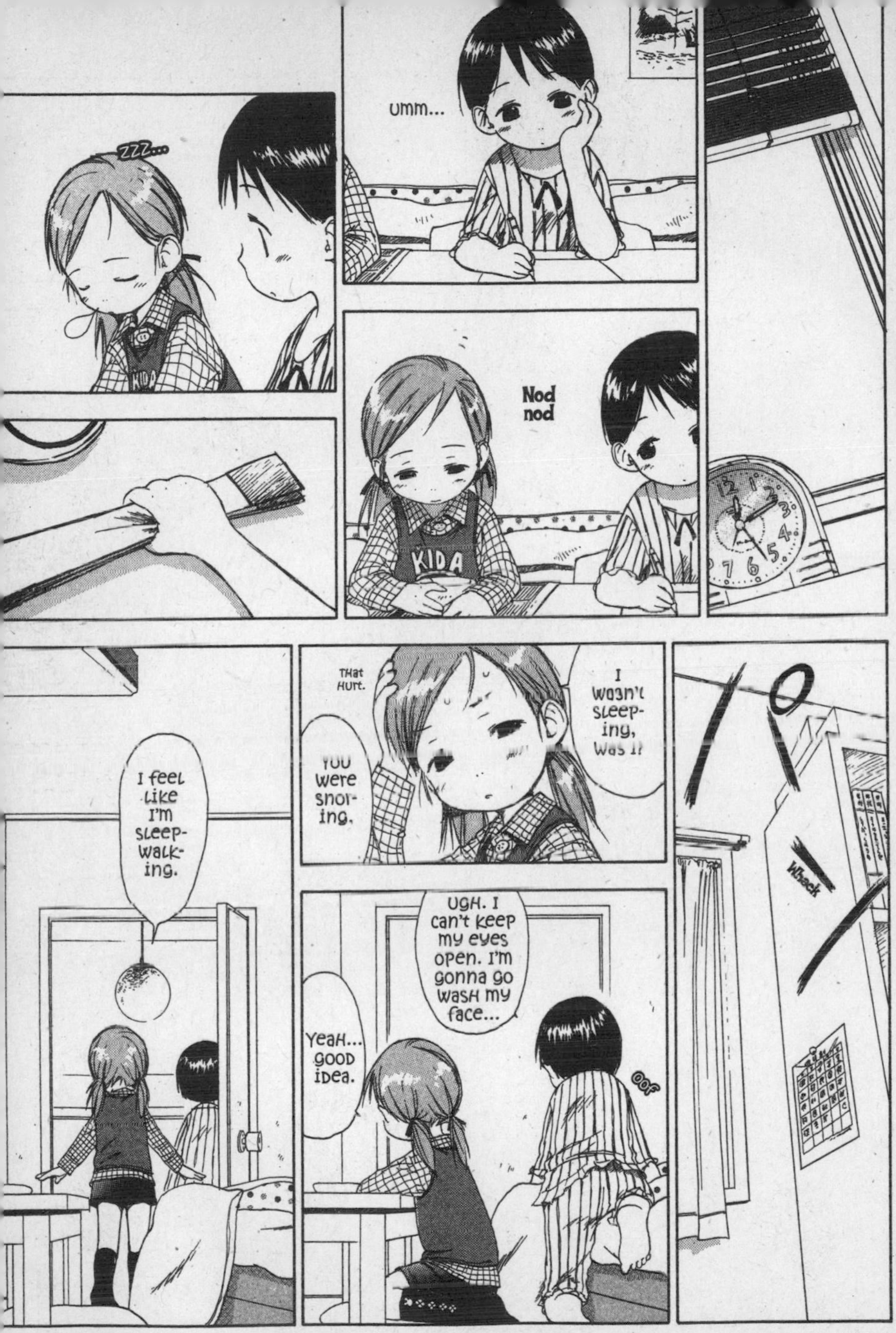
umm...
zzz...
Nod nod
Whack
I wasn't sleeping, was I?
That hurt.
You were snoring.
Ugh. I can't keep my eyes open. I'm gonna go wash my face...
oof
Yeah... good idea.
I feel like I'm sleepwalking.

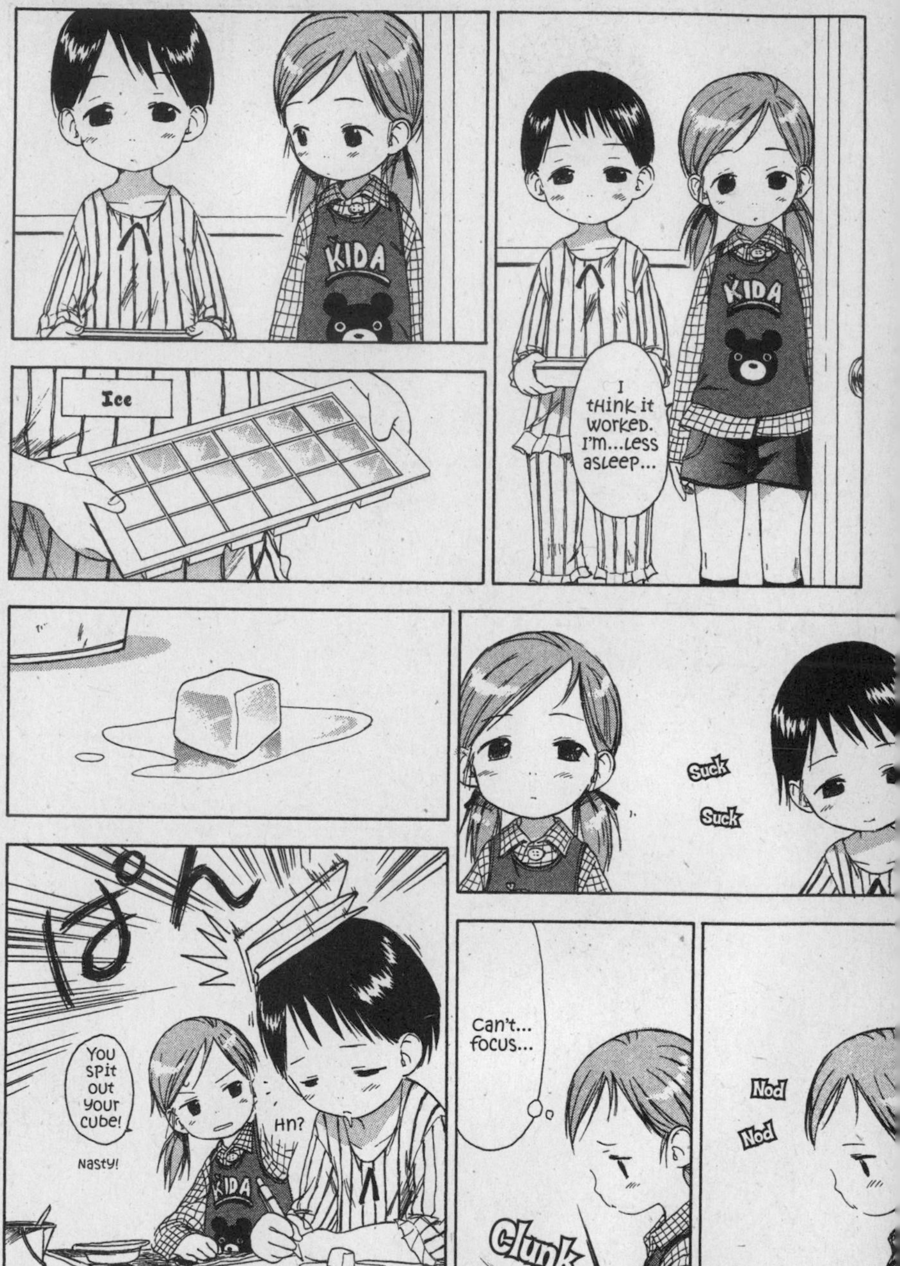

I think it worked. I'm...less asleep...
Ice
Suck
Suck
Nod
Nod
Can't... focus...
Clunk
ぱん
Hn?
You spit out your cube!
Nasty!

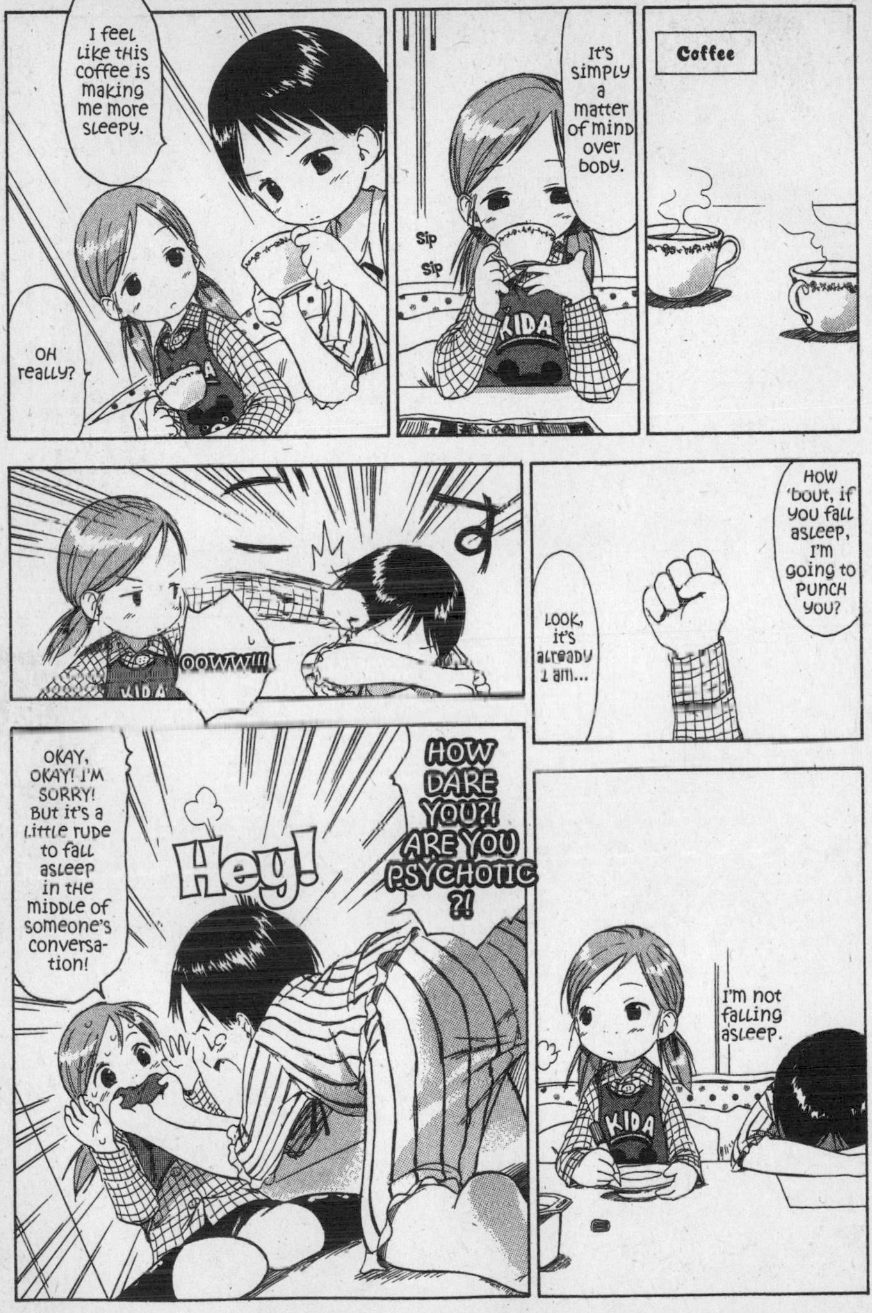

Coffee
It's simply a matter of mind over body.
Sip
Sip
I feel like this coffee is making me more sleepy.
Oh really?
How 'bout, if you fall asleep, I'm going to punch you?
Look, it's already I am...
OOWW!!!
I'm not falling asleep.
HOW DARE YOU?! ARE YOU PSYCHOTIC?!
Hey!
OKAY, OKAY! I'M SORRY! But it's a little rude to fall asleep in the middle of someone's conversation!

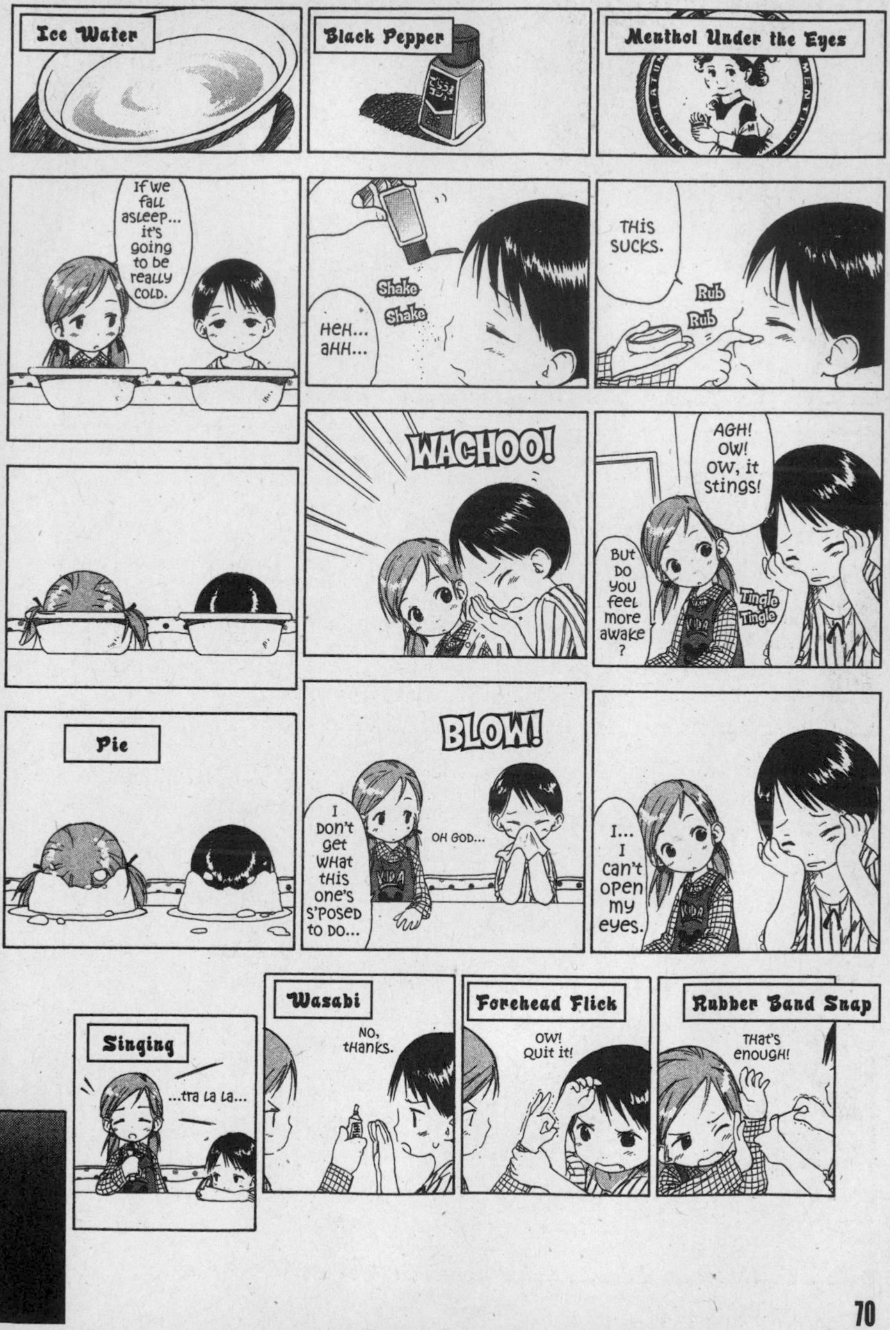
Menthol Under the Eyes
THIS SUCKS.
Rub
Rub
AGH! OW! OW, it stings!
But DO you feel more awake?
Tingle
Tingle
I... I can't open my eyes.
Black Pepper
Shake
Shake
HeH... aHH...
WACHOO!
BLOW!
OH GOD...
I Don't get WHat tHis one's s'posed to Do...
Ice Water
If we fall asleep... it's going to be really COLD.
Pie
Rubber Band Snap
THat's enougH!
Forehead Flick
OW! Quit it!
Wasabi
NO, tHanks.
Singing
...tra la la...

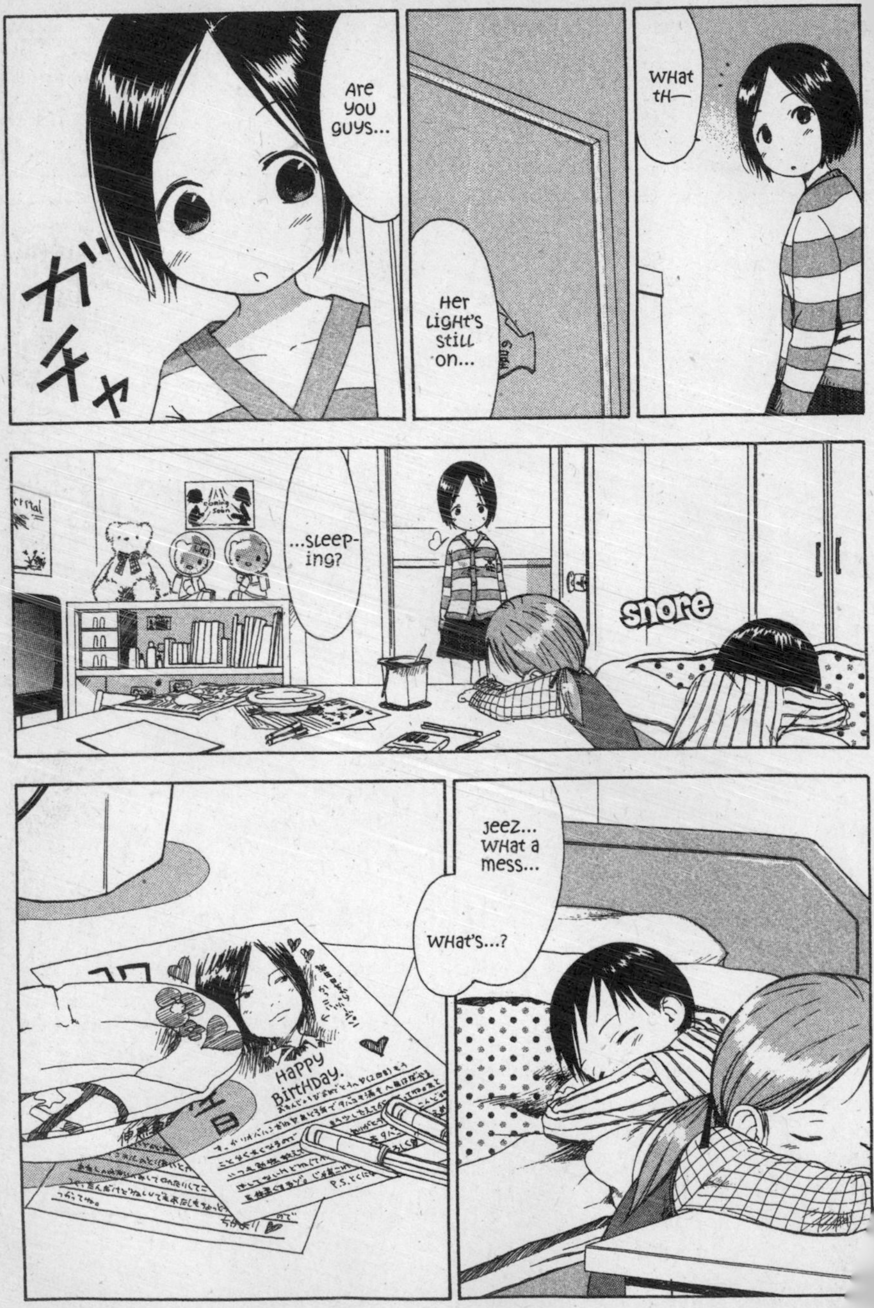

WHAT TH—
Her LIGHT'S still on...
Are YOU GUYS...
ガチャ
...SLEEP-ING?
snore
JEEZ... WHAT A mess...
WHAT'S...?
HAPPY BIRTHDAY.

PAGE 74

name	*season*
☐NOBUE	☐SPRING
☐CHIKA	■SUMMER
☐MIU	☐AUTUMN
■MATSURI	☐WINTER

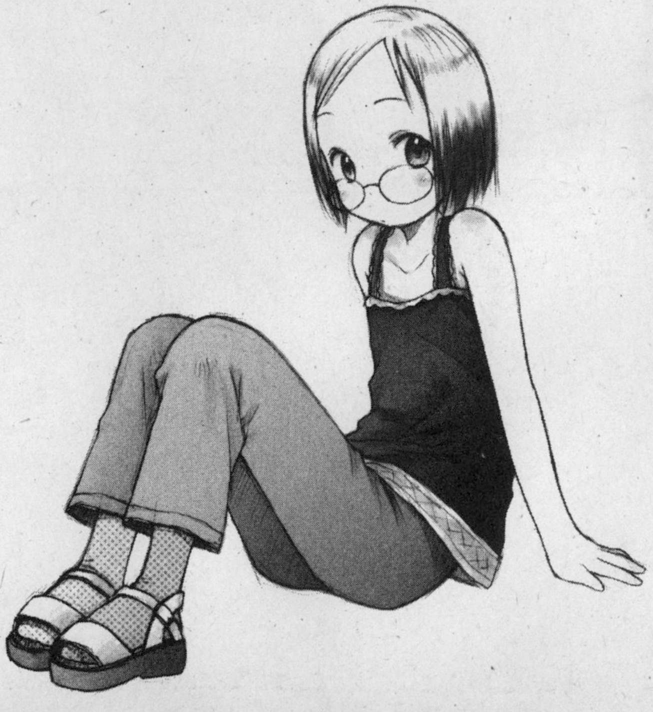

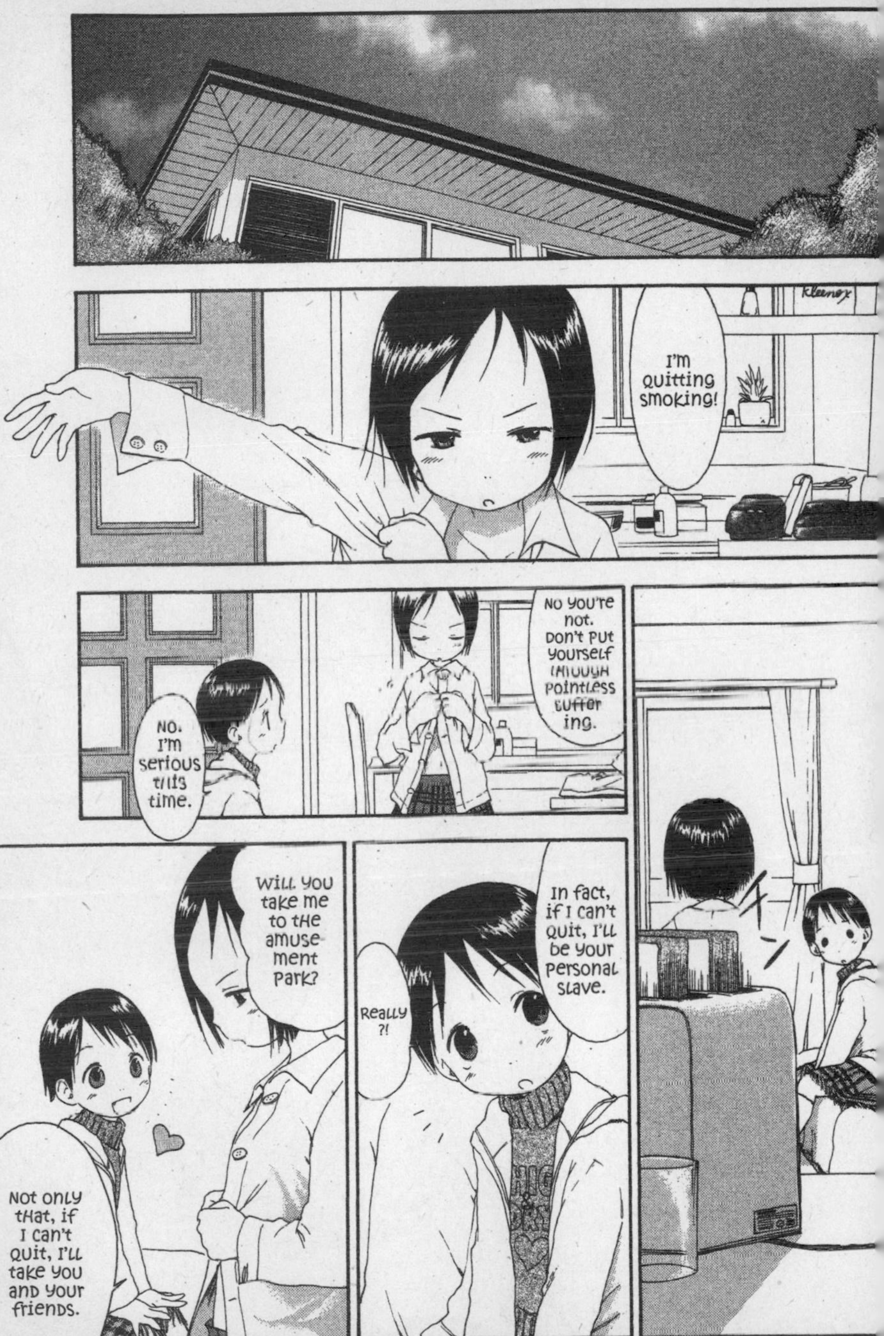
Kleenex
I'm quitting smoking!
No you're not. Don't put yourself through pointless suffering.
No. I'm serious this time.
In fact, if I can't quit, I'll be your personal slave.
Really?!
Will you take me to the amusement park?
Not only that, if I can't quit, I'll take you and your friends.

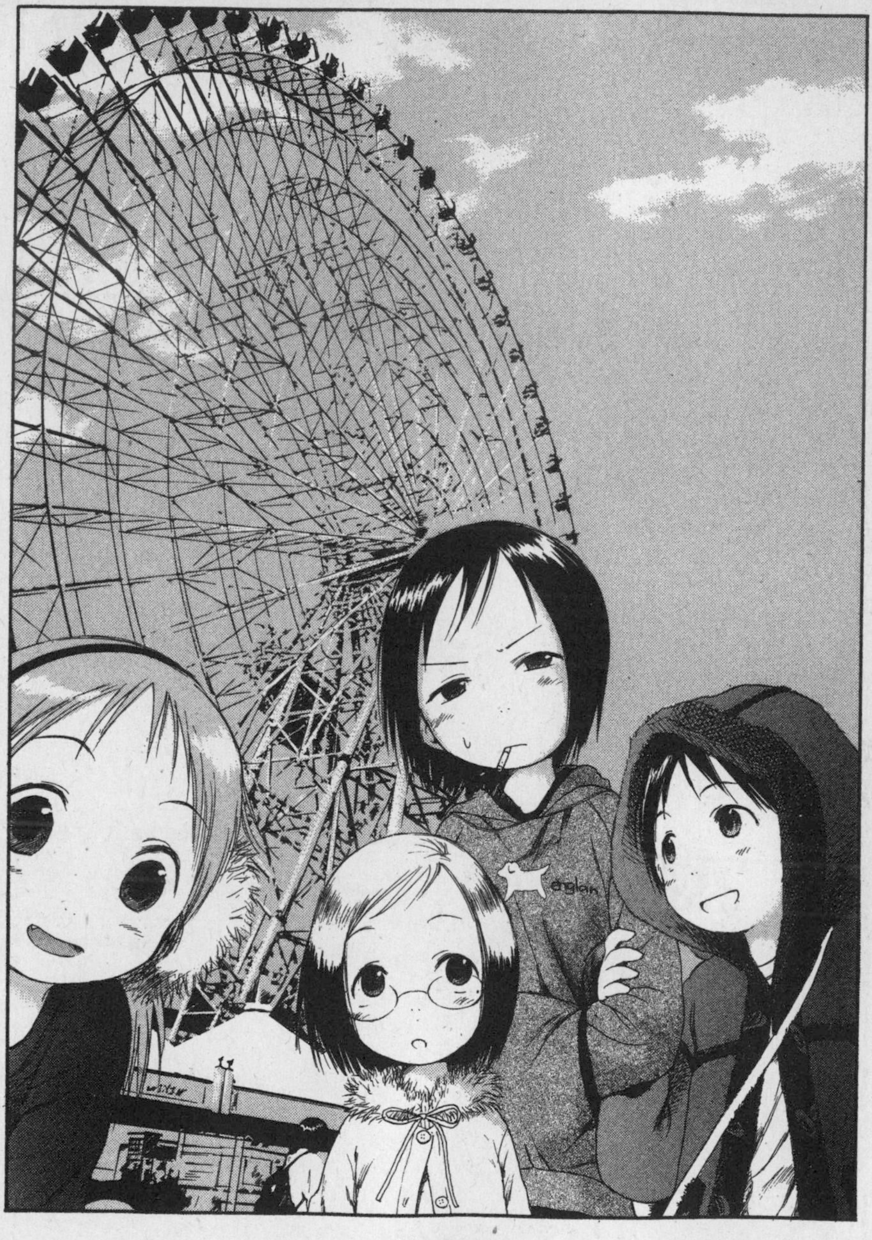

Episode.5
BURNT TURKEY

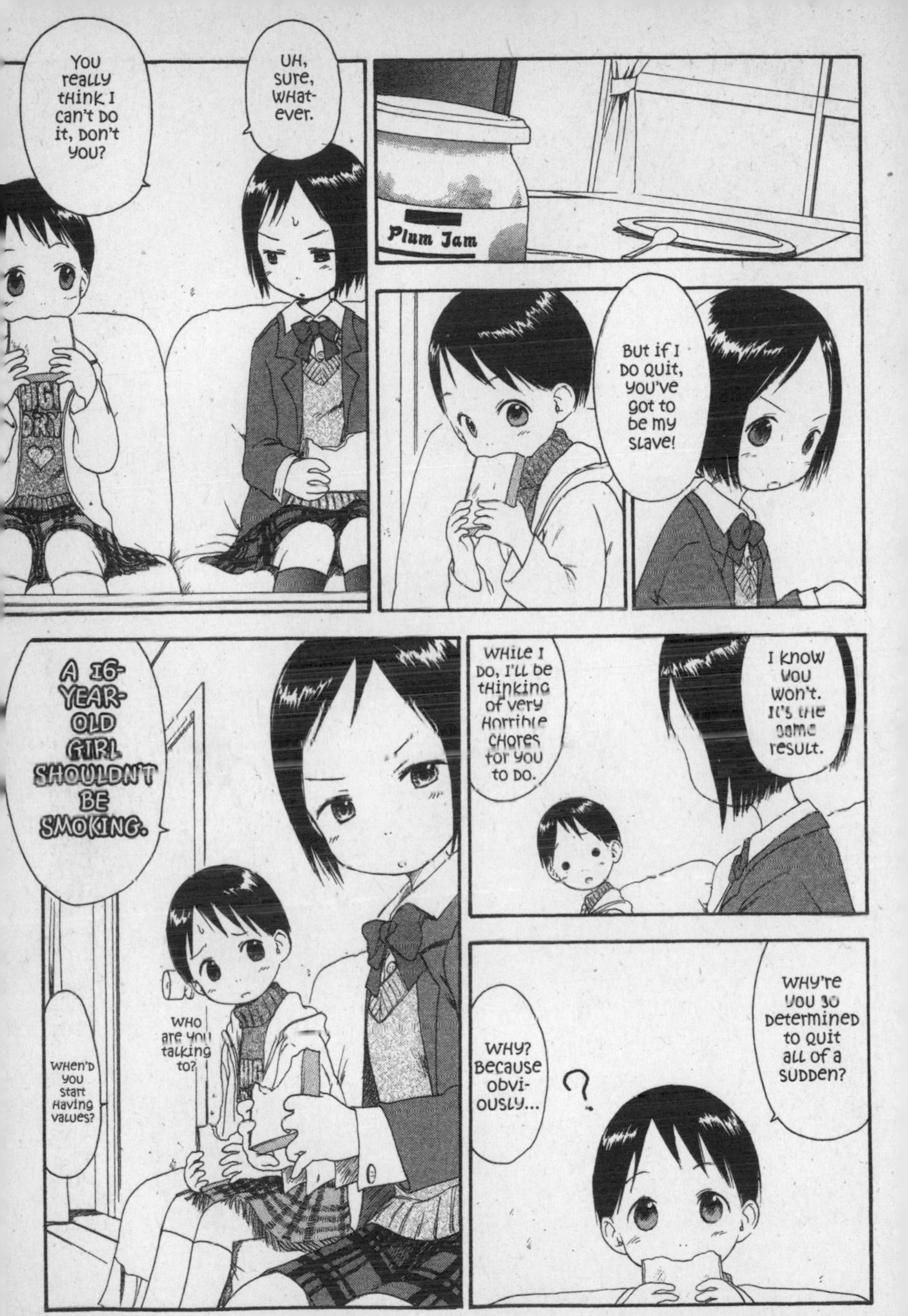
Plum Jam
But if I do quit, you've got to be my slave!
Uh, sure, whatever.
You really think I can't do it, don't you?
I know you won't. It's the same result.
While I do, I'll be thinking of very horrible chores for you to do.
Why're you so determined to quit all of a sudden?
Why? Because obviously...
?
A 16-year-old girl shouldn't be smoking.
Who are you talking to?
When'd you start having values?

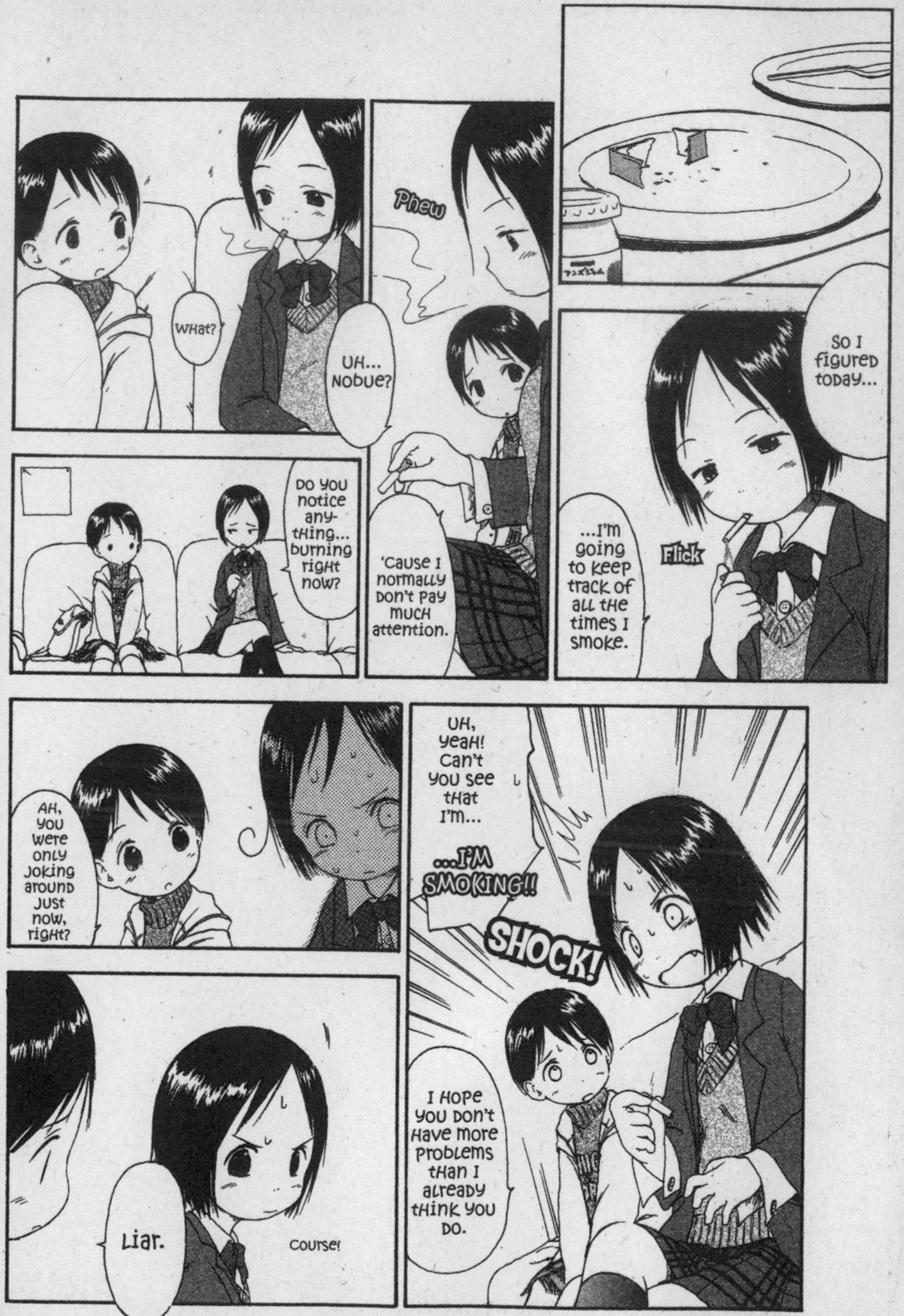

So I figured today...
...I'm going to keep track of all the times I smoke.
Flick
Phew
Uh... Nobue?
'Cause I normally don't pay much attention.
What?
Do you notice anything... burning right now?
Uh, yeah! Can't you see that I'm...
...I'M SMOKING!!
SHOCK!
I hope you don't have more problems than I already think you do.
Ah, you were only joking around just now, right?
Course!
Liar.

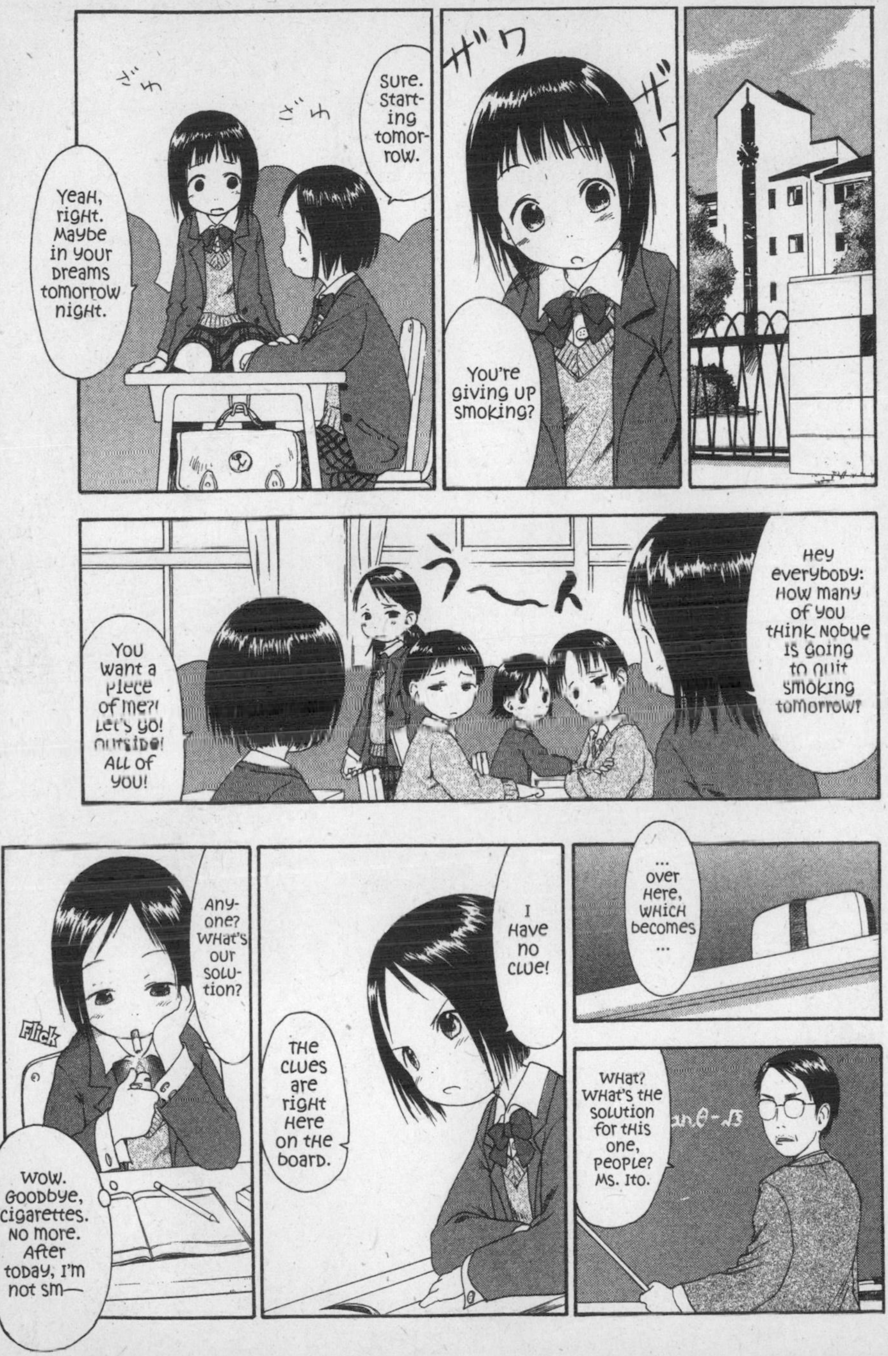
ザワ
ザワ
You're giving up smoking?
Sure. Starting tomorrow.
ざわ
ざわ
Yeah, right. Maybe in your dreams tomorrow night.
Hey everybody: How many of you think Nobue is going to quit smoking tomorrow?
う〜ん
You want a piece of me?! Let's go! Outside! All of you!
... over here, which becomes ...
What? What's the solution for this one, people? Ms. Ito.
I have no clue!
The clues are right here on the board.
Anyone? What's our solution?
Flick
Wow. Goodbye, cigarettes. No more. After today, I'm not sm—

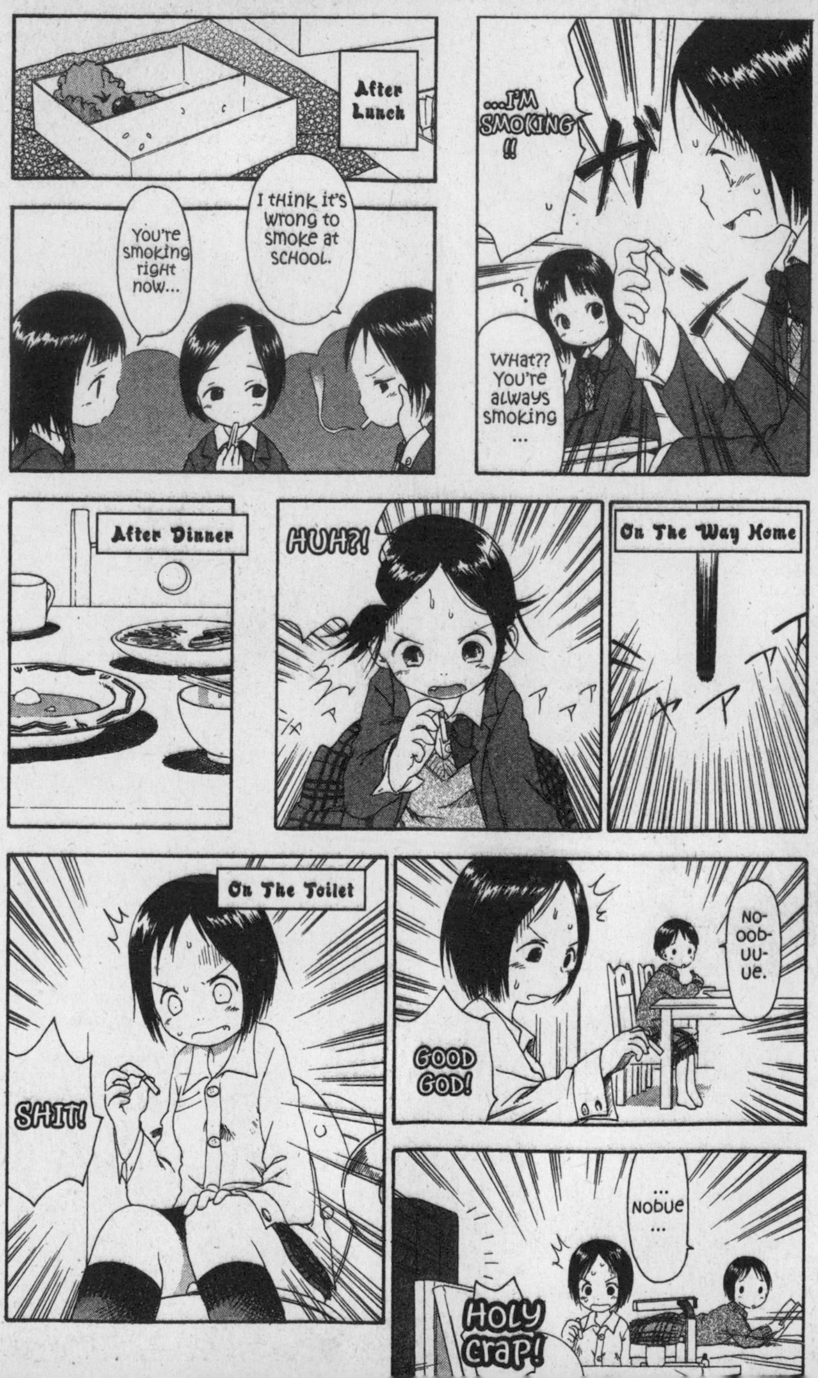
After Lunch
I think it's wrong to smoke at school.
You're smoking right now...
...I'M SMOKING!!
WHAT?? You're always smoking...
After Dinner
HUH?!
On The Way Home
On The Toilet
SHIT!
NO-OOB-UUU-UE.
GOOD GOD!
...NOBUE...
HOLY CRAP!

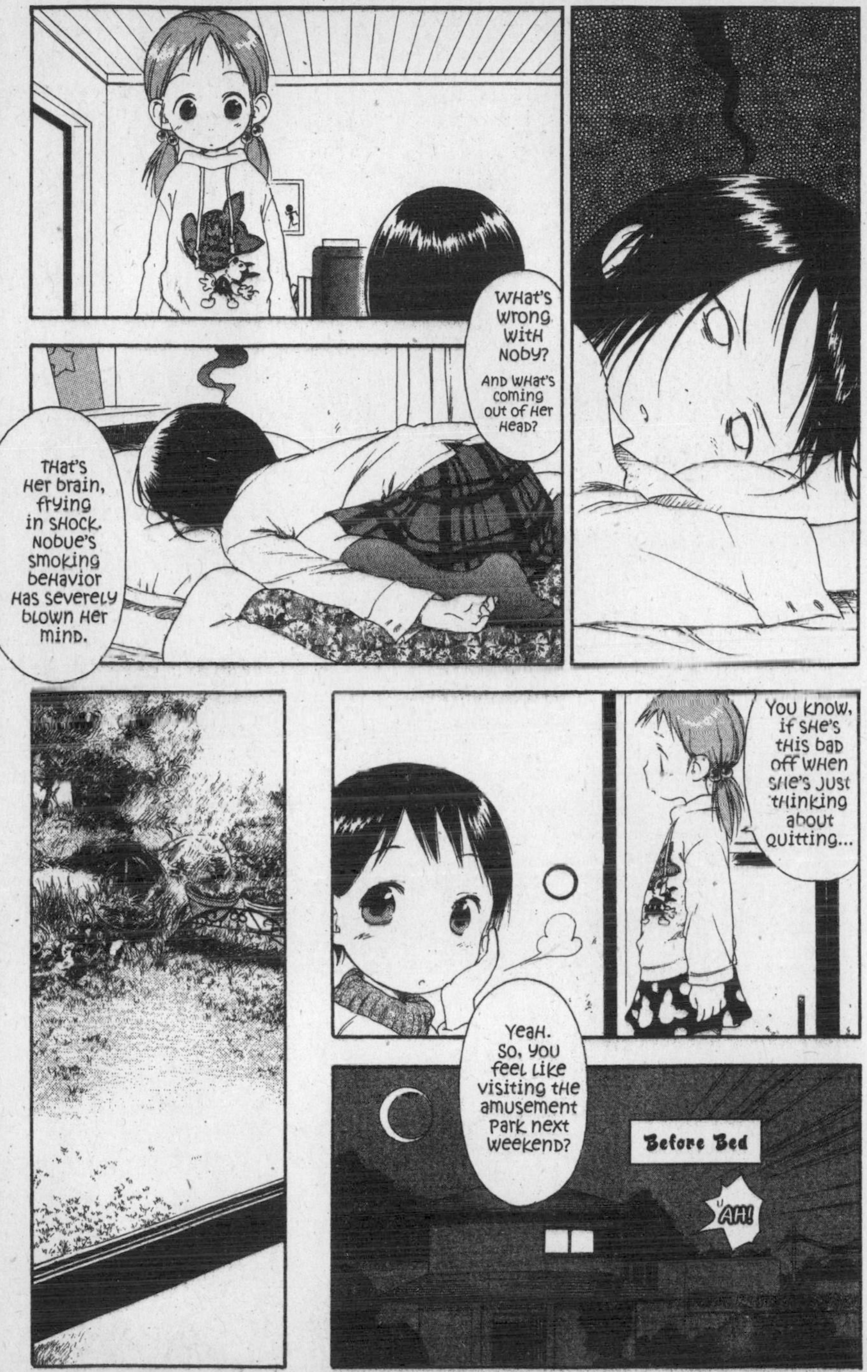

What's wrong with Noby?
And what's coming out of her head?
That's her brain, frying in shock. Nobue's smoking behavior has severely blown her mind.
You know, if she's this bad off when she's just thinking about quitting...
Yeah. So, you feel like visiting the amusement park next weekend?
Before Bed
AH!

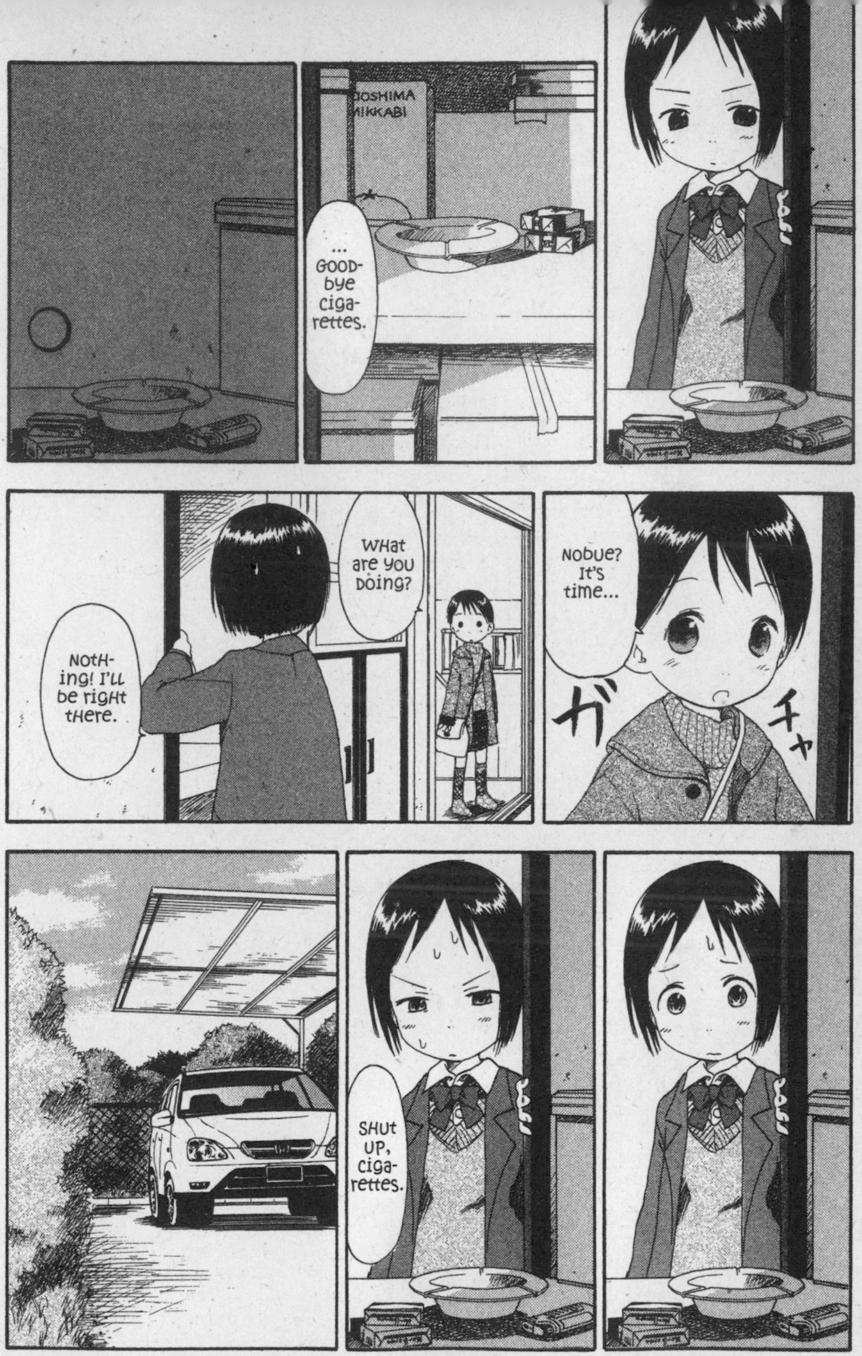

OOSHIMA
MIKKABI
... GOOD-bye ciga-rettes.
Nobue? It's time...
ガ
チャ
What are you Doing?
Noth-ing! I'll be right there.
SHUt UP, ciga-rettes.

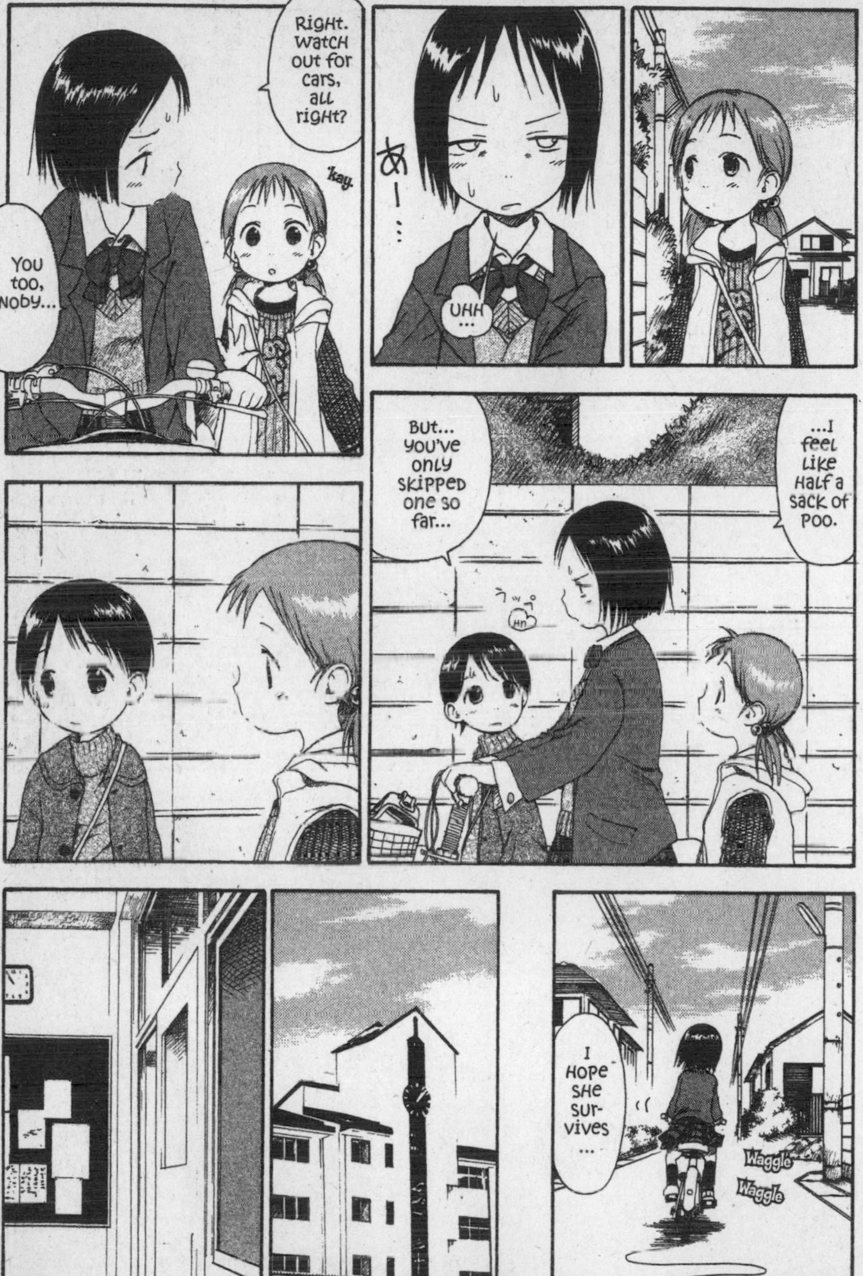
あー…
UHH...
Right. Watch out for cars, all right?
'kay.
You too, Noby...
...I feel like half a sack of poo.
But... you've only skipped one so far...
HN
I hope she survives...
Waggle
Waggle

You're really going through with it?

Yes...

Ito!

What?

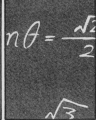

$$n\theta = \frac{\sqrt{2}}{2}$$

$$\sqrt{3}$$

$\measuredangle\theta \leqq 180° \cap x^3$

$\sin\theta = \frac{\sqrt{2}}{2}$

$\theta = \frac{\sqrt{2}}{2}t$

How about digging in on this one?

Yummy.

HA!

Ito... what on earth are you doing?

What?

OH GOD.

Are you okay?

Don't hurt yourself...

NO prob.

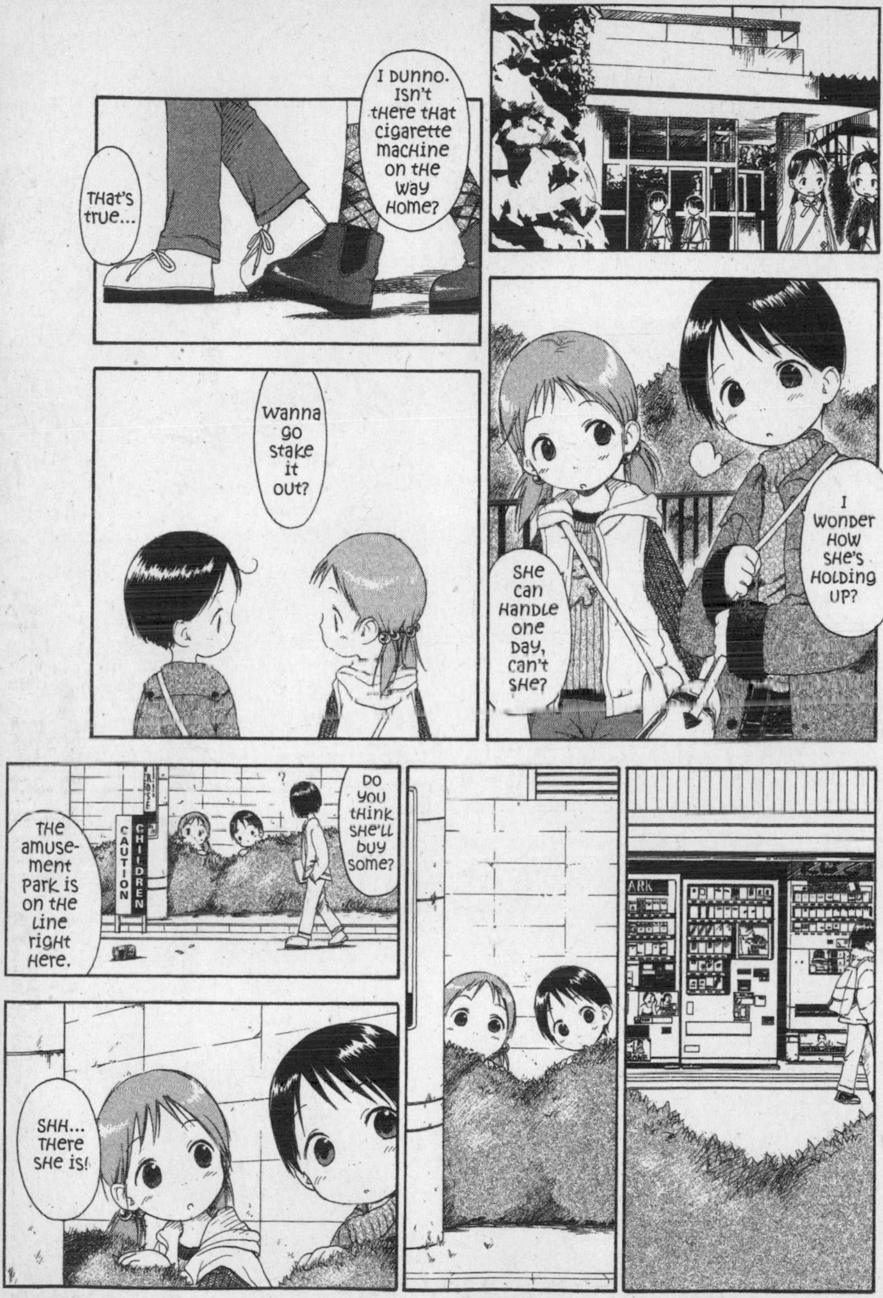
I wonder how she's holding up?
She can handle one day, can't she?
I dunno. Isn't there that cigarette machine on the way home?
That's true...
Wanna go stake it out?
Do you think she'll buy some?
CAUTION
CHILDREN
The amusement park is on the line right here.
SHH... There she is!

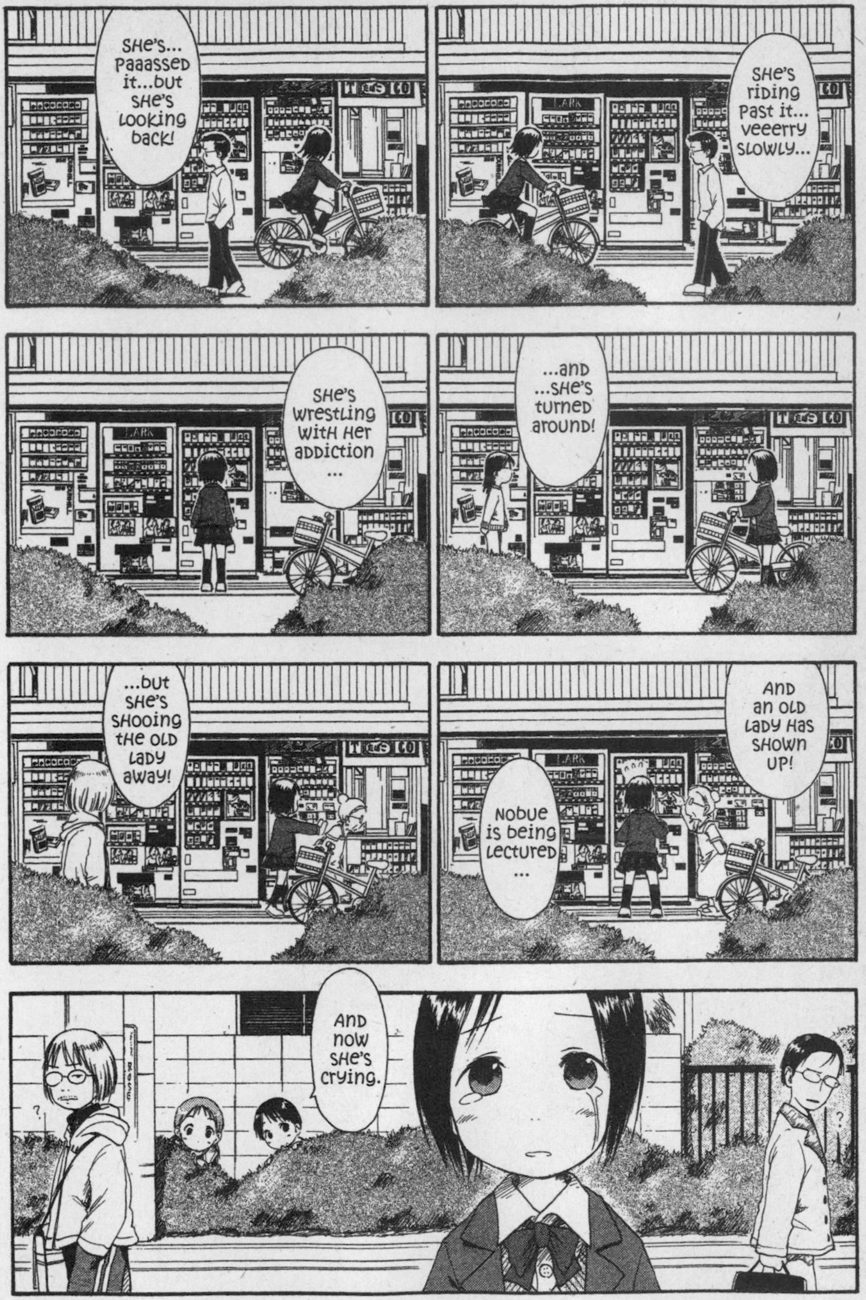
SHE's riding past it... veeerry slowly...
SHE's... paaassed it...but SHE's looking back!
...and ...SHE's turned around!
SHE's wrestling with her addiction ...
And an old lady has shown up!
Nobue is being lectured ...
...but SHE's shooing the old lady away!
And now SHE's crying.

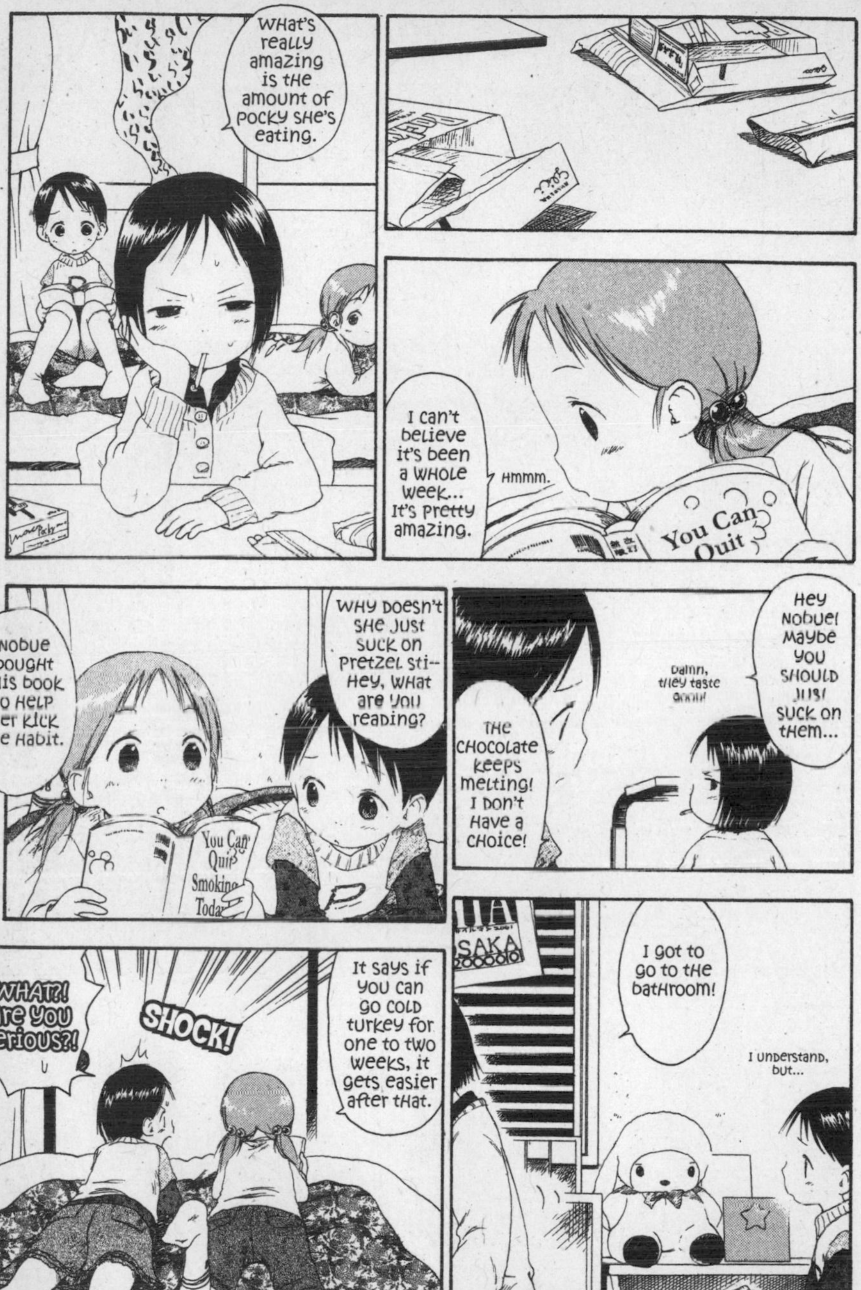
Hmmm.
I can't believe it's been a whole week... It's pretty amazing.
You Can Quit
What's really amazing is the amount of Pocky she's eating.
Hey Nobue! Maybe you should just suck on them...
Damn, they taste good!
The chocolate keeps melting! I don't have a choice!
Why doesn't she just suck on pretzel sti-- Hey, what are you reading?
Nobue bought this book to help her kick the habit.
You Can Quit Smoking
I got to go to the bathroom!
I understand, but...
It says if you can go cold turkey for one to two weeks, it gets easier after that.
SHOCK!
WHAT?! Are you serious?!

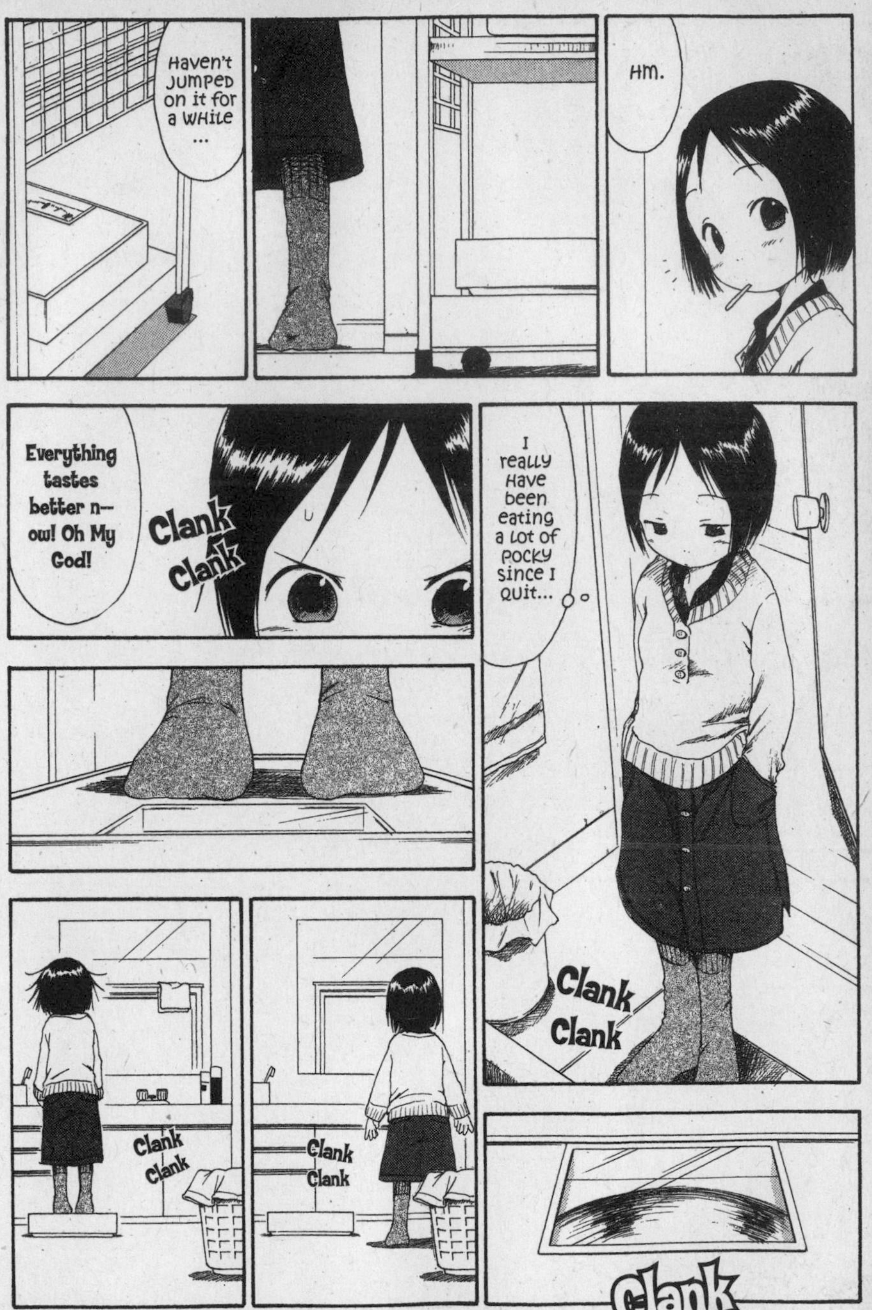

Hm.
Haven't jumped on it for a while ...
I really have been eating a lot of pocky since I quit...
Clank
Clank
Everything tastes better n--ow! Oh my God!
Clank
Clank
clank
Clank
Clank
Clank
Clank

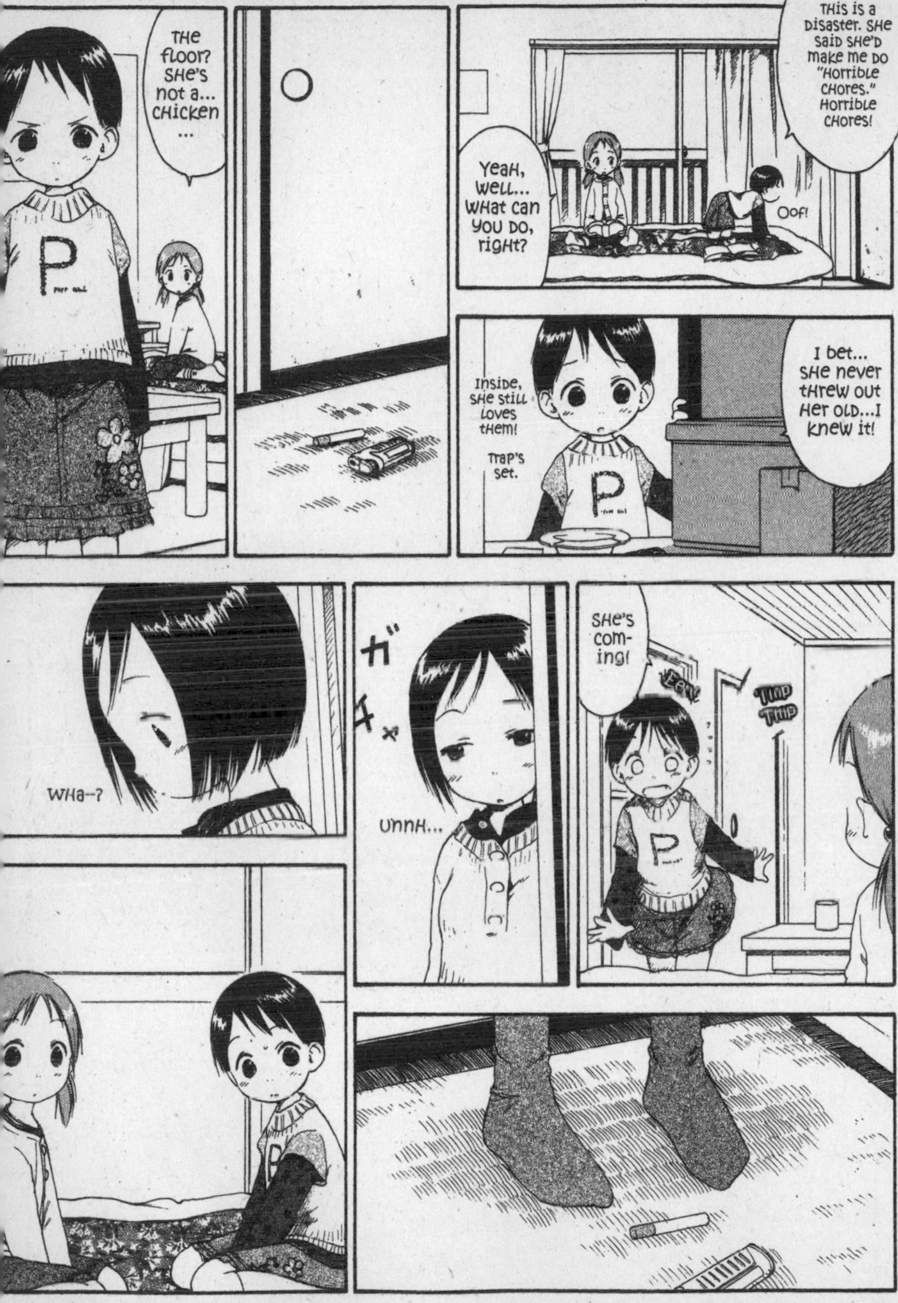
This is a disaster. She said she'd make me do "Horrible chores." Horrible chores!
Oof!
Yeah, well... What can you do, right?
I bet... She never threw out her old...I knew it!
Inside, she still loves them!
Trap's set.
The floor? She's not a... chicken ...
She's com-ing!
THIP THIP
ガ
Unnh...
Wha--?

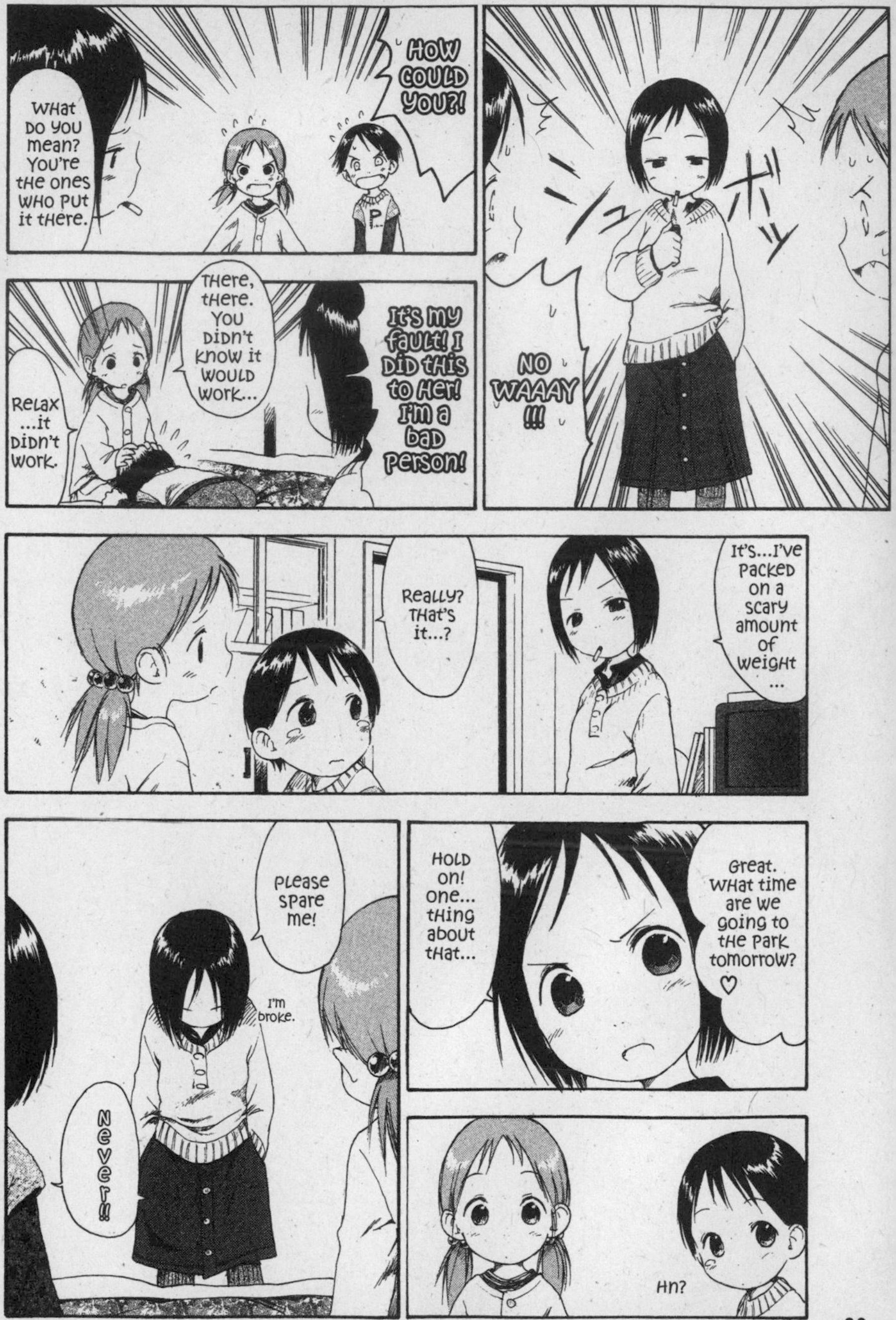
シュ
ボッ
NO WAAAY !!!
HOW COULD YOU?!
What do you mean? You're the ones who put it there.
It's my fault! I did this to her! I'm a bad person!
There, there. You didn't know it would work...
Relax ...it didn't work.
It's...I've packed on a scary amount of weight ...
Really? That's it...?
Great. What time are we going to the park tomorrow? ♡
Hold on! One... thing about that...
Hn?
Please spare me!
I'm broke.
Never!!

PAGE 91

name	*season*
☑NOBUE	☐SPRING
☐CHIKA	☐SUMMER
☐MIU	☑AUTUMN
☐MATSURI	☐WINTER

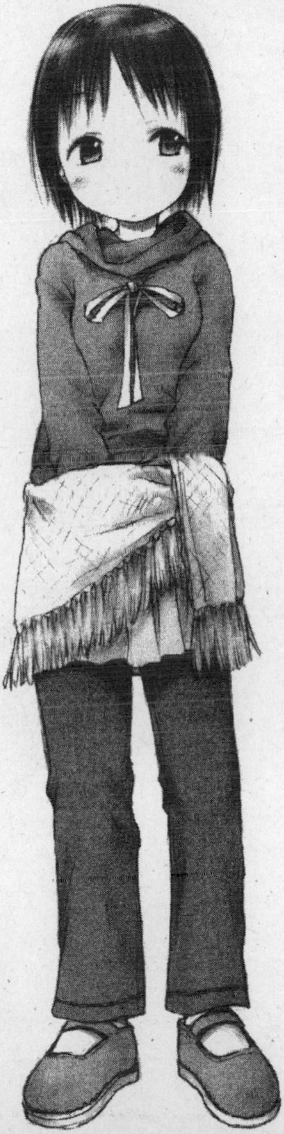

PAGE 92

name	*season*
□NOBUE	□SPRING
□CHIKA	□SUMMER
□MIU	□AUTUMN
□MATSURI	□WINTER

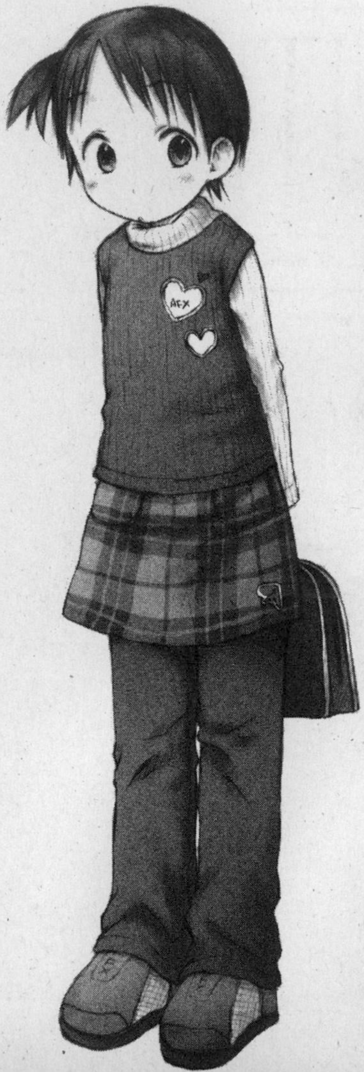

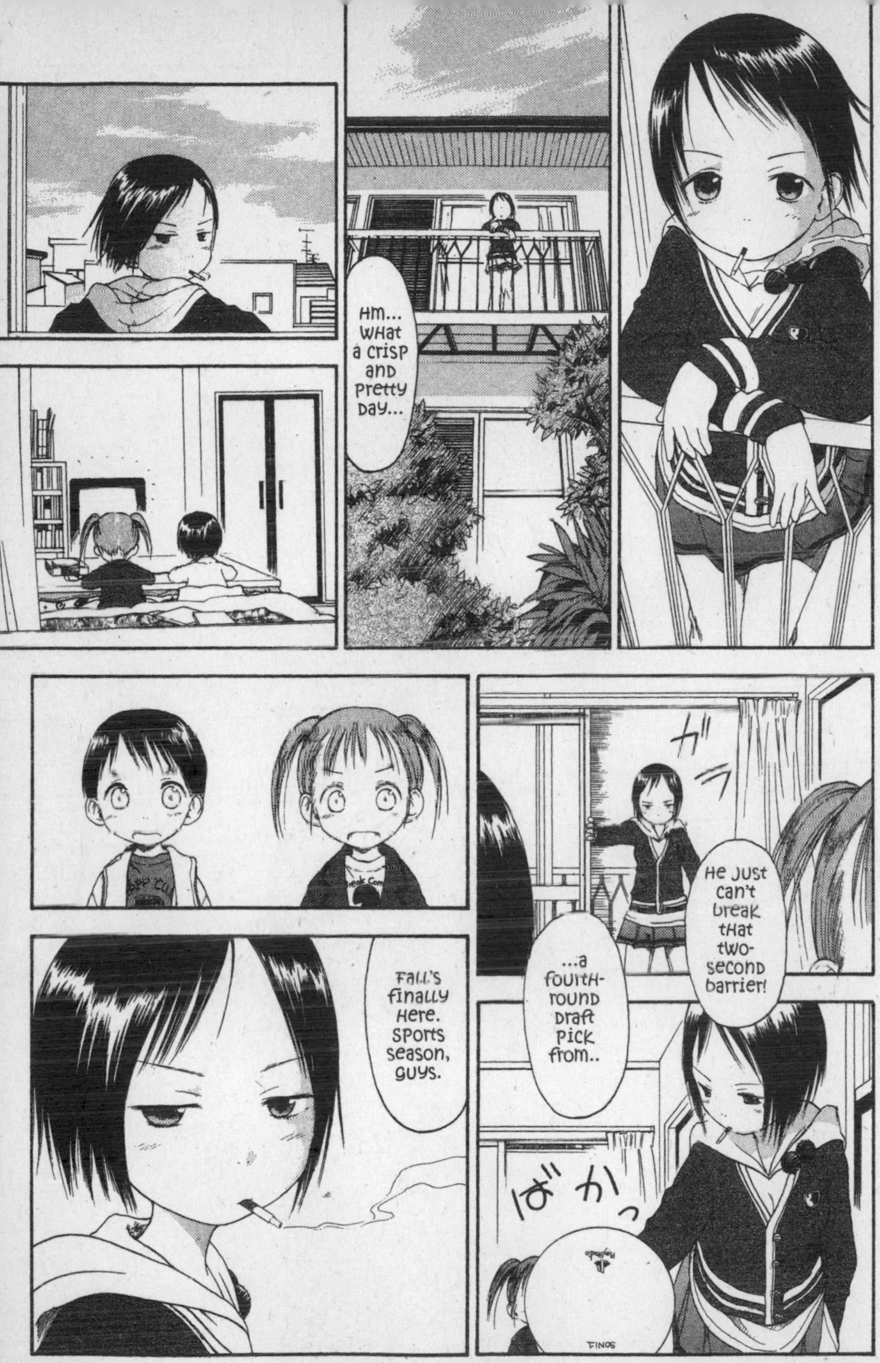
Hm... what a crisp and pretty day...
ガラ
He just can't break that two-second barrier!
...a fourth-round draft pick from..
ばかっ
Fall's finally here. Sports season, guys.

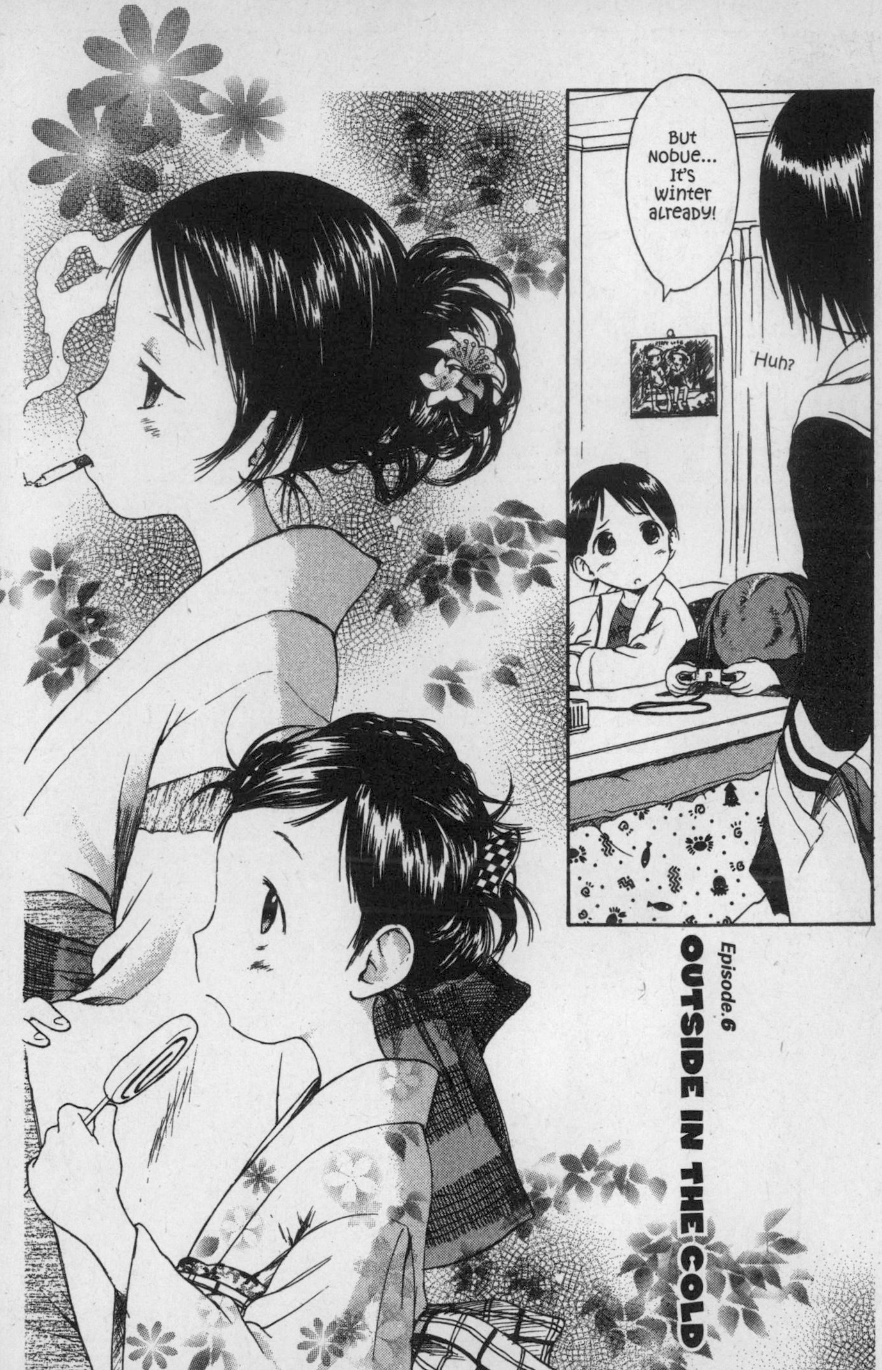
But Nobue... It's winter already!
Huh?
Episode.6
OUTSIDE IN THE COLD

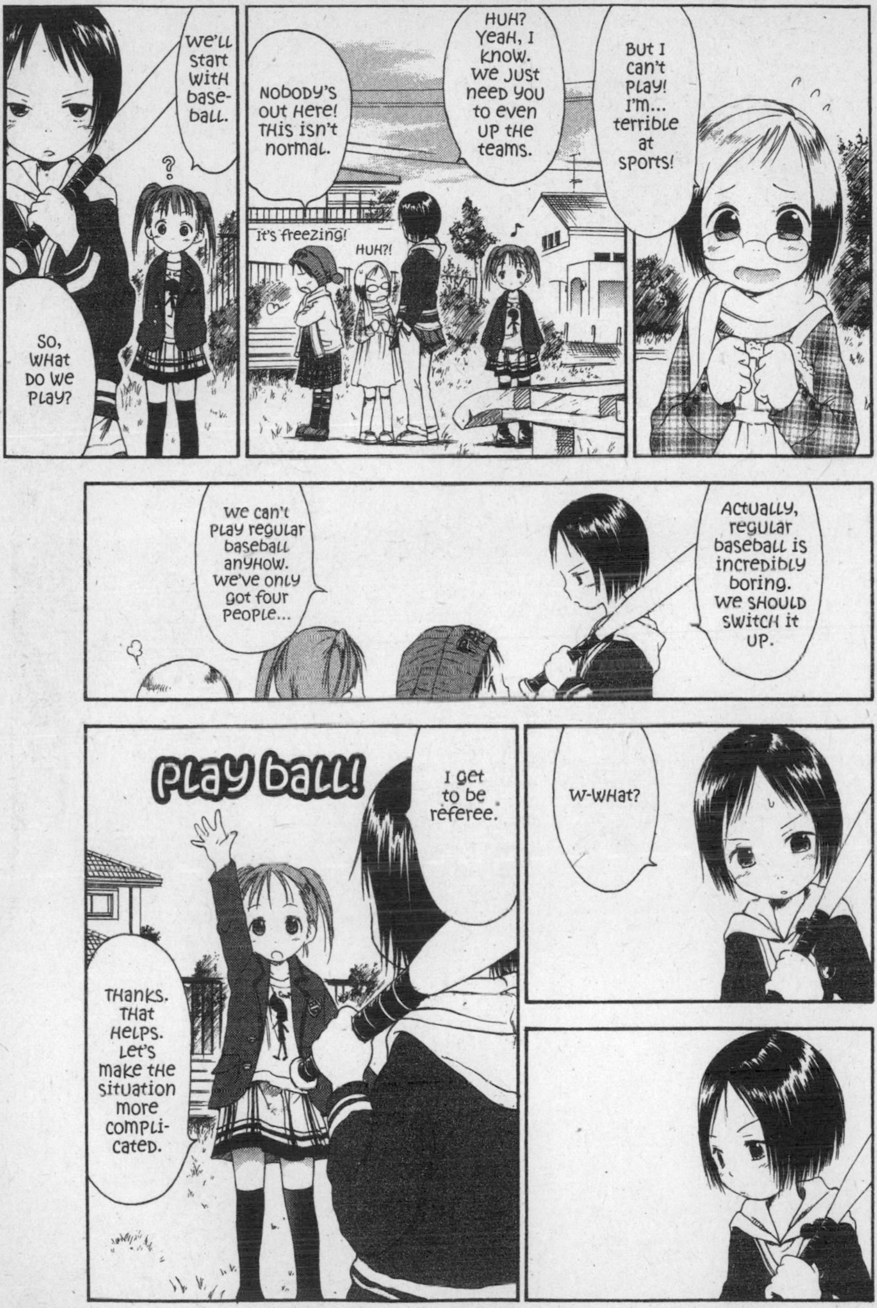
But I can't play! I'm... terrible at sports!
HUH? YeaH, I know. We just need you to even up the teams.
Nobody's out here! This isn't normal.
HUH?!
It's freezing!
We'll start with base-ball.
So, what do we play?
Actually, regular baseball is incredibly boring. We should switch it up.
We can't play regular baseball anyhow. We've only got four people...
W-What?
I get to be referee.
Play ball!
Thanks. That helps. Let's make the situation more compli-cated.

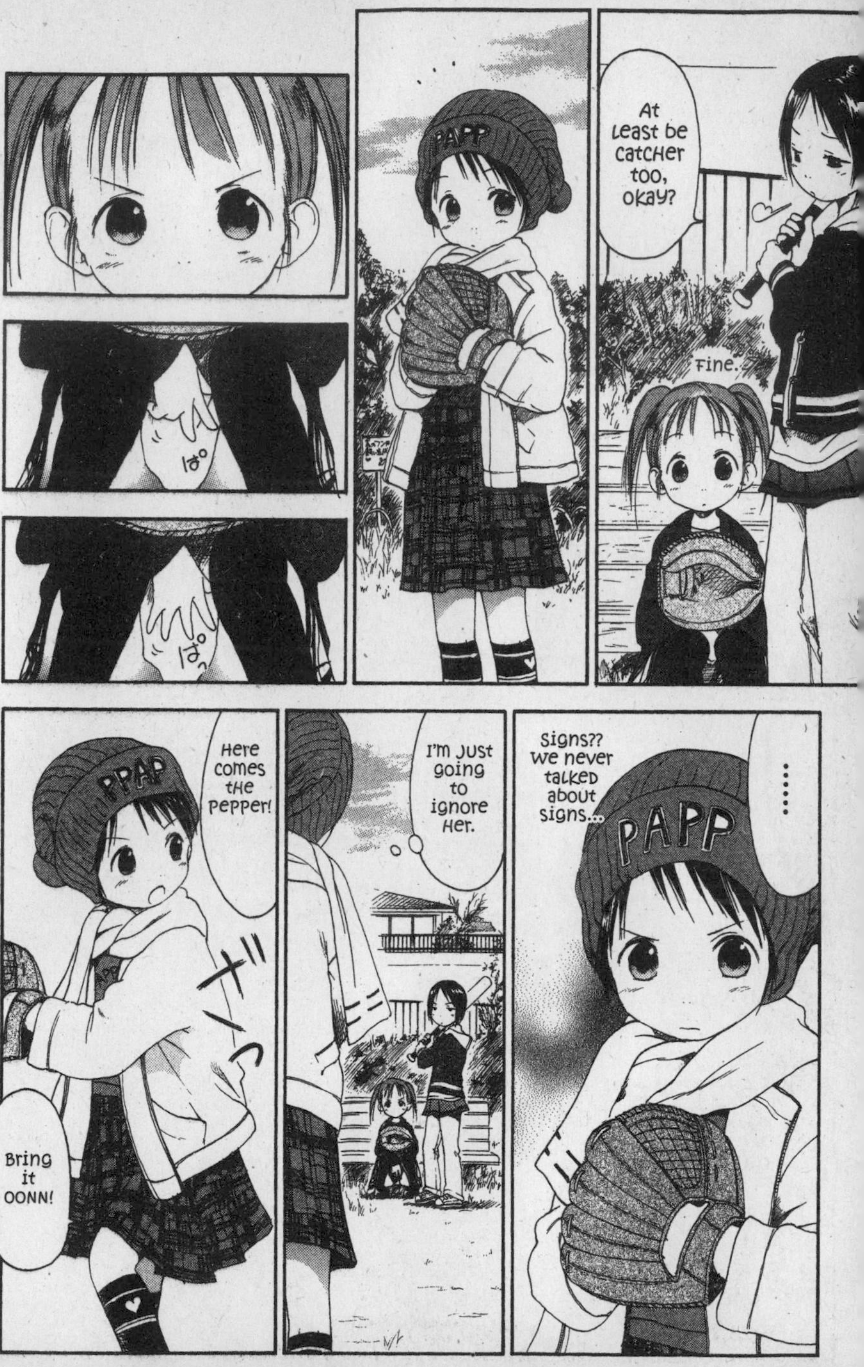
At least be catcher too, okay?
Fine.
ぱ
ぱっ
......
Signs?? We never talked about signs...
I'm just going to ignore her.
Here comes the pepper!
Bring it OONN!

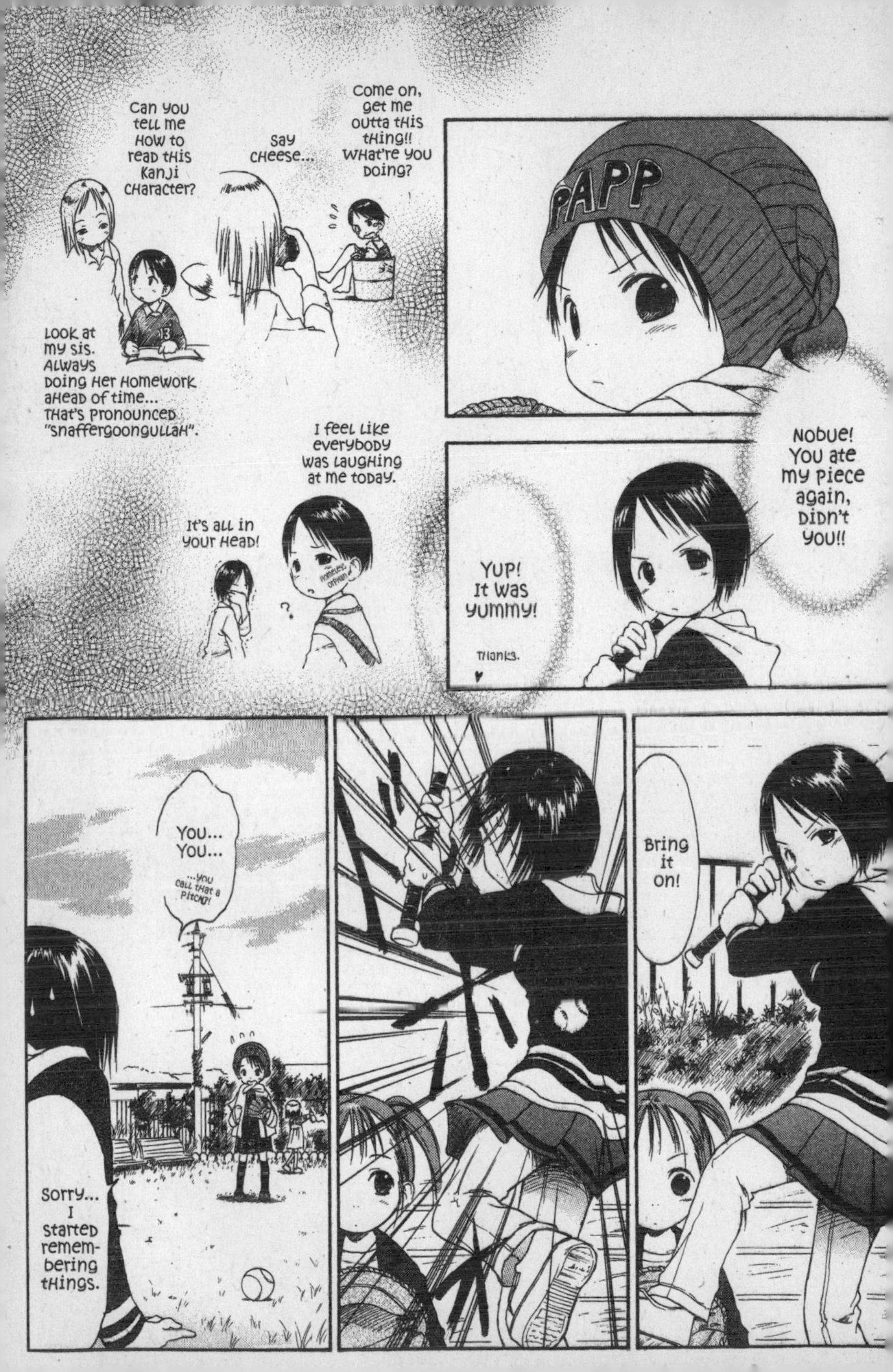
Nobue! You ate my piece again, Didn't you!!
Yup! It was yummy!
Thanks.
Come on, get me outta this thing!! What're you doing?
Say cheese...
Can you tell me how to read this kanji character?
Look at my sis. Always doing her homework ahead of time... That's pronounced "snaffergoongullah".
I feel like everybody was laughing at me today.
It's all in your head!
Bring it on!
You... You...
...You call that a pitch?!
Sorry... I started remembering things.

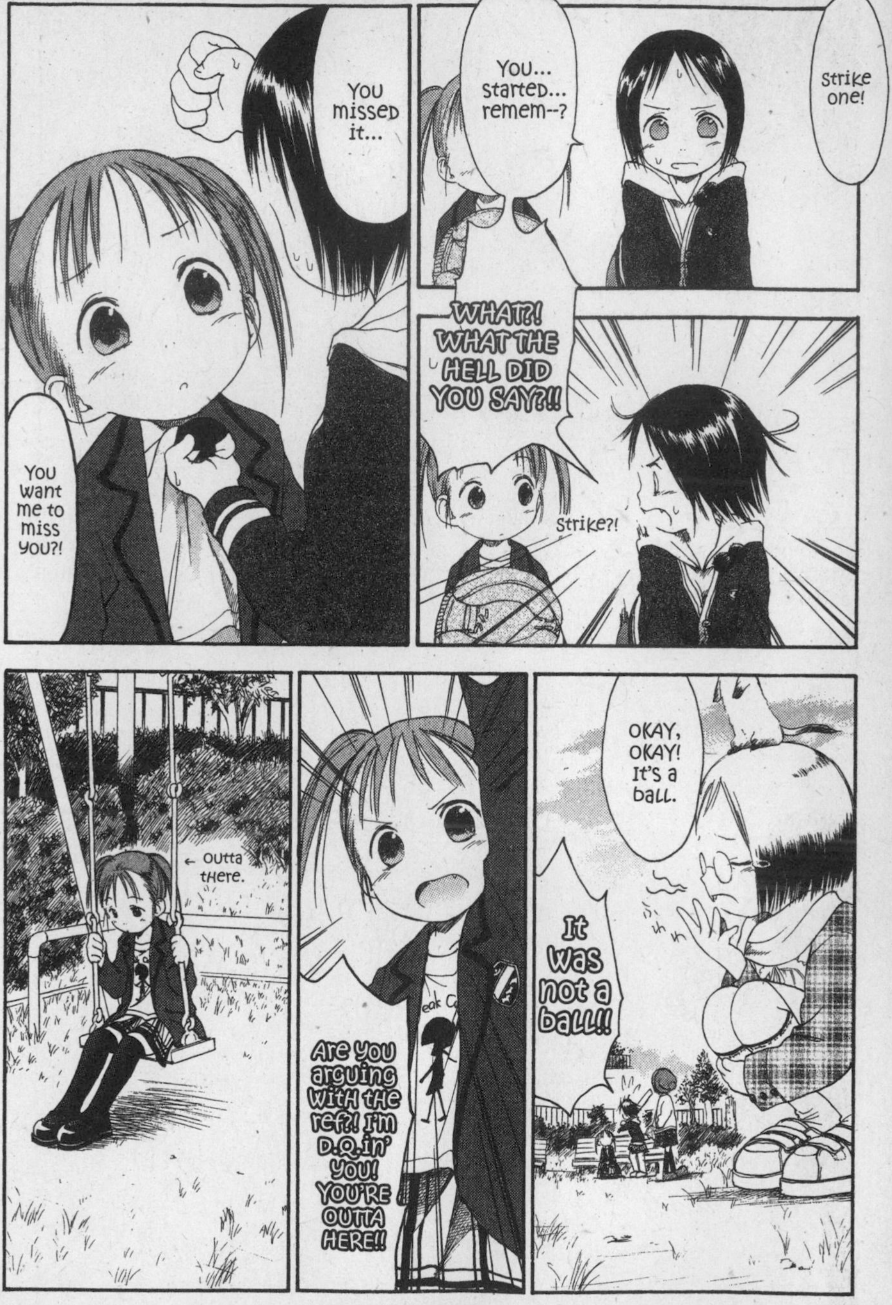
Strike one!
You... started... remem--?
WHAT?! WHAT THE HELL DID YOU SAY?!!
Strike?!
You missed it...
You want me to miss you?!
OKAY, OKAY! It's a ball.
It was not a ball!!
Are you arguing with the ref?! I'm D.Q.in' you! YOU'RE OUTTA HERE!!
← Outta there.

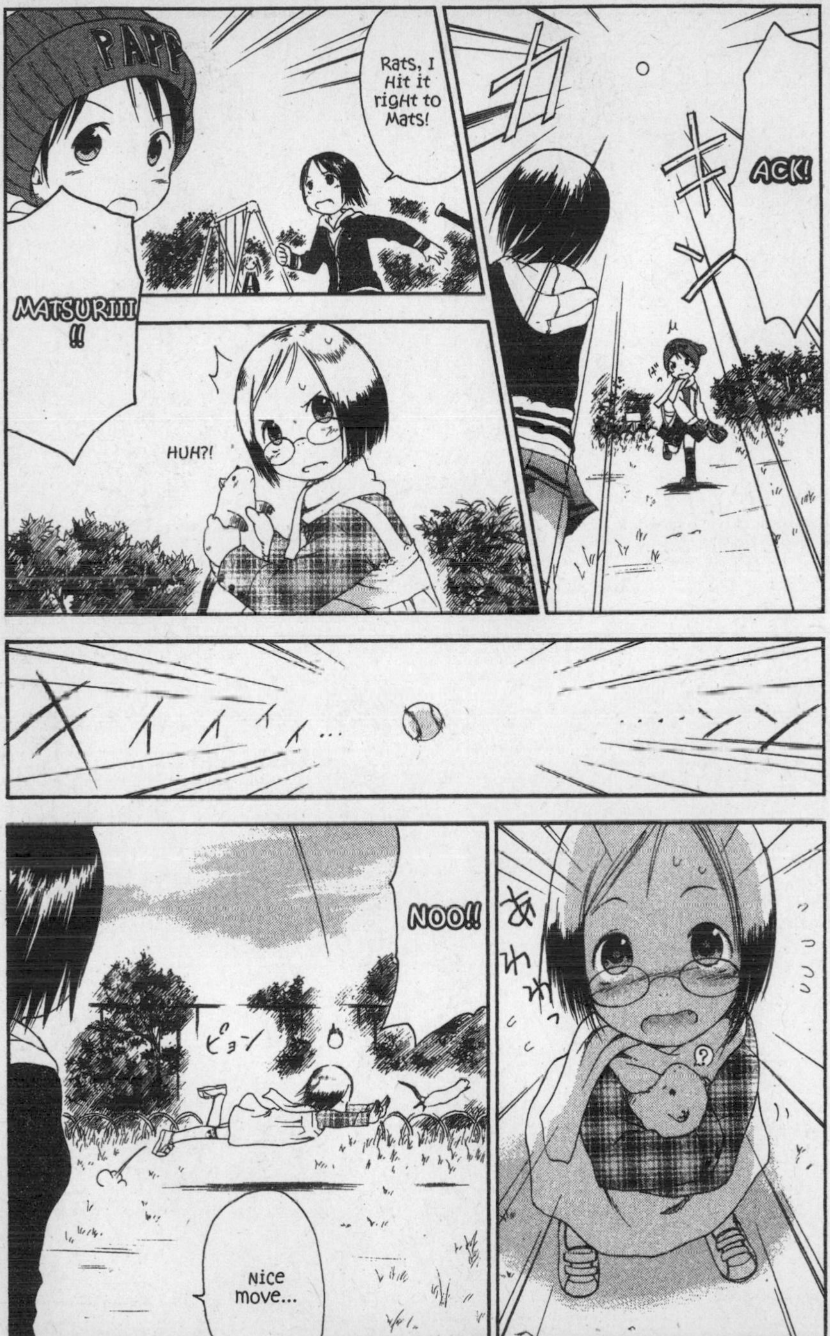

ACK!
Rats, I Hit it right to Mats!
MATSURIII !!
HUH?!
イイイ…
…ンン
あわわっ
NOO!!
ピョン
Nice move...

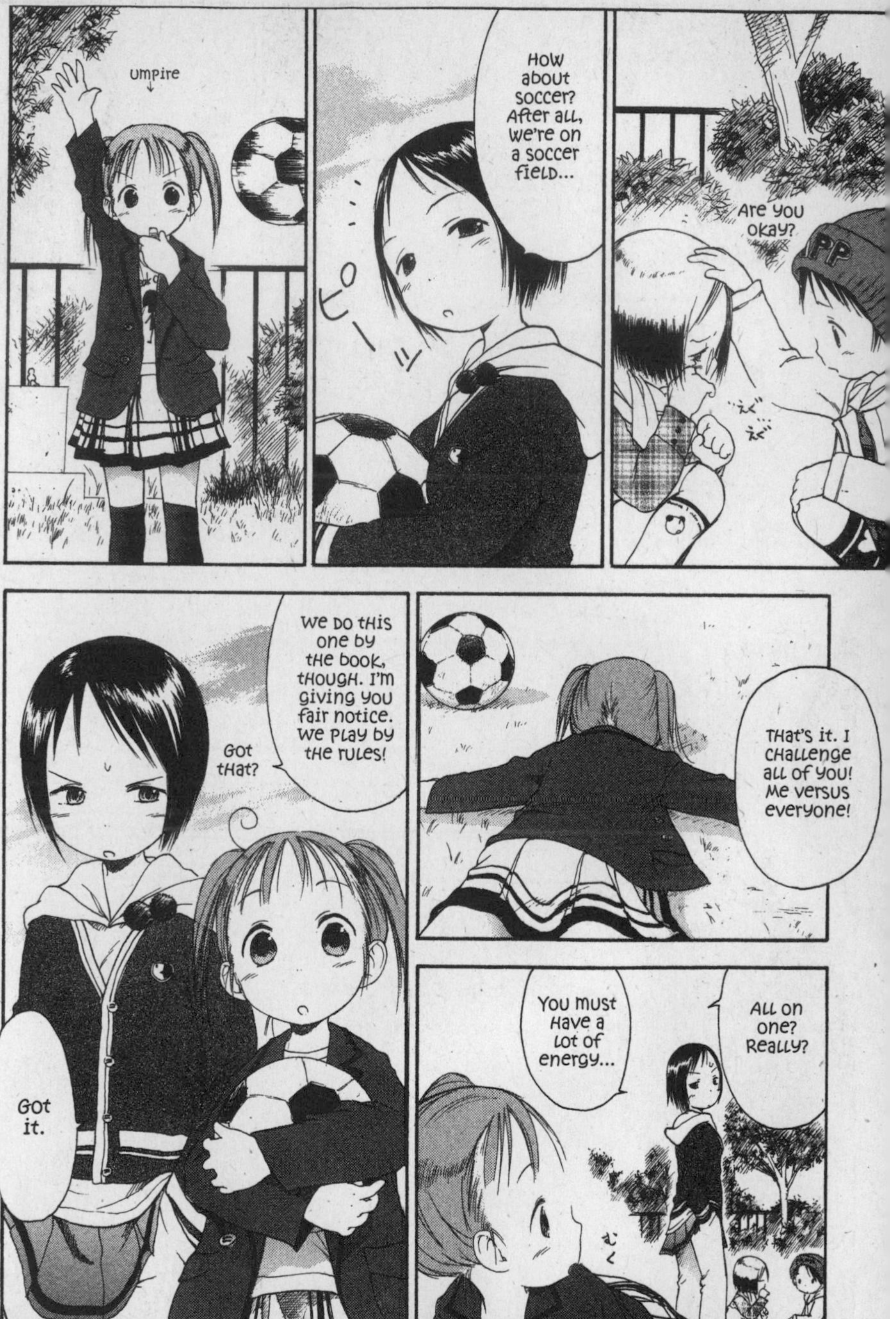

Are you okay?
How about soccer? After all, we're on a soccer field...
ピーーッ
umpire ↓
That's it. I challenge all of you! Me versus everyone!
All on one? Really?
You must have a lot of energy...
むく
We do this one by the book, though. I'm giving you fair notice. We play by the rules!
Got that?
Got it.

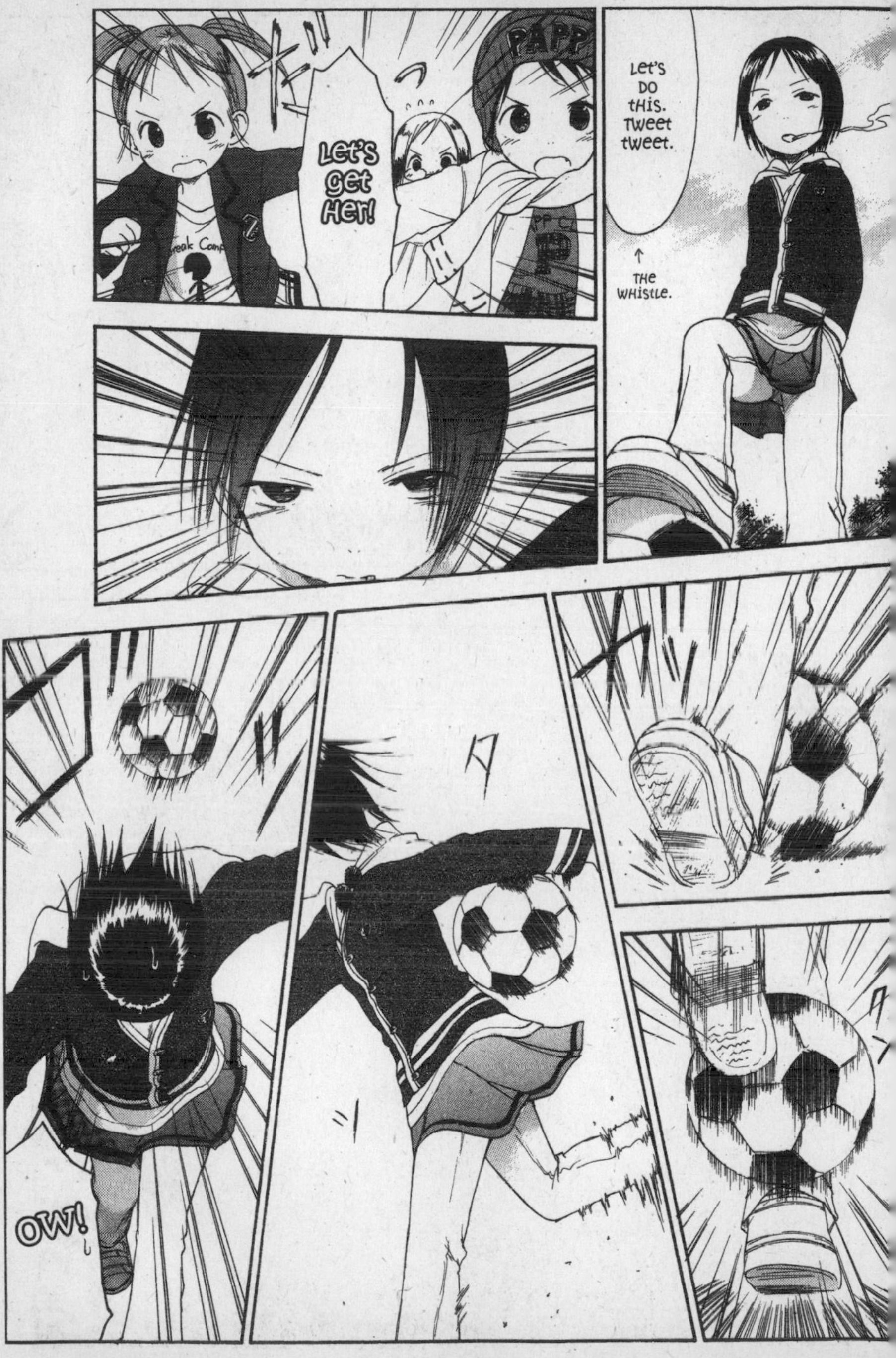
Let's DO tHis. Tweet tweet.
↑ THe whistle.
PAPP
Let's get Her!
Freak Camp
OW!

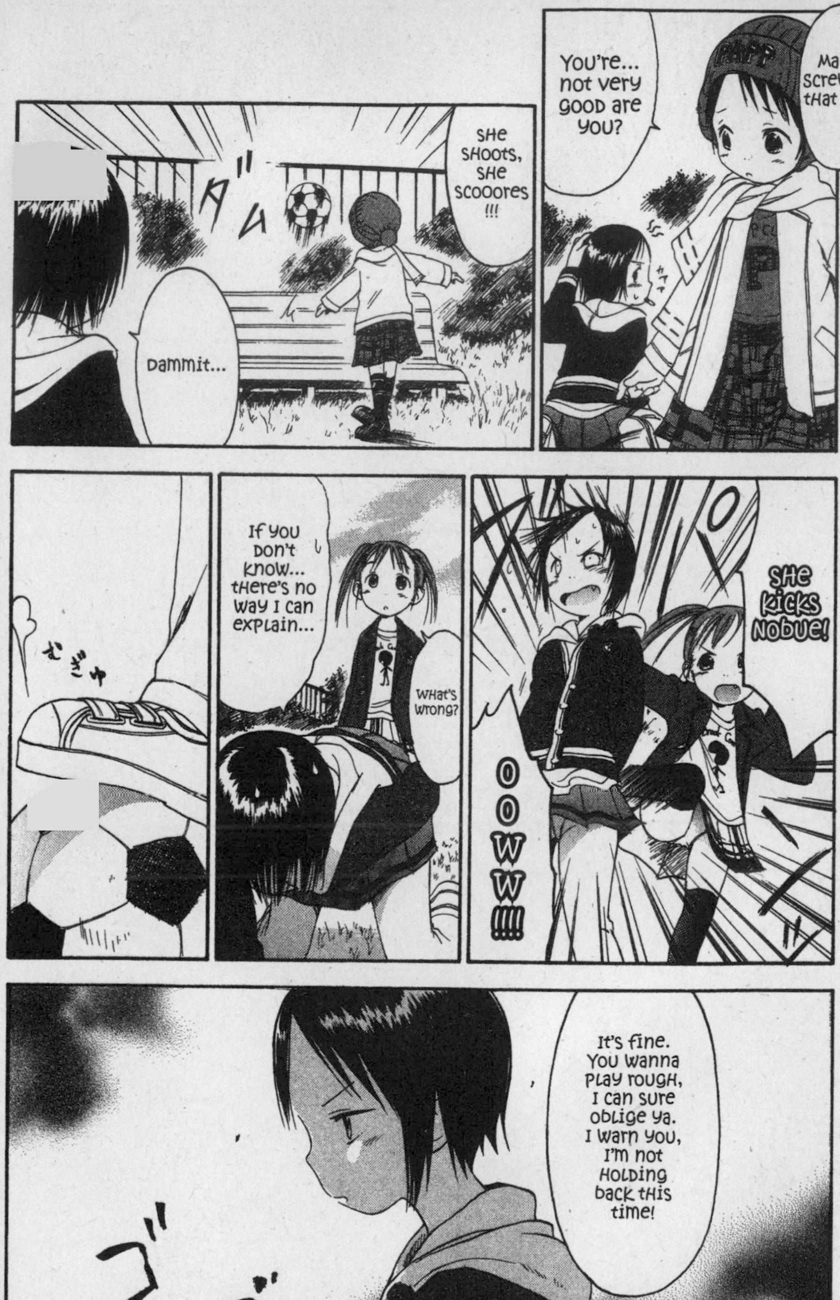
Man. Screwed that up.
You're... not very good are you?
She shoots, she scooores!!!
ダム
Dammit...
She kicks Nobue!
OOWW!!!!
If you don't know... there's no way I can explain...
What's wrong?
むぎゅ
It's fine. You wanna play rough, I can sure oblige ya. I warn you, I'm not holding back this time!
ゴゴ

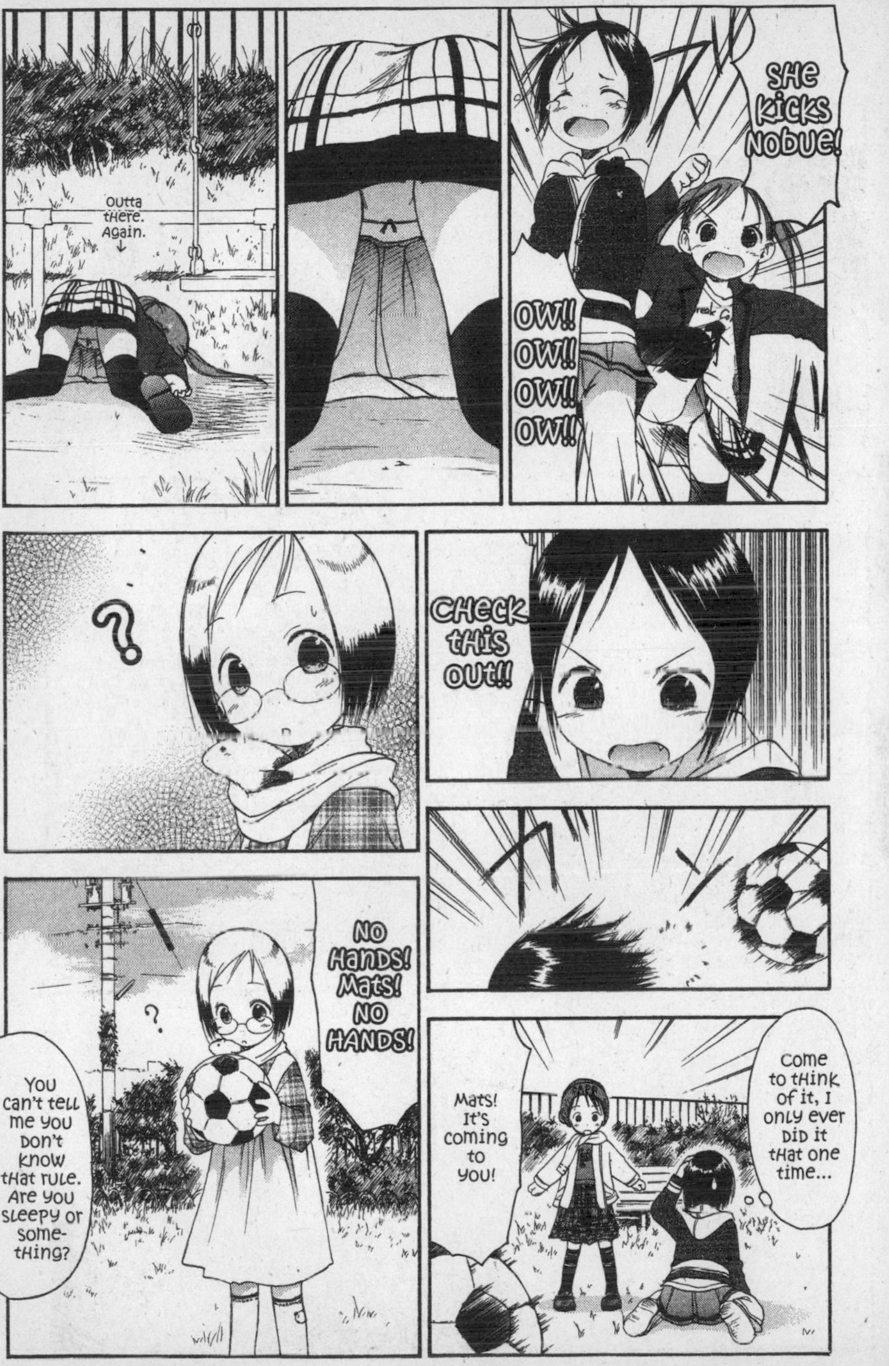
SHE KICKS NOBUE!
OW!! OW!! OW!! OW!!
Outta there. Again.
CHECK THIS OUT!!
?
Come to think of it, I only ever did it that one time...
Mats! It's coming to you!
?
NO HANDS! Mats! NO HANDS!
You can't tell me you don't know that rule. Are you sleepy or some-thing?

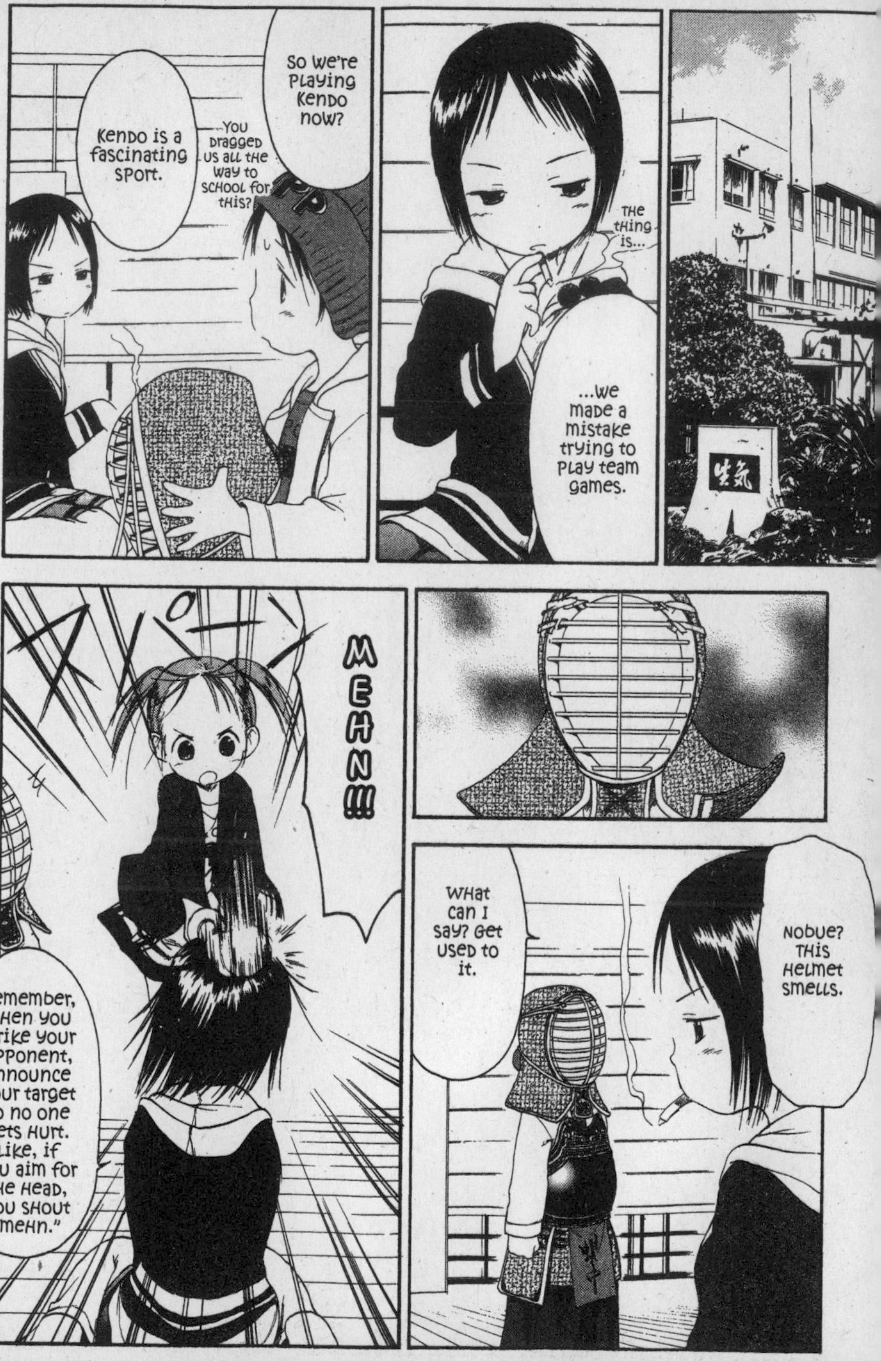
The thing is...
...we made a mistake trying to play team games.
So we're playing kendo now?
You dragged us all the way to school for this?
Kendo is a fascinating sport.
Nobue? This helmet smells.
What can I say? Get used to it.
MEHN!!!
Remember, when you strike your opponent, announce your target so no one gets hurt. Like, if you aim for the head, you shout "mehn."

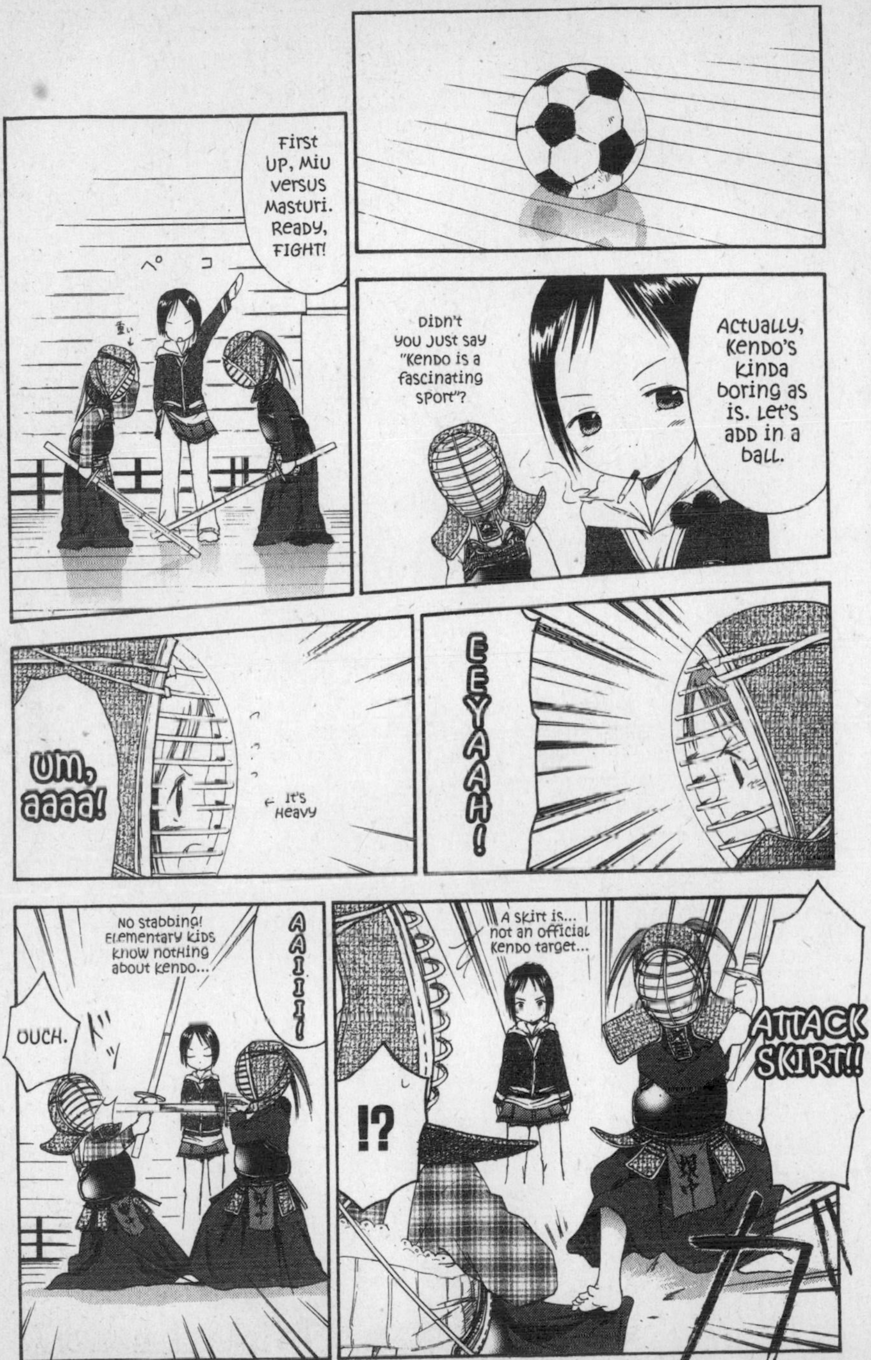
Actually, Kendo's kinda boring as is. Let's add in a ball.
Didn't you just say "Kendo is a fascinating sport"?
First up, Miu versus Masturi. Ready, FIGHT!
ペコ
重い
EEYAAAH!
um, aaaa!
← It's Heavy
ATTACK SKIRT!!
A skirt is... not an official Kendo target...
!?
AAIIII!
No stabbing! Elementary kids know nothing about kendo...
OUCH.
ドッ

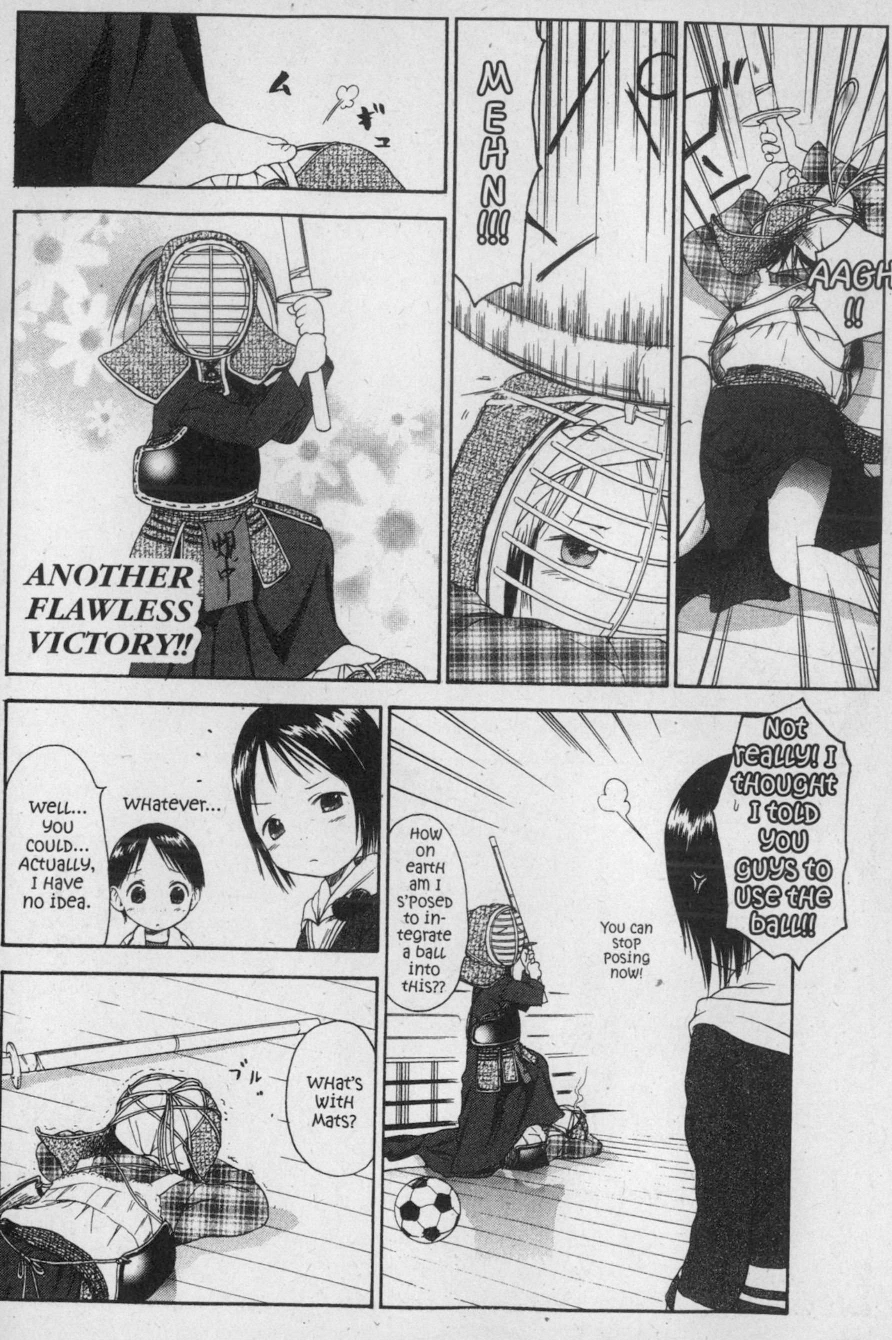
AAGH !!
MEHN!!!
ム ギュ
ANOTHER FLAWLESS VICTORY!!
Not really! I thought I told you guys to use the ball!!
You can stop posing now!
How on earth am I s'posed to integrate a ball into this??
Whatever...
Well... you could... Actually, I have no idea.
ブル
What's with Mats?

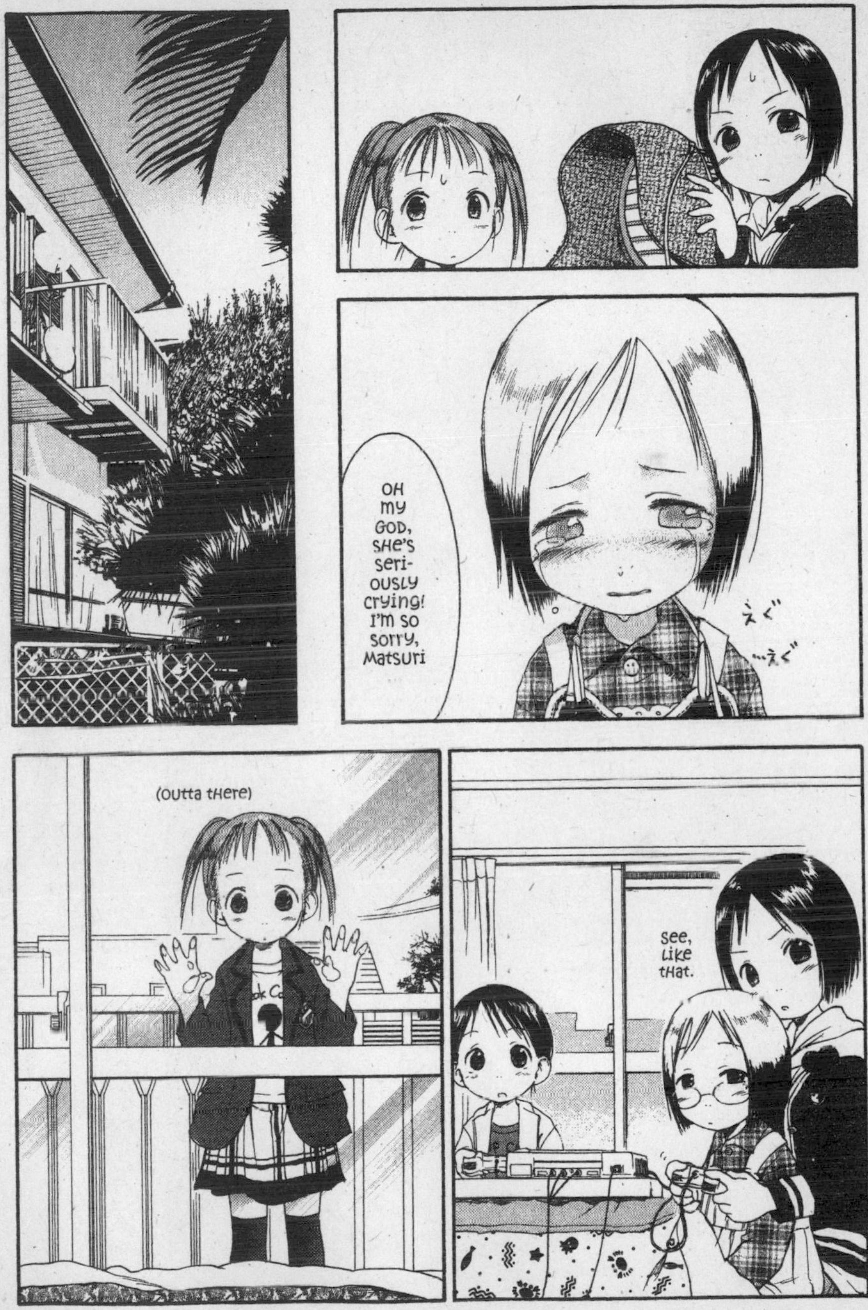
OH my GOD, SHE's seri-OUSLY crying! I'm SO SORRY, Matsuri...
えぐ
…えぐ
see, like tHat.
(OUTTA tHERE)

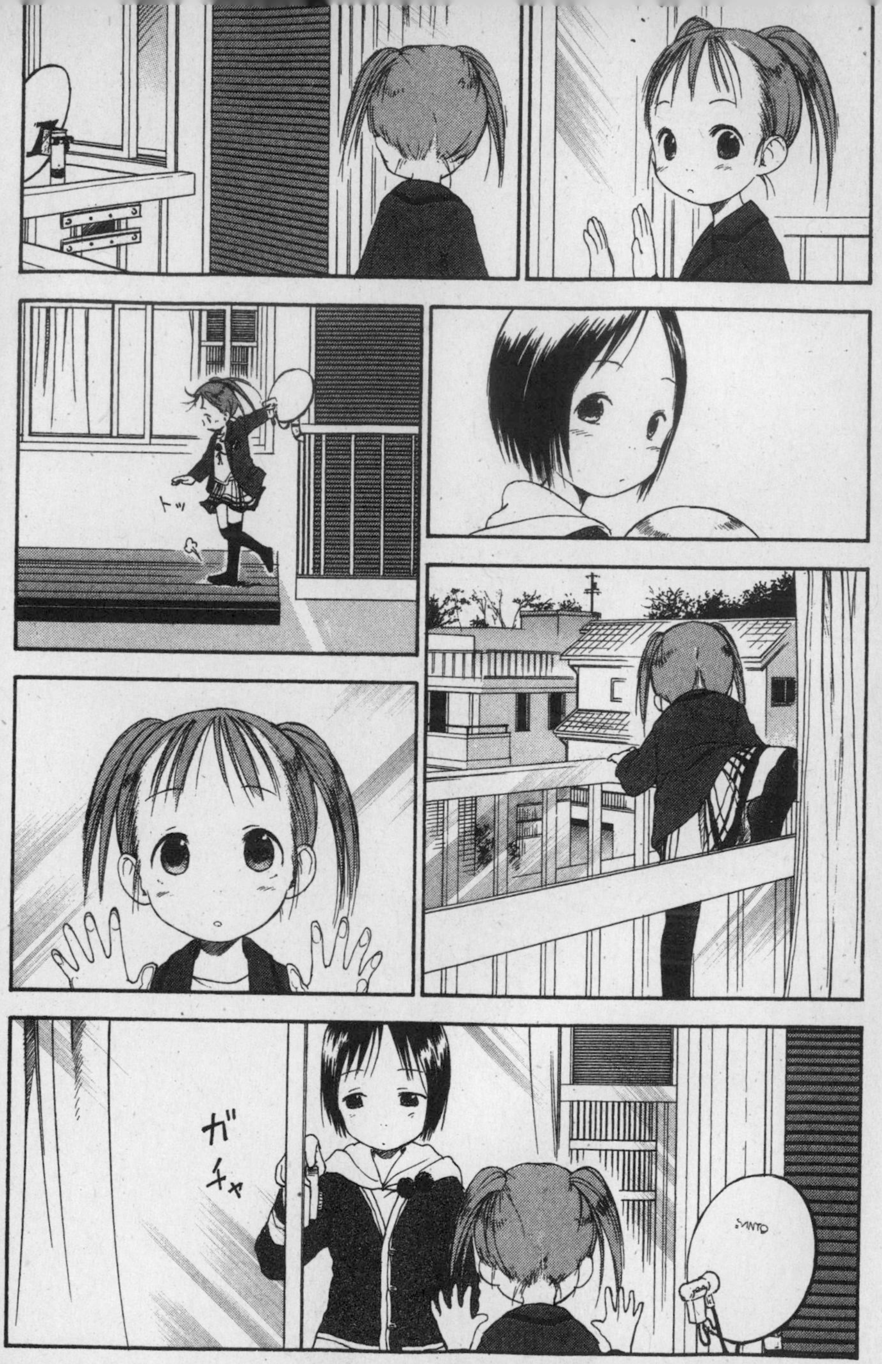
トッ
ガチャ

PAGE 109

name	*season*
☐NOBUE	☐SPRING
☐CHIKA	☐SUMMER
☐MIU	☐AUTUMN
☐MATSURI	☐WINTER

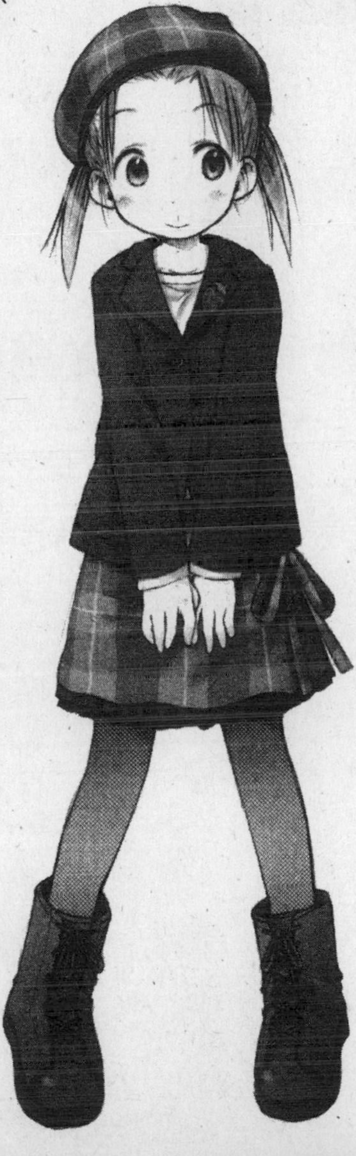

PAGE 110

name	season
□NOBUE	□SPRING
□CHIKA	□SUMMER
□MIU	■AUTUMN
■MATSURI	□WINTER

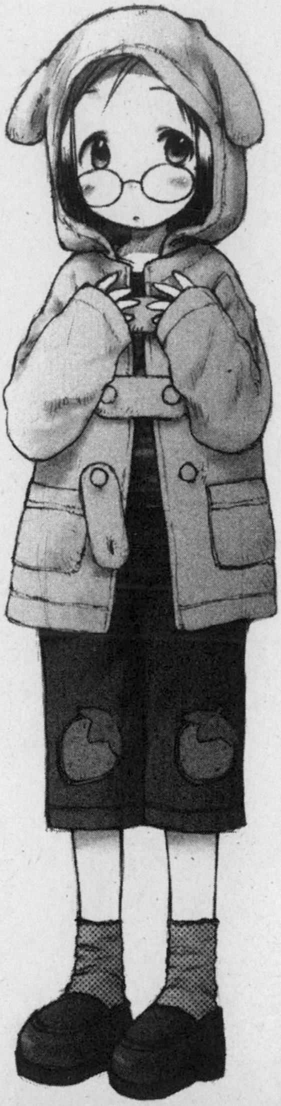

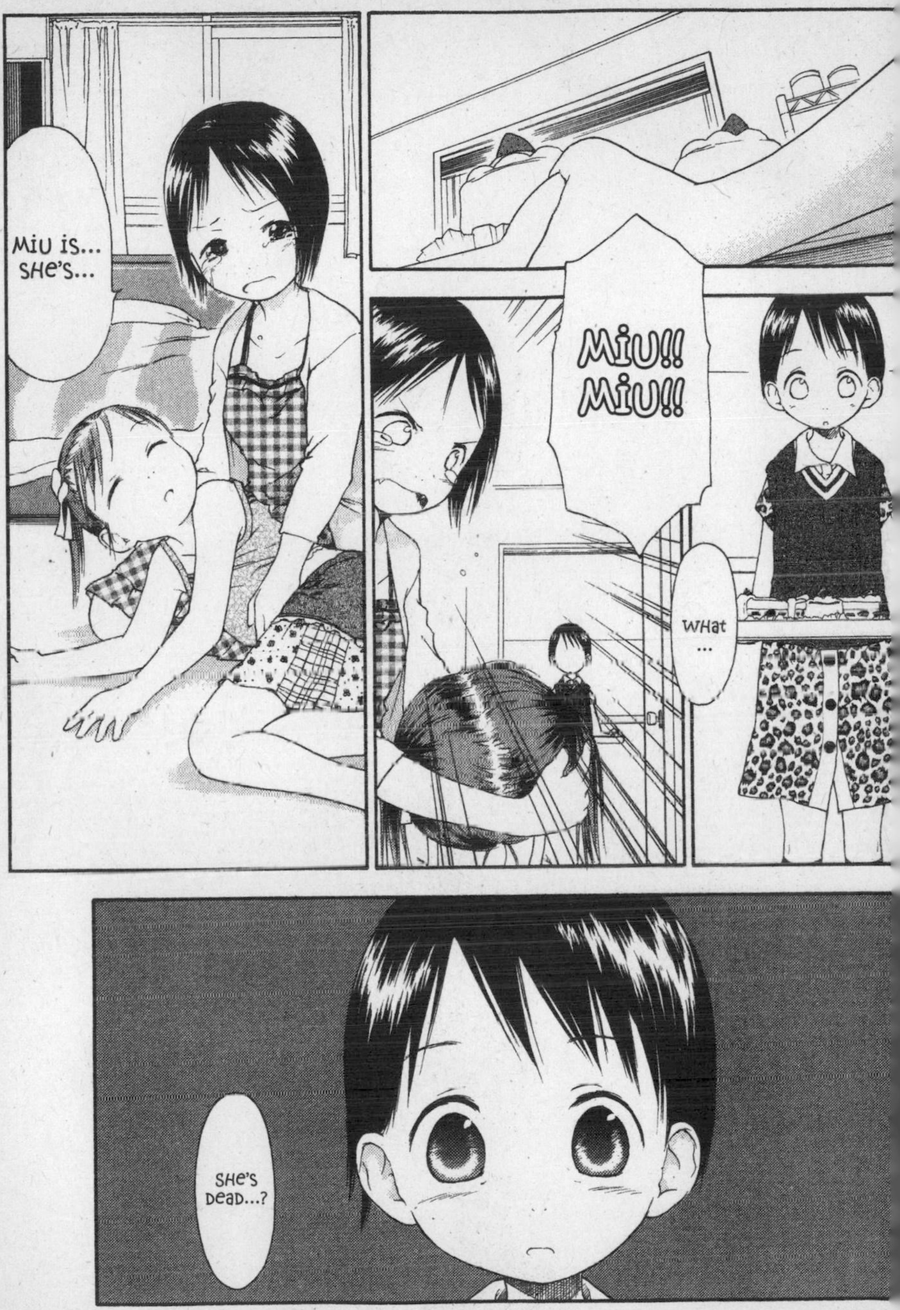
WHat ...
MIU!! MIU!!
MIU IS... SHE'S...
SHE'S DEAD...?

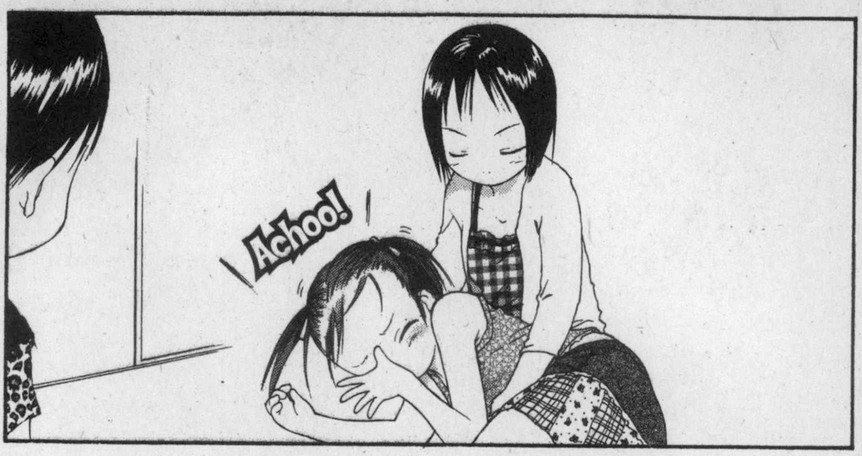
Achoo!

Episode.7

Determined Dead!

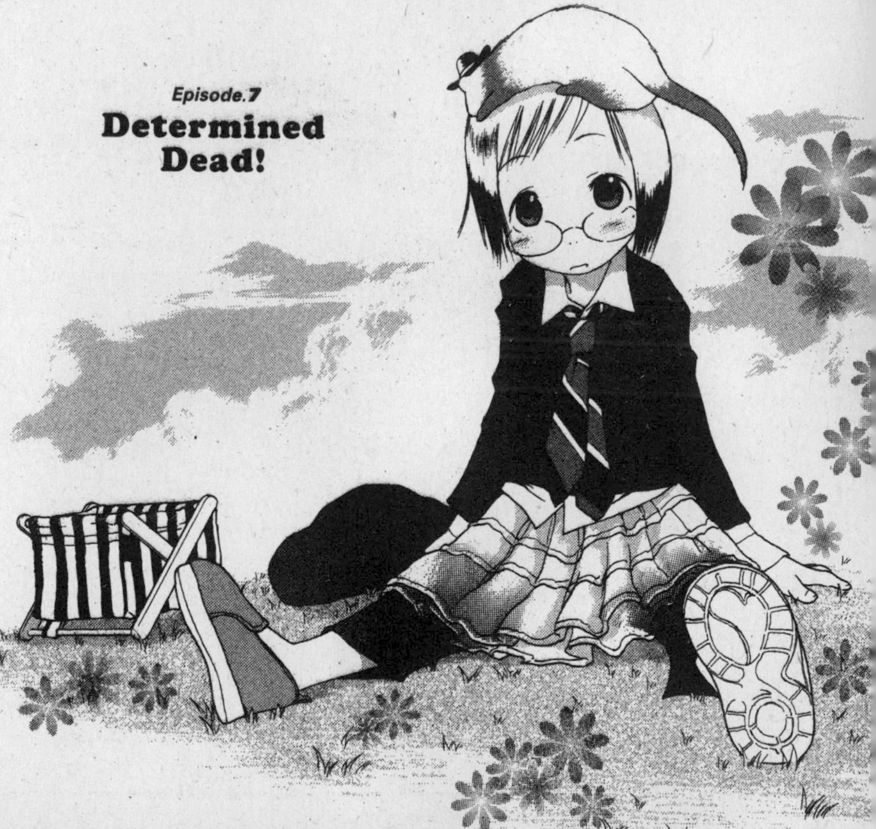

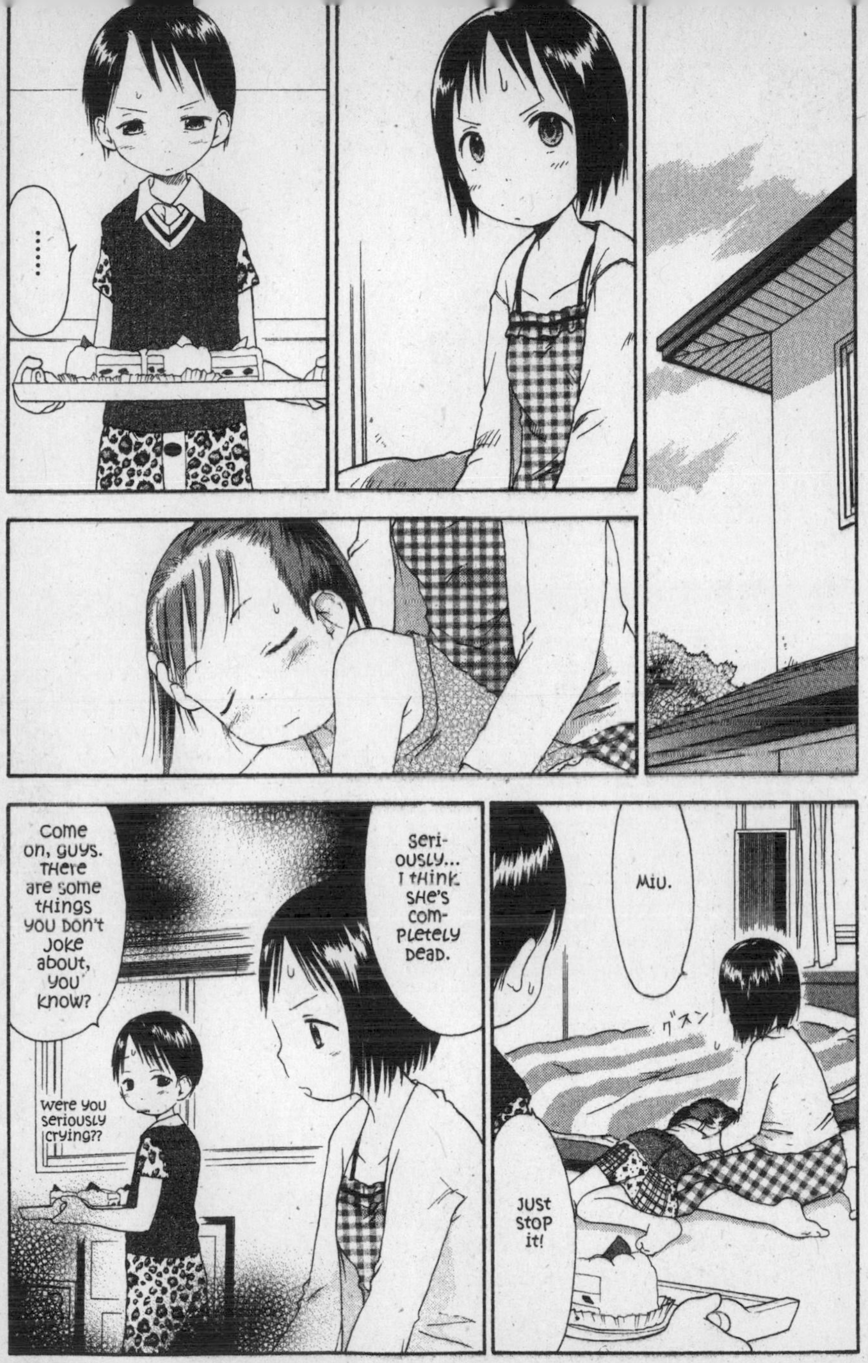
......
Miu.
グスン
Just stop it!
Seri-ously... I think she's com-pletely dead.
Come on, guys. There are some things you don't joke about, you know?
Were you seriously crying??

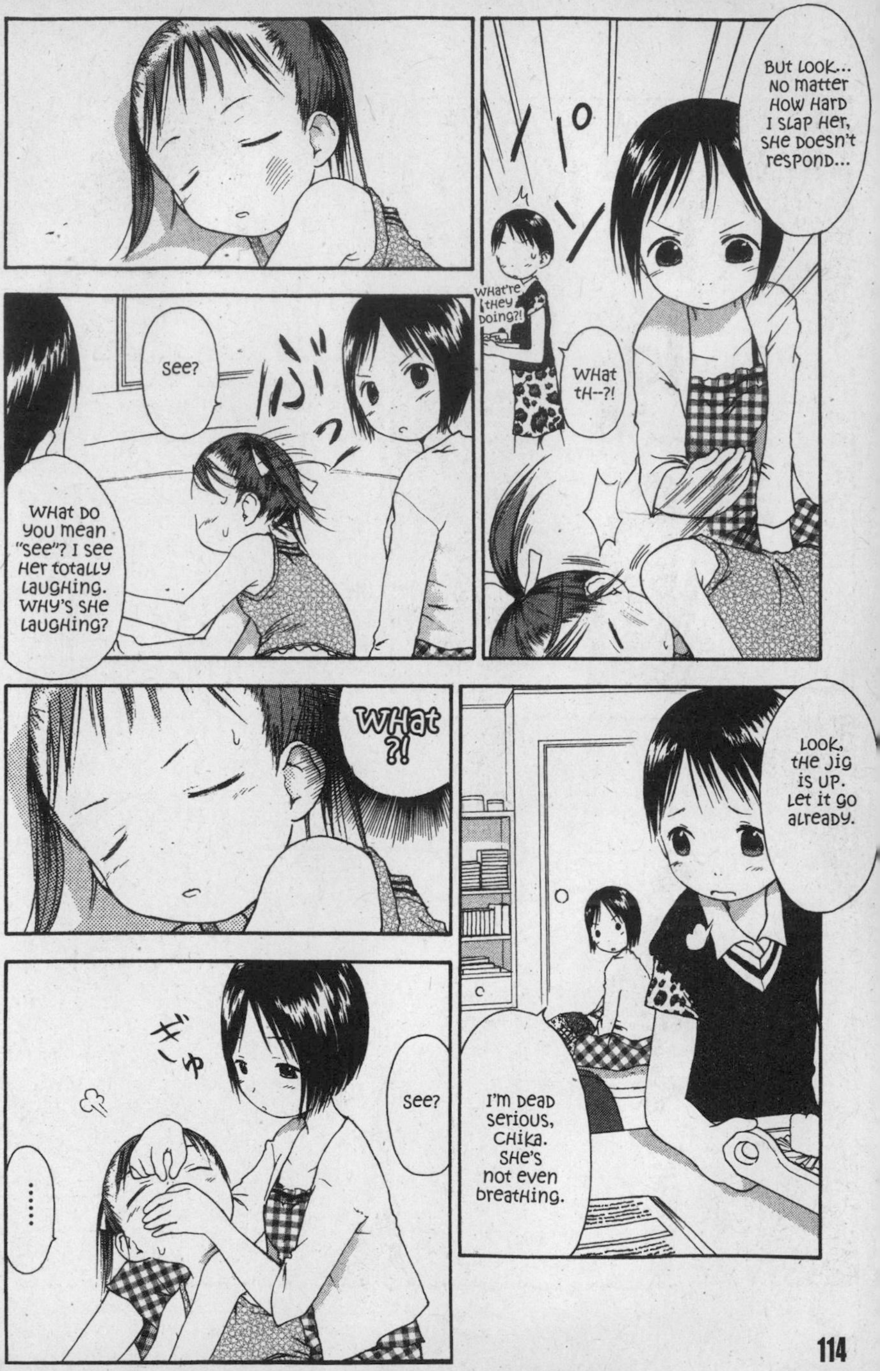

But look... no matter how hard I slap her, she doesn't respond...
What're they doing?!
What th--?!
See?
ぶっ
What do you mean "see"? I see her totally laughing. Why's she laughing?
Look, the jig is up. Let it go already.
I'm dead serious, Chika. She's not even breathing.
WHAT ?!
ぎゅ
See?
......

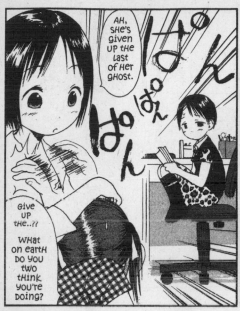

Hey... that's enough ...
ぱん
ぱん
ぱん
Ah, she's given up the last of her ghost.
Give up the..?? What on earth do you two think you're doing?
Her body is a lifeless shell now.
I'm telling you! This is the deadest girl!
I don't think she's given up any of her ghost...
Seriously. Her body won't even respond to the most severe tickling!
......

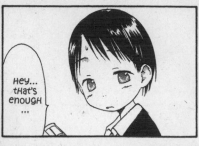

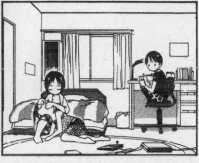

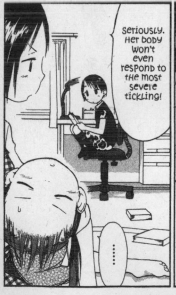

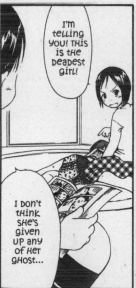

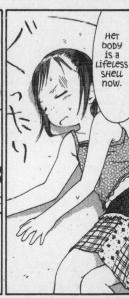

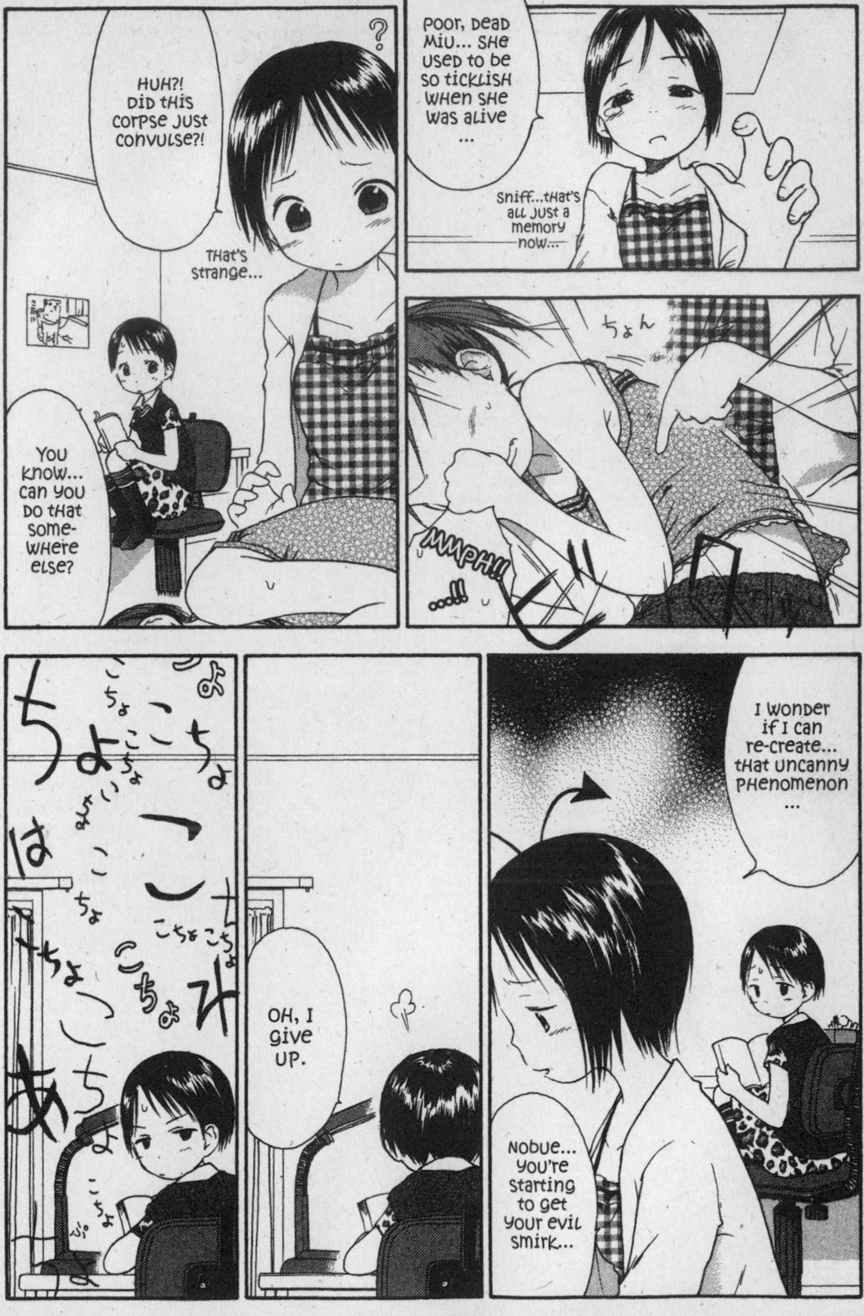

Poor, dead Miu... she used to be so ticklish when she was alive ...
Sniff...that's all just a memory now...
ちょん
MMPH!!
...!!
?
Huh?! Did this corpse just convulse?!
That's strange...
You know... can you do that some-where else?
I wonder if I can re-create... that uncanny phenomenon ...
Nobue... you're starting to get your evil smirk...
Oh, I give up.

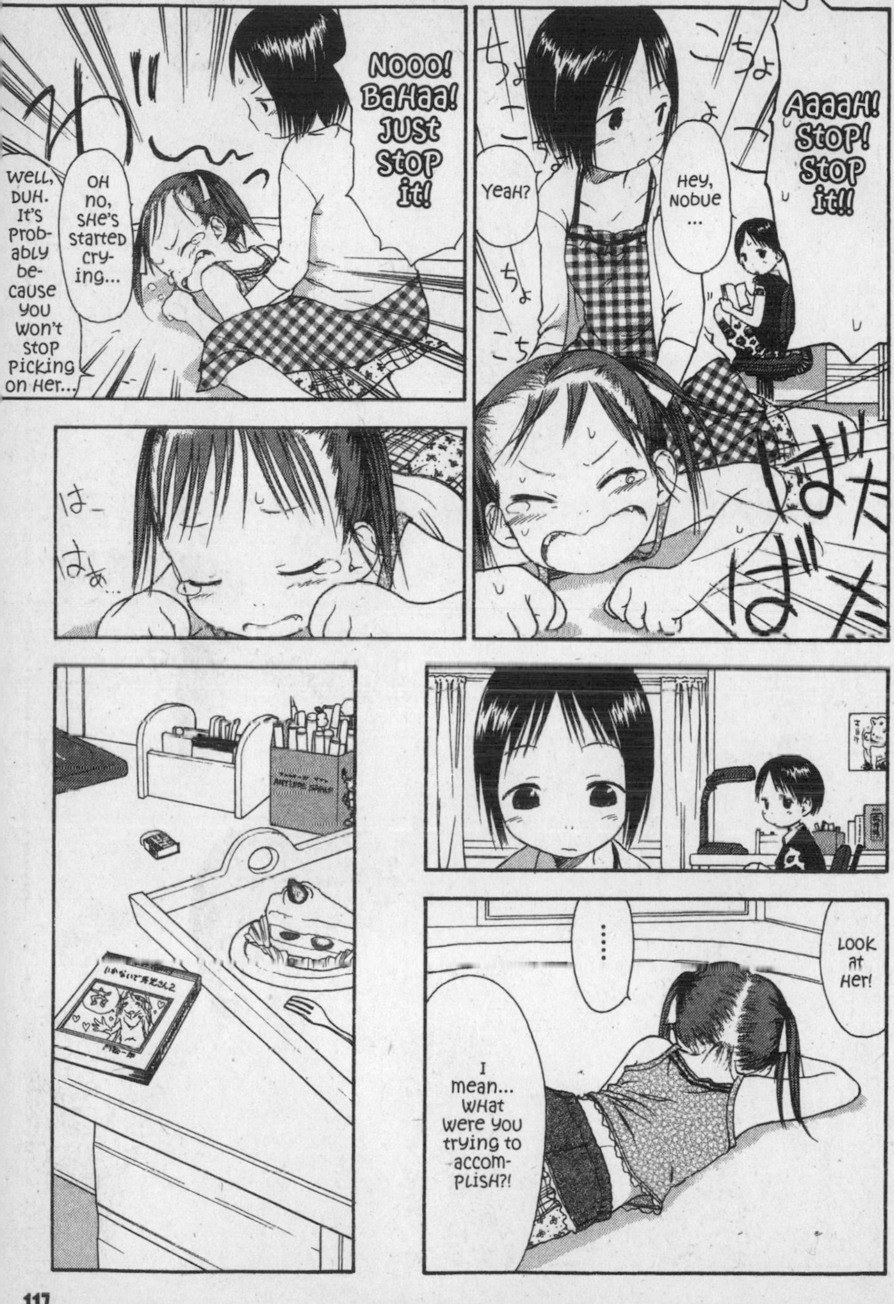
AaaaH! Stop! Stop it!!
Hey, Nobue ...
Yeah?
ばたばた
NOOO! BaHaa! JUST Stop it!
OH no, SHE's started crying...
Well, DUH. It's probably because you won't stop picking on Her...
はーはぁ...
Look at Her!
.....
I mean... What were you trying to accomplish?!

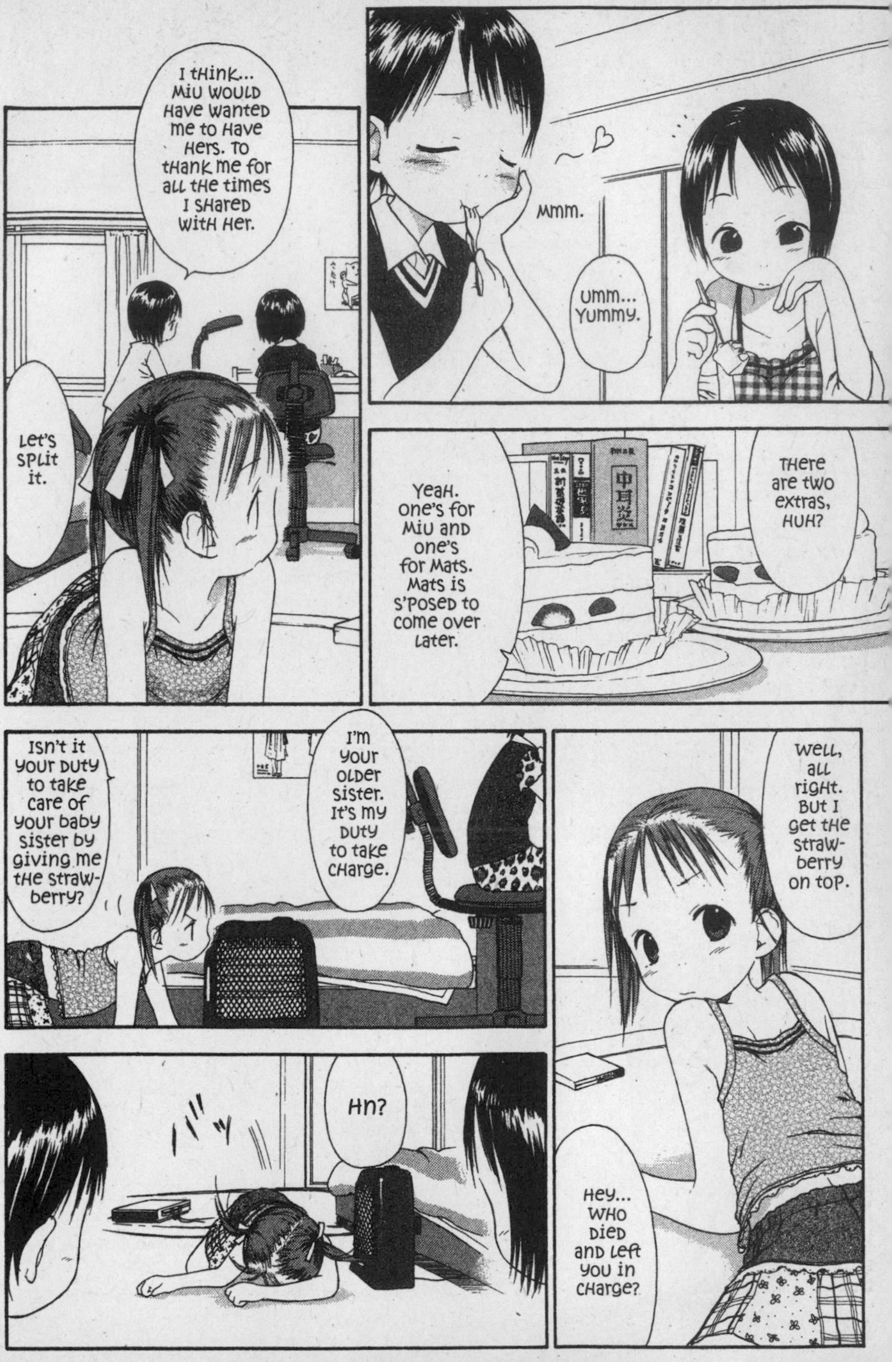
~♡
Mmm.
Umm... Yummy.
There are two extras, huh?
Yeah. One's for Miu and one's for Mats. Mats is s'posed to come over later.
I think... Miu would have wanted me to have hers. To thank me for all the times I shared with her.
Let's split it.
Well, all right. But I get the strawberry on top.
Hey... who died and left you in charge?
I'm your older sister. It's my duty to take charge.
Isn't it your duty to take care of your baby sister by giving me the strawberry?
Hn?
バッ

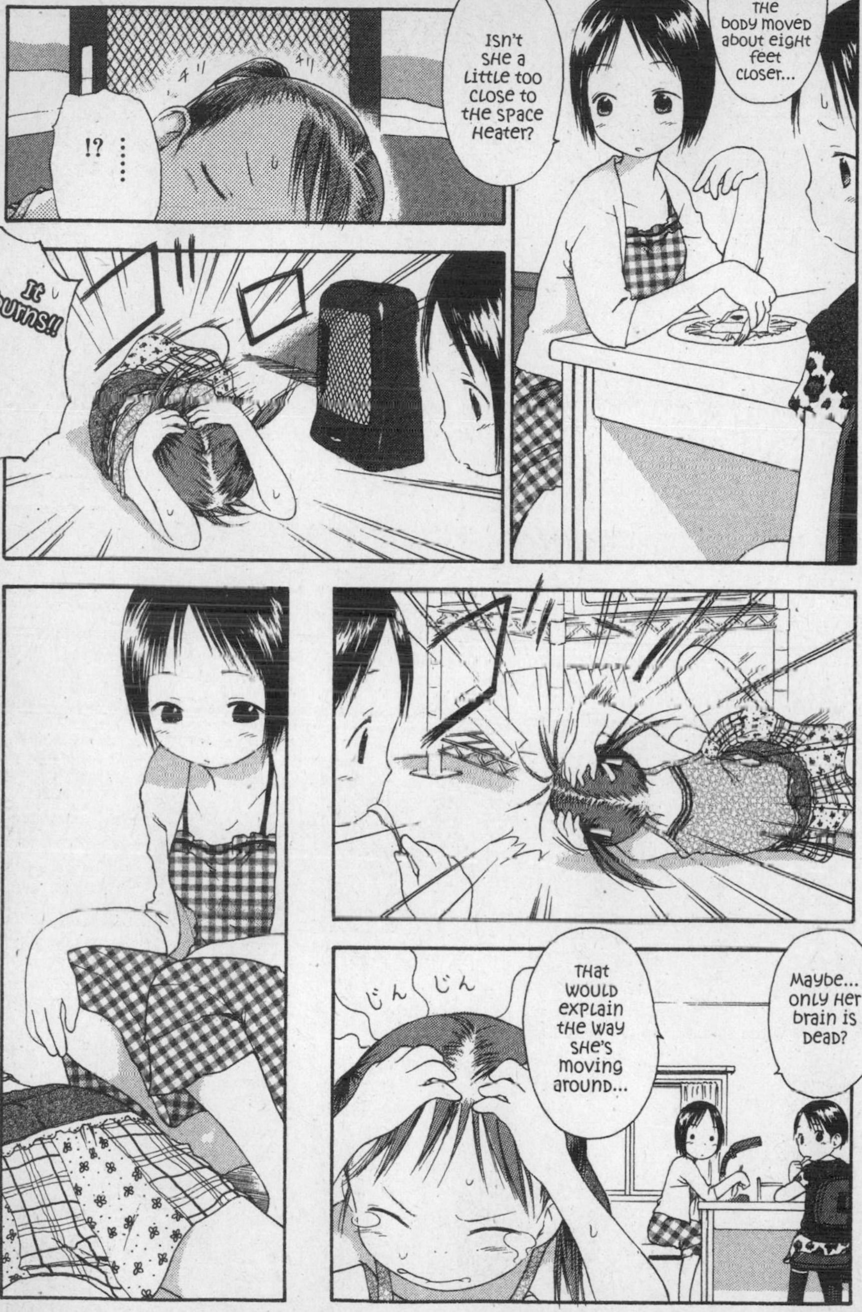
The body moved about eight feet closer...
Isn't she a little too close to the space heater?
チリ チリ
!? ……
It burns!!
Maybe... only her brain is dead?
That would explain the way she's moving around...
じん じん

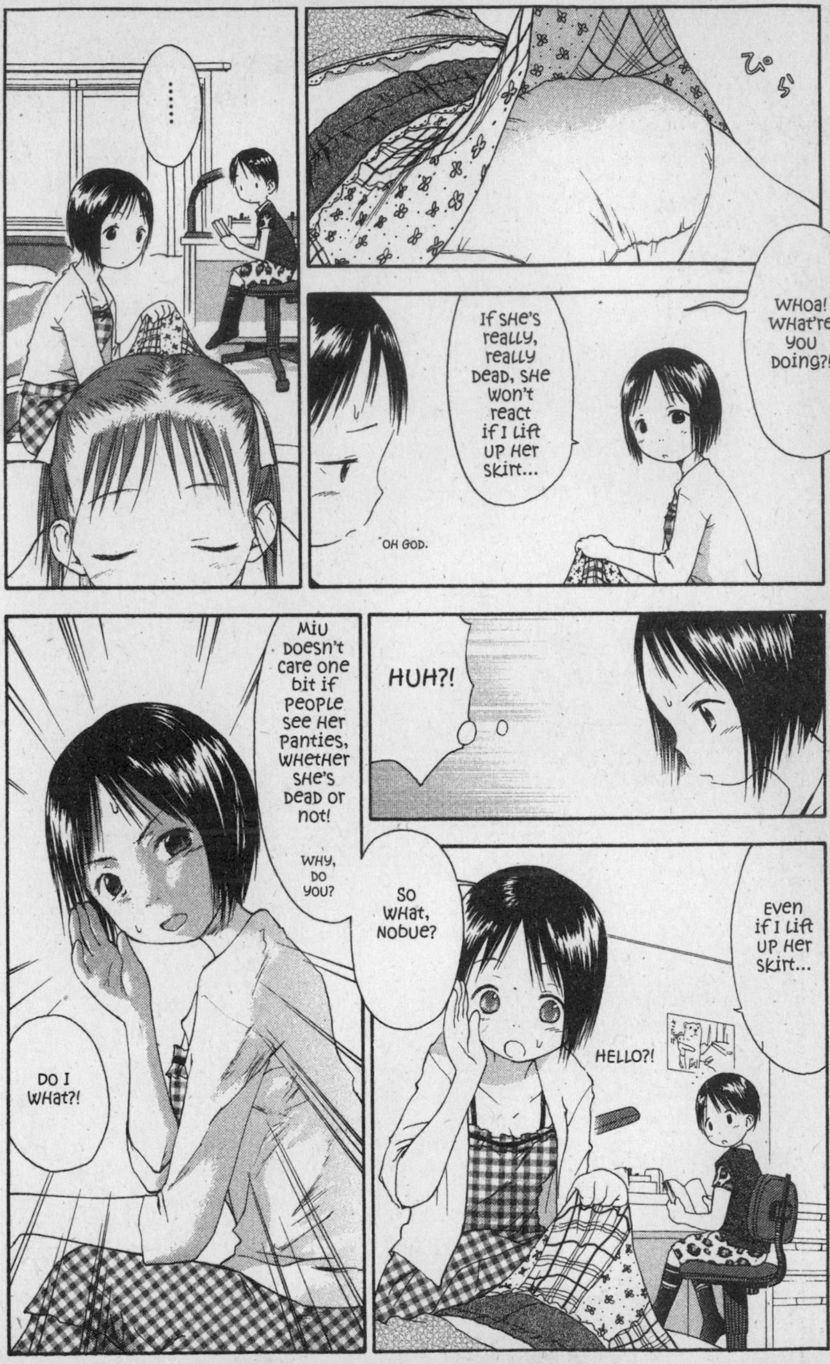
ぴら
WHOA! WHAT'RE YOU DOING?!
IF SHE'S REALLY, REALLY DEAD, SHE WON'T REACT IF I LIFT UP HER SKIRT...
OH GOD.
......
HUH?!
EVEN IF I LIFT UP HER SKIRT...
HELLO?!
SO WHAT, NOBUE?
MIU DOESN'T CARE ONE BIT IF PEOPLE SEE HER PANTIES, WHETHER SHE'S DEAD OR NOT!
WHY, DO YOU?
DO I WHAT?!

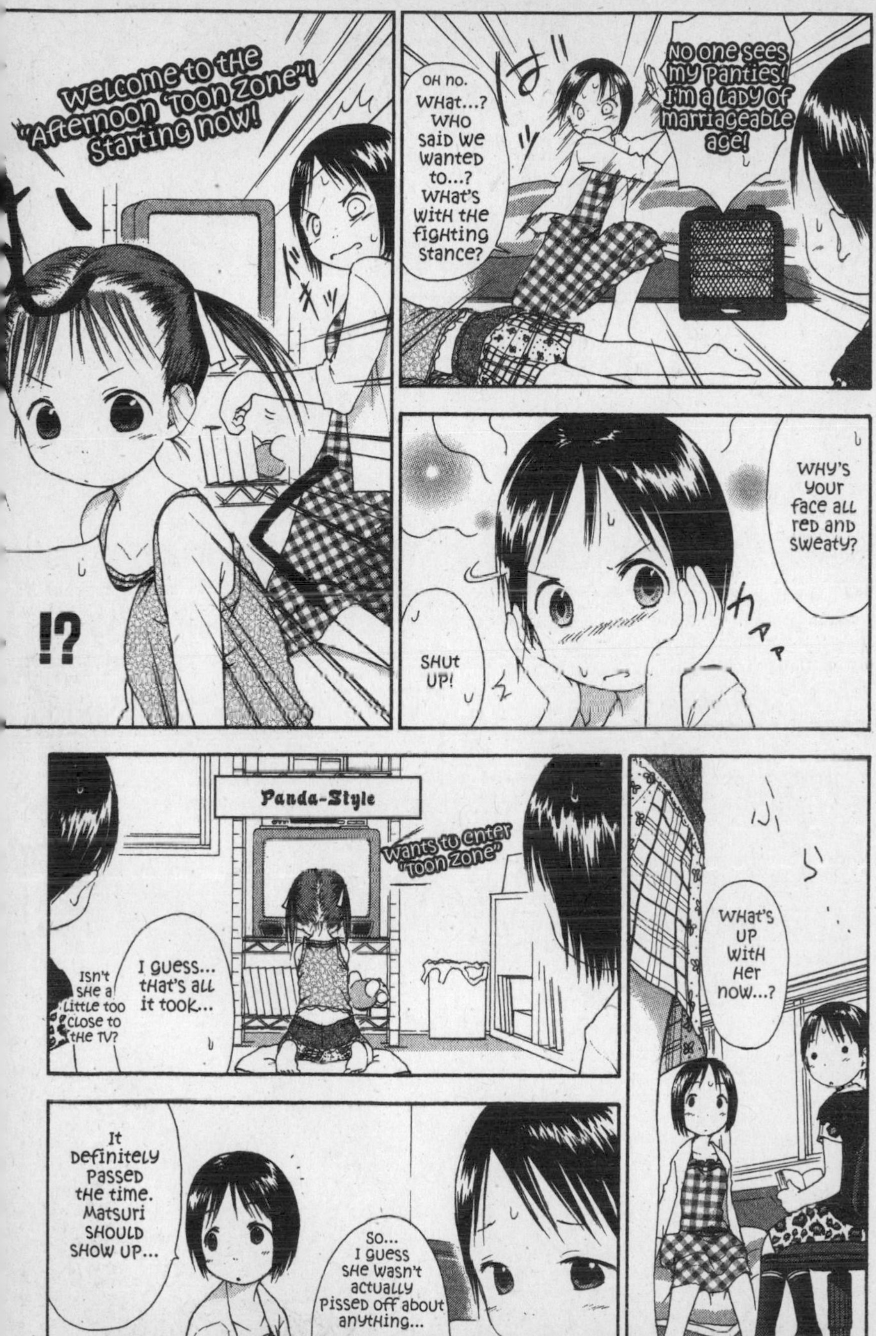
No one sees my panties! I'm a lady of marriageable age!
Oh no. What...? Who said we wanted to...? What's with the fighting stance?
Why's your face all red and sweaty?
Shut up!
Welcome to the "Afternoon 'Toon Zone"! Starting now!
!?
What's up with her now...?
Panda-Style
Wants to enter "'Toon Zone"
I guess... that's all it took...
Isn't she a little too close to the TV?
So... I guess she wasn't actually pissed off about anything...
She was just... bored?
It definitely passed the time. Matsuri should show up...

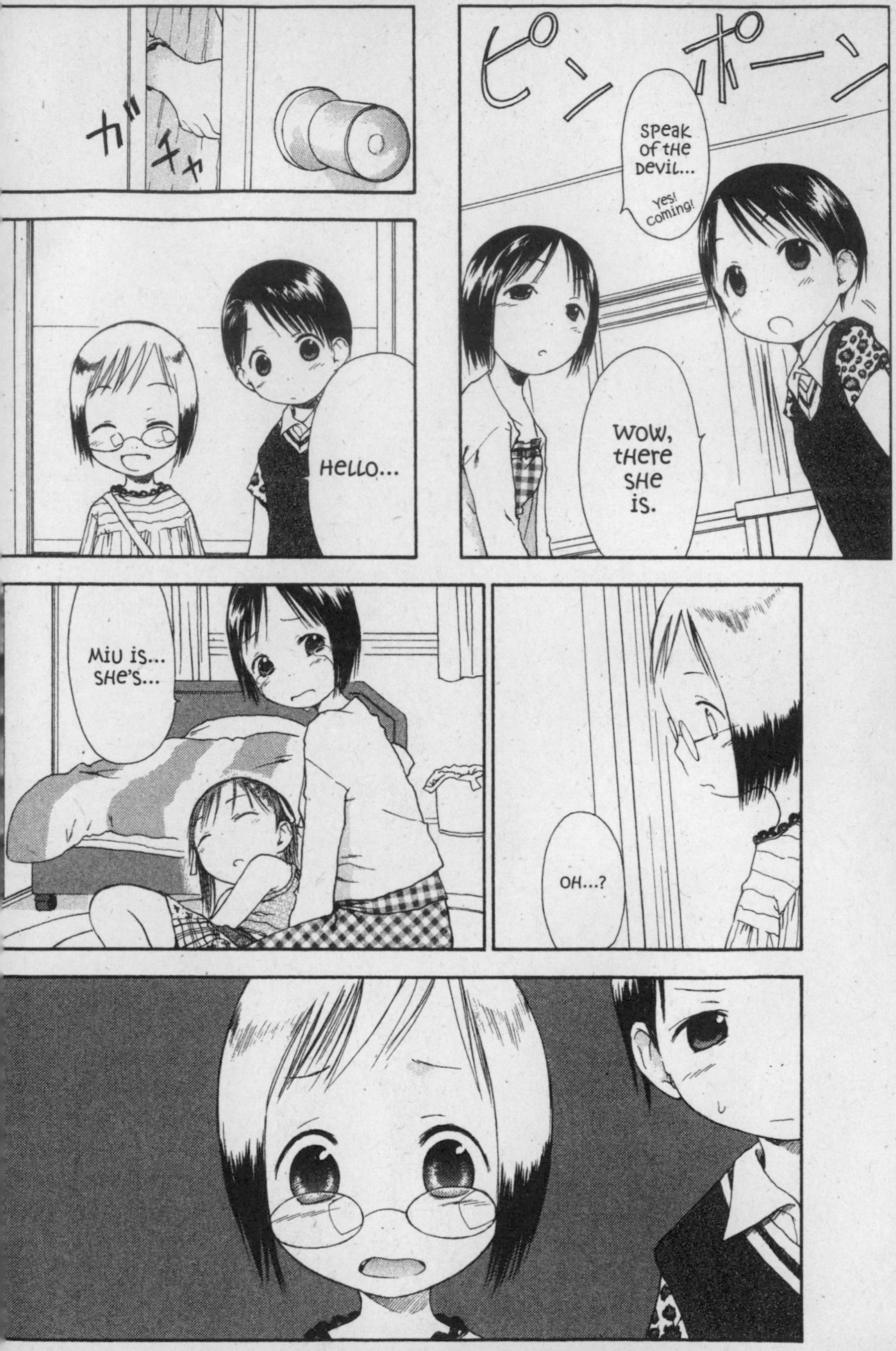
ピンポーン
SPEAK OF THE DEVIL...
YES! COMING!
WOW, THERE SHE IS.
ガチャ
HELLO...
OH...?
MIU IS... SHE'S...

PAGE 123

name	season
☑NOBUE	☐SPRING
☐CHIKA	☐SUMMER
☐MIU	☐AUTUMN
☐MATSURI	☑WINTER

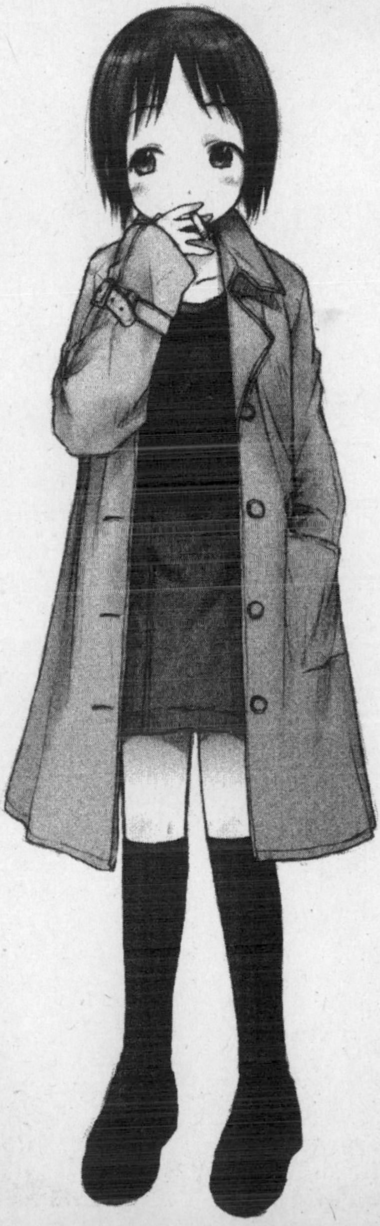

PAGE 124

name

☐NOBUE
☑CHIKA
☐MIU
☐MATSURI

season

☐SPRING
☐SUMMER
☐AUTUMN
☑WINTER

は　ぁ…

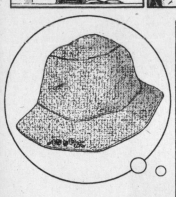

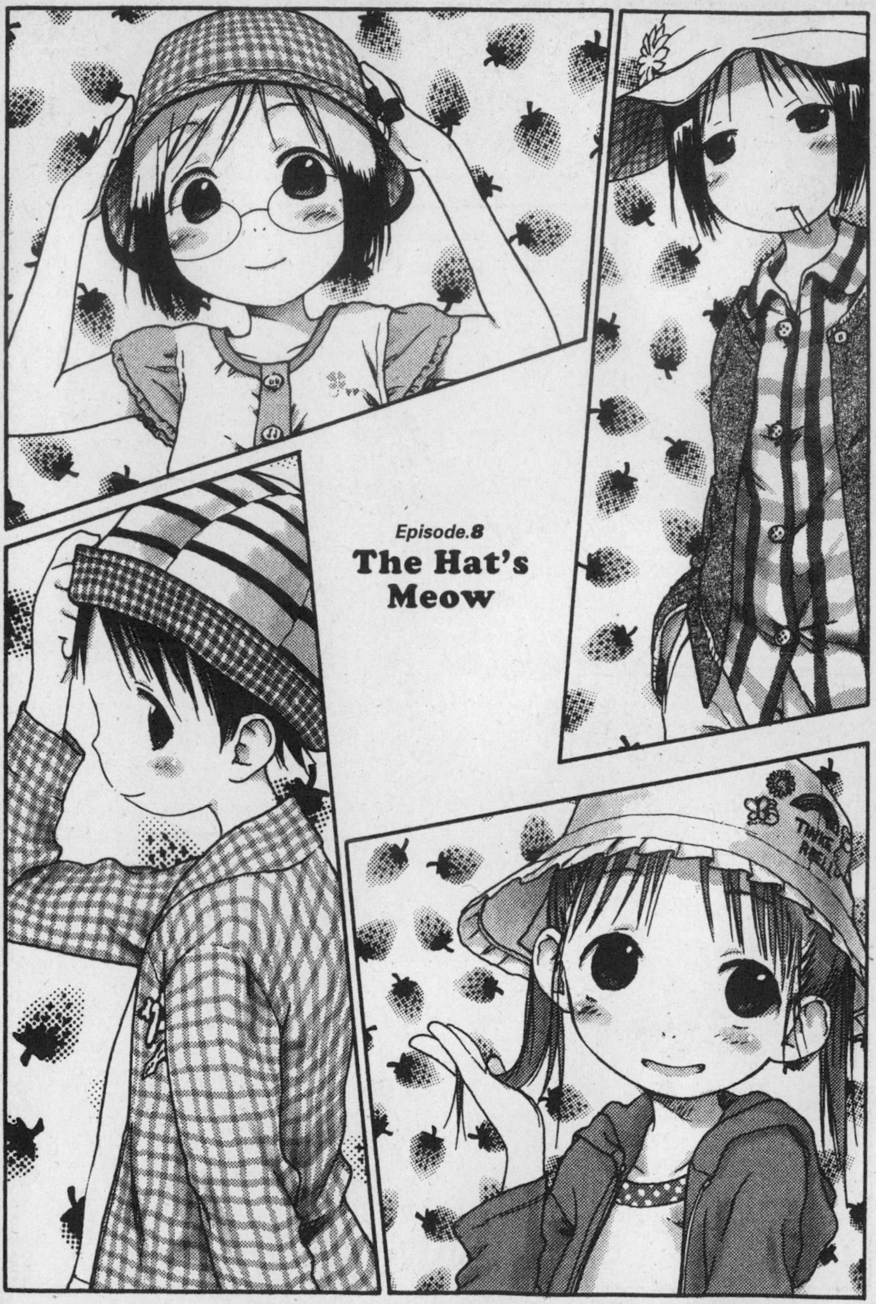

Episode.8

The Hat's Meow

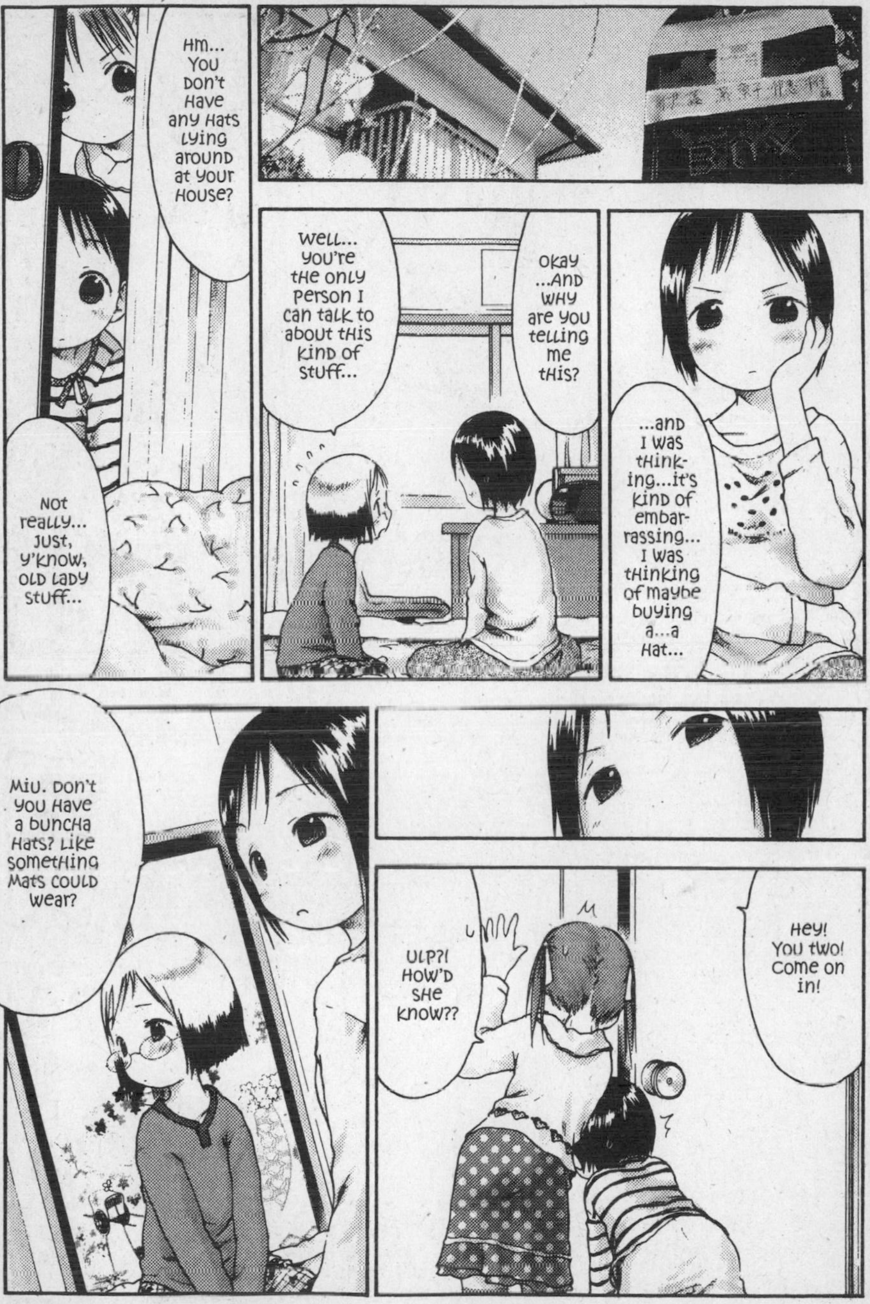
...and I was thinking...it's kind of embarrassing... I was thinking of maybe buying a...a hat...
Okay ...and why are you telling me this?
Well... you're the only person I can talk to about this kind of stuff...
Hm... You don't have any hats lying around at your house?
Not really... just, y'know, old lady stuff...
Hey! You two! Come on in!
Ulp?! How'd she know??
Miu. Don't you have a buncha hats? Like something Mats could wear?

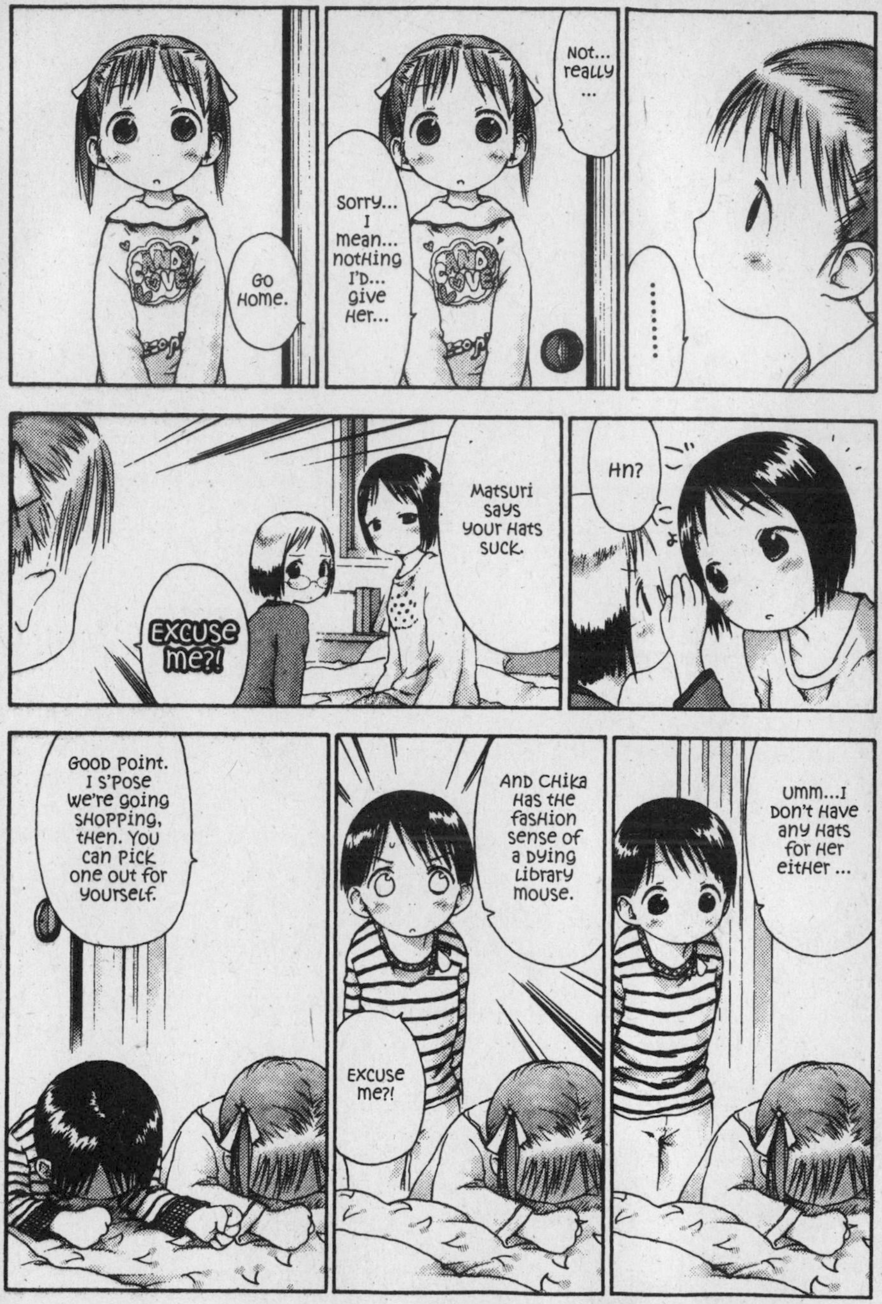
......
Not... really ...
Sorry... I mean... nothing I'd... give her...
Go home.
Hn?
Matsuri says your hats suck.
EXCUSE me?!
Umm...I don't have any hats for her either ...
And Chika has the fashion sense of a dying library mouse.
EXCUSE me?!
Good point. I s'pose we're going shopping, then. You can pick one out for yourself.

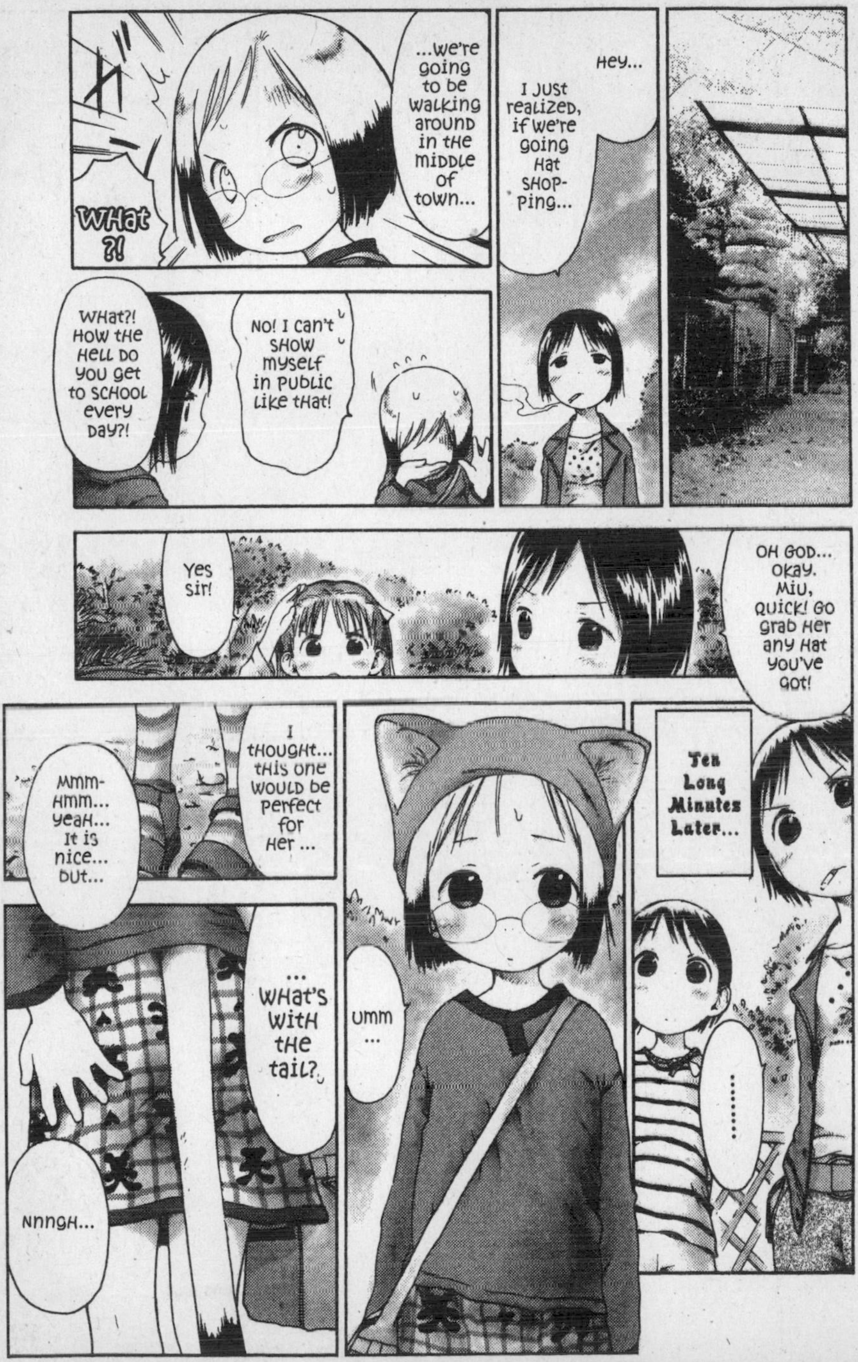
Hey...
I just realized, if we're going hat shop-ping...
...we're going to be walking around in the middle of town...
WHat ?!
No! I can't show myself in public like that!
WHat?! How the hell do you get to school every day?!
OH GOD... Okay. Miu, quick! Go grab her any hat you've got!
Yes sir!
Ten Long Minutes Later...
......
umm ...
I thought... this one would be perfect for her ...
Mmm-hmm... yeah... It is nice... but...
... What's with the tail?
Nnngh...

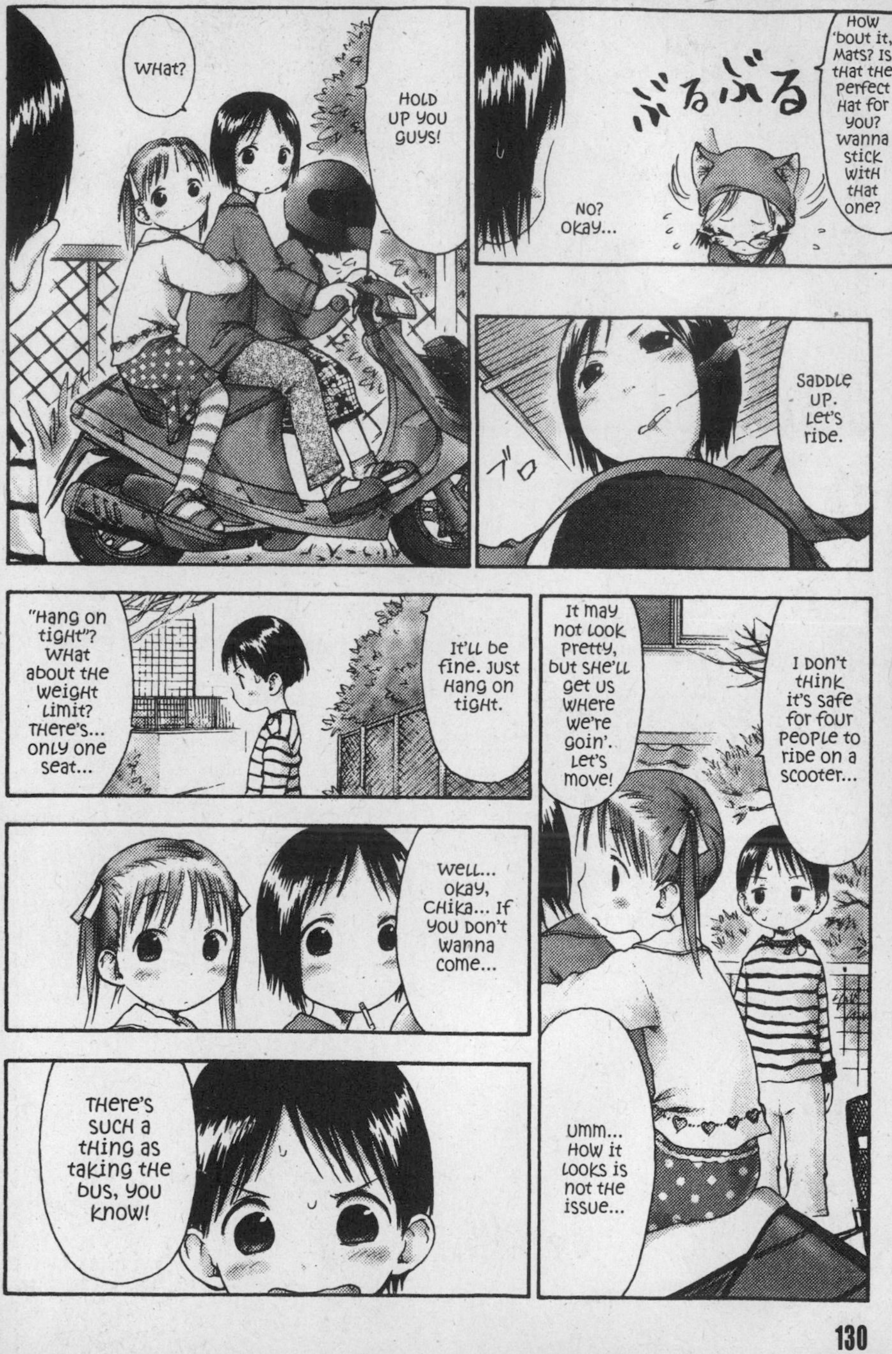
How 'bout it, Mats? Is that the perfect hat for you? Wanna stick with that one?
ぶるぶる
No? Okay...
Saddle up. Let's ride.
ブロ
Hold up you guys!
What?
I don't think it's safe for four people to ride on a scooter...
It may not look pretty, but she'll get us where we're goin'. Let's move!
Umm... How it looks is not the issue...
It'll be fine. Just hang on tight.
"Hang on tight"? What about the weight limit? There's... only one seat...
Well... okay, Chika... If you don't wanna come...
There's such a thing as taking the bus, you know!

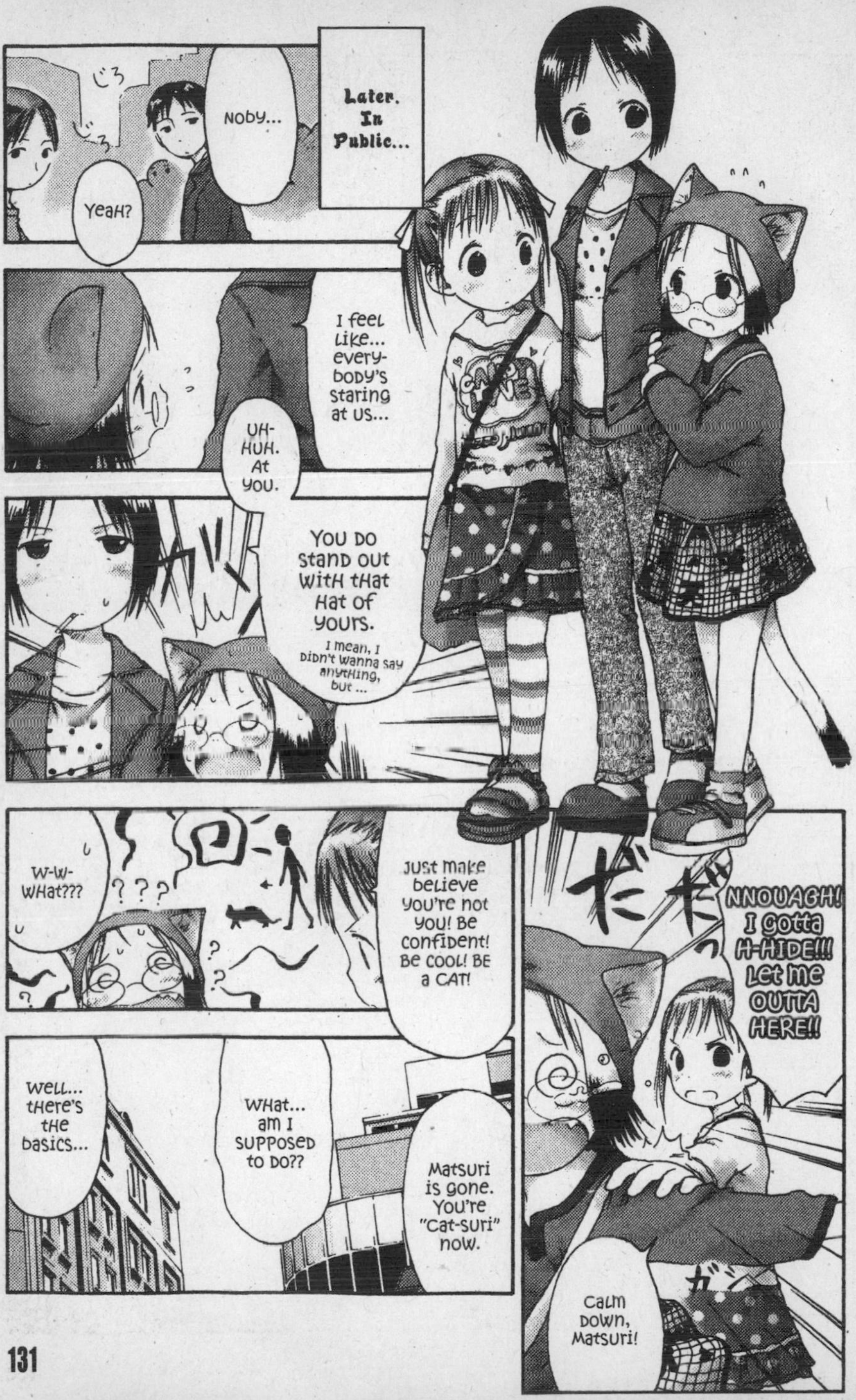
Later. In Public...
Noby...
Yeah?
じろ じろ
I feel like... every-body's staring at us...
Uh-huh. At you.
You do stand out with that hat of yours.
I mean, I didn't wanna say anything, but ...
NNOUAGH! I gotta H-HIDE!!! Let me OUTTA HERE!!
Calm down, Matsuri!
What... am I supposed to do??
Well... there's the basics...
Matsuri is gone. You're "Cat-suri" now.
Just make believe you're not you! Be confident! Be cool! Be a cat!
W-W-What???

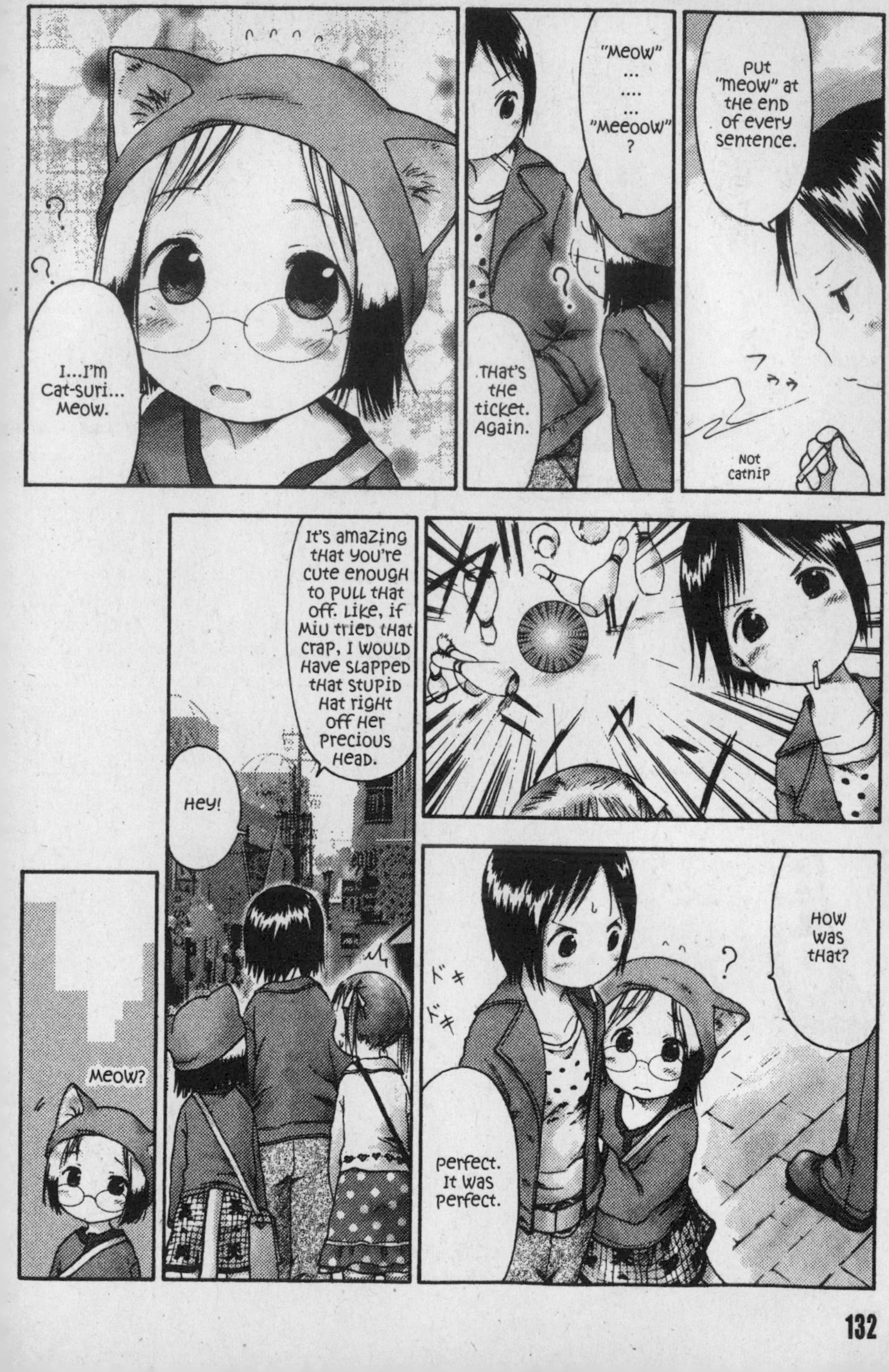

Put "meow" at the end of every sentence.
Not catnip
"Meow" ... . "Meeoow" ?
That's the ticket. Again.
I...I'm Cat-suri... Meow.
How was that?
Perfect. It was perfect.
It's amazing that you're cute enough to pull that off. Like, if Miu tried that crap, I would have slapped that stupid hat right off her precious head.
Hey!
Meow?

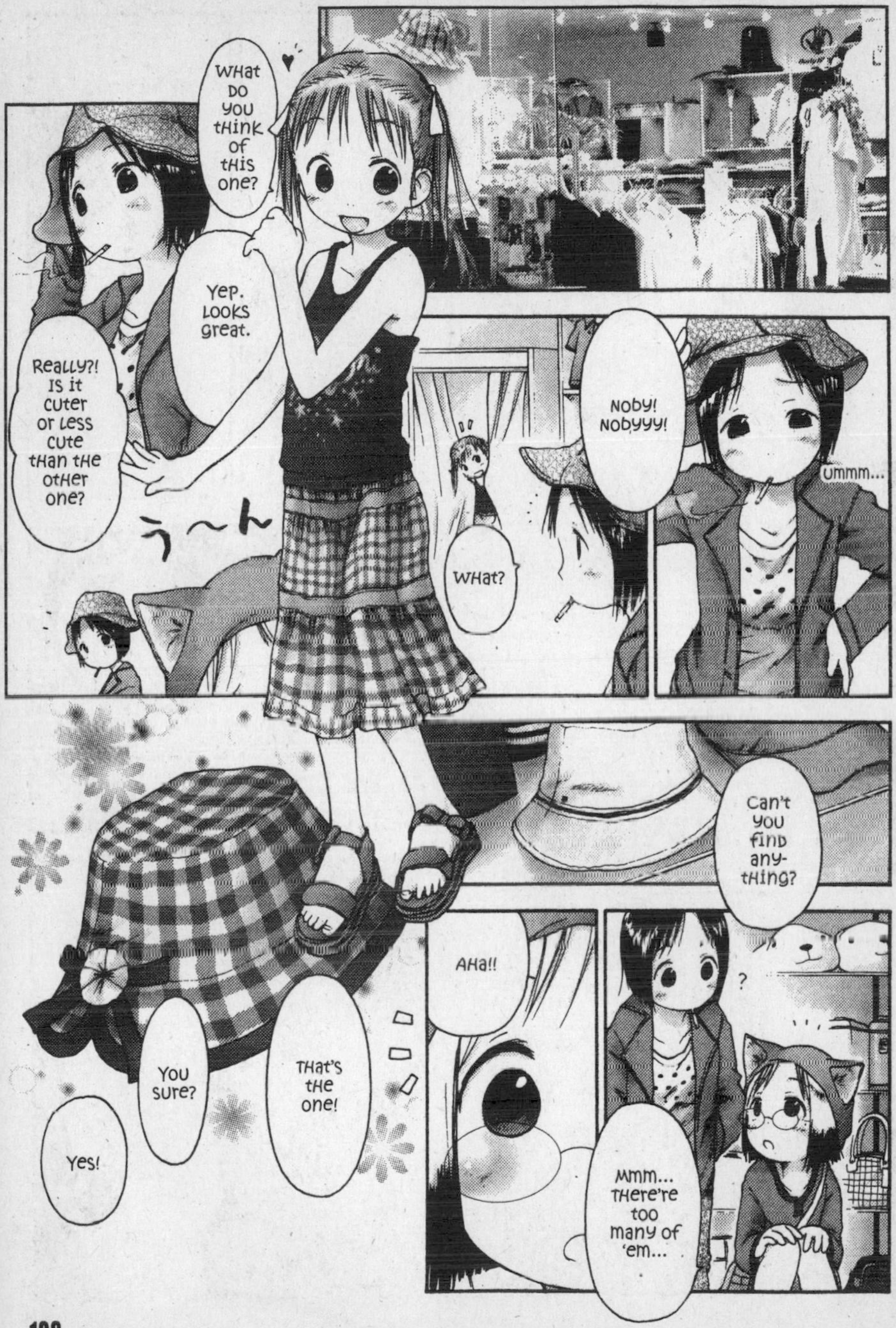
Noby! Nobyyy!
Ummm...
What?
What do you think of this one?
Yep. Looks great.
Really?! Is it cuter or less cute than the other one?
うーん
Can't you find any-thing?
?
Mmm... There're too many of 'em...
AHa!!
That's the one!
You sure?
Yes!

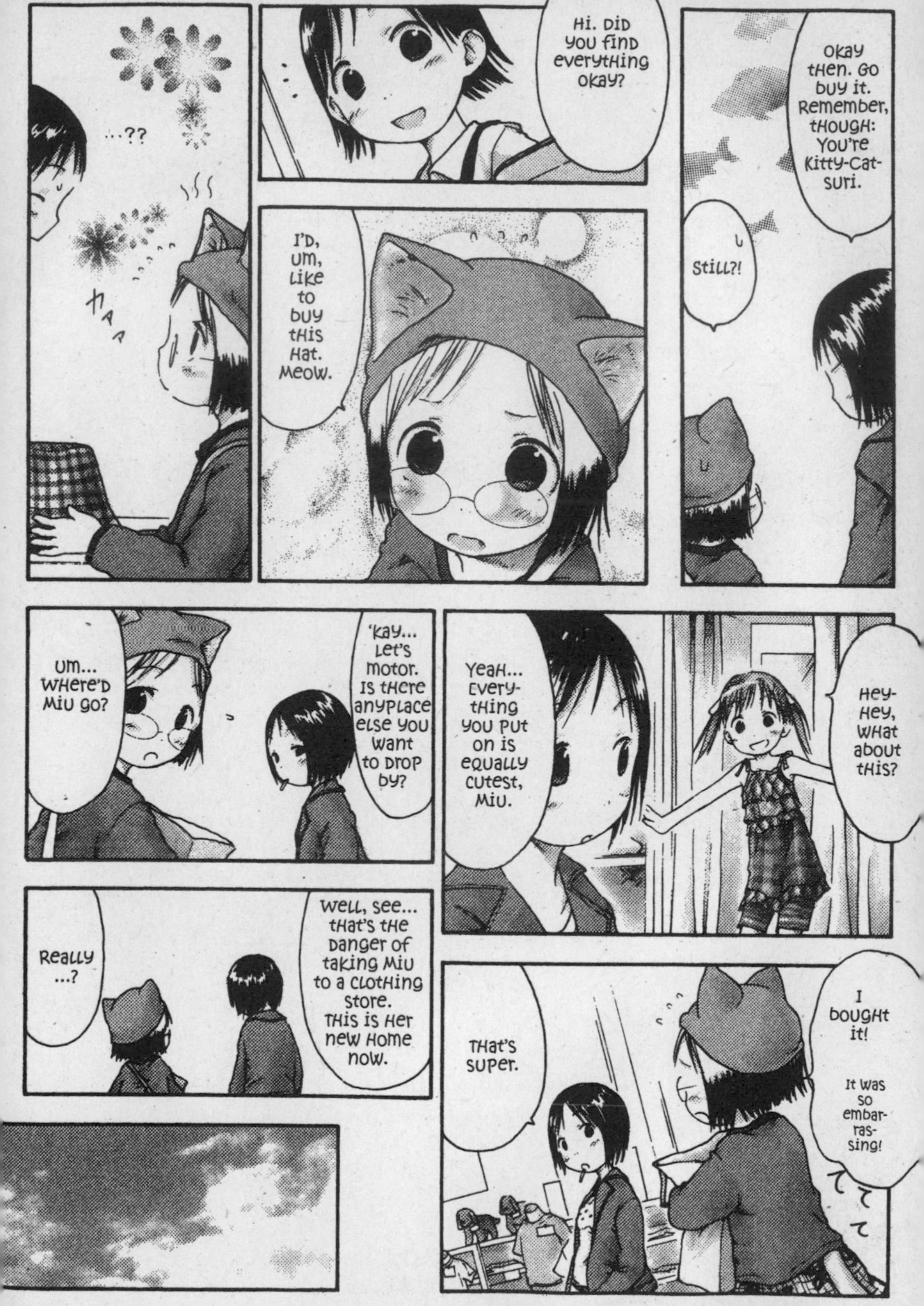
Okay then. Go buy it. Remember, though: You're Kitty-Cat-suri.
Still?!
Hi. Did you find everything okay?
I'd, um, like to buy this hat. Meow.
...??
Hey-hey, what about this?
Yeah... Every-thing you put on is equally cutest, Miu.
'Kay... Let's motor. Is there anyplace else you want to drop by?
Um... where'd Miu go?
I bought it!
It was so embar-rassing!
That's super.
Well, see... that's the danger of taking Miu to a clothing store. This is her new home now.
Really ...?

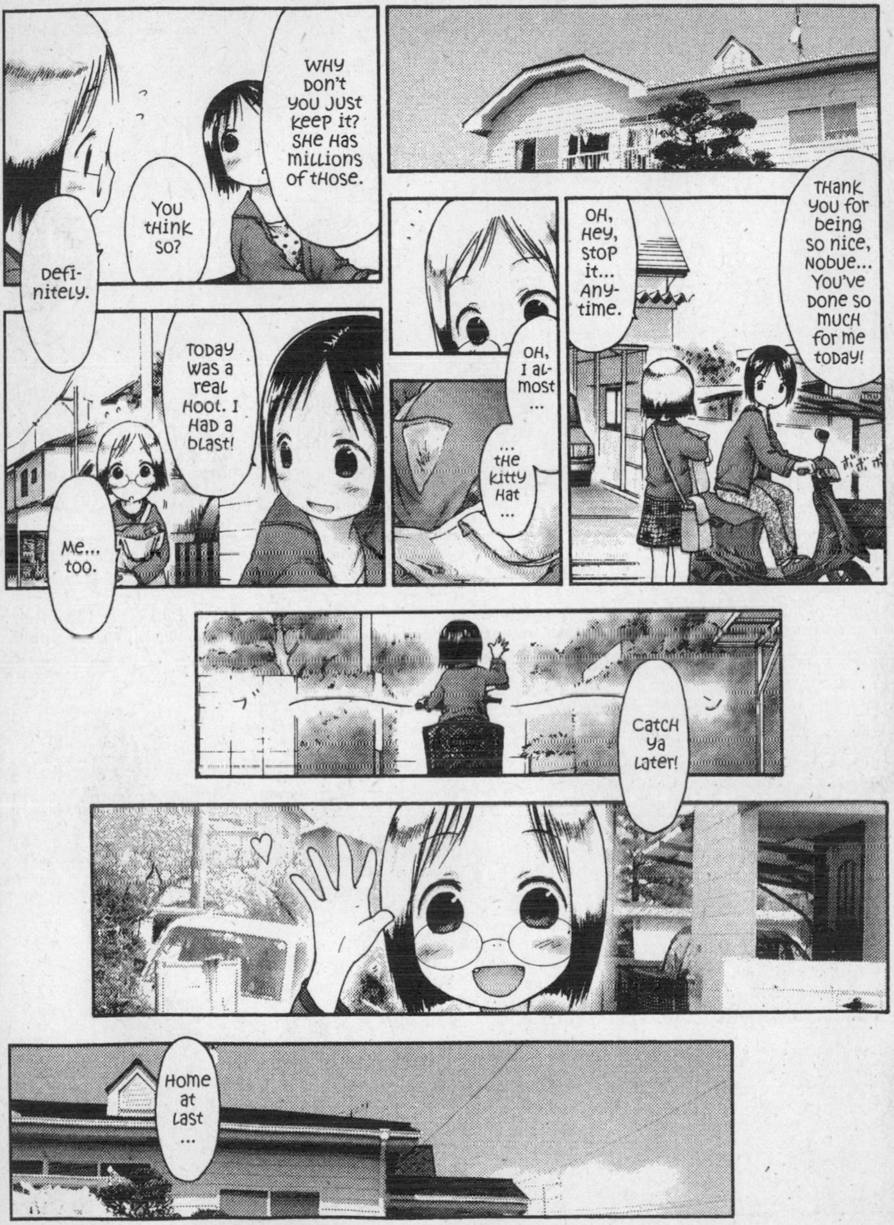
WHY Don't you JUST keep it? SHE HAS millions of tHOSE.
You tHINK so?
Defi-nitely.
THANK you for being so nice, NOBUE... You've Done so MUCH for me toDAY!
OH, HEy, stop it... Any-time.
OH, I al-most ...
... tHe kitty Hat ...
toDAY was a real Hoot. I HAD a blast!
Me... too.
CatcH ya Later!
Home at Last ...

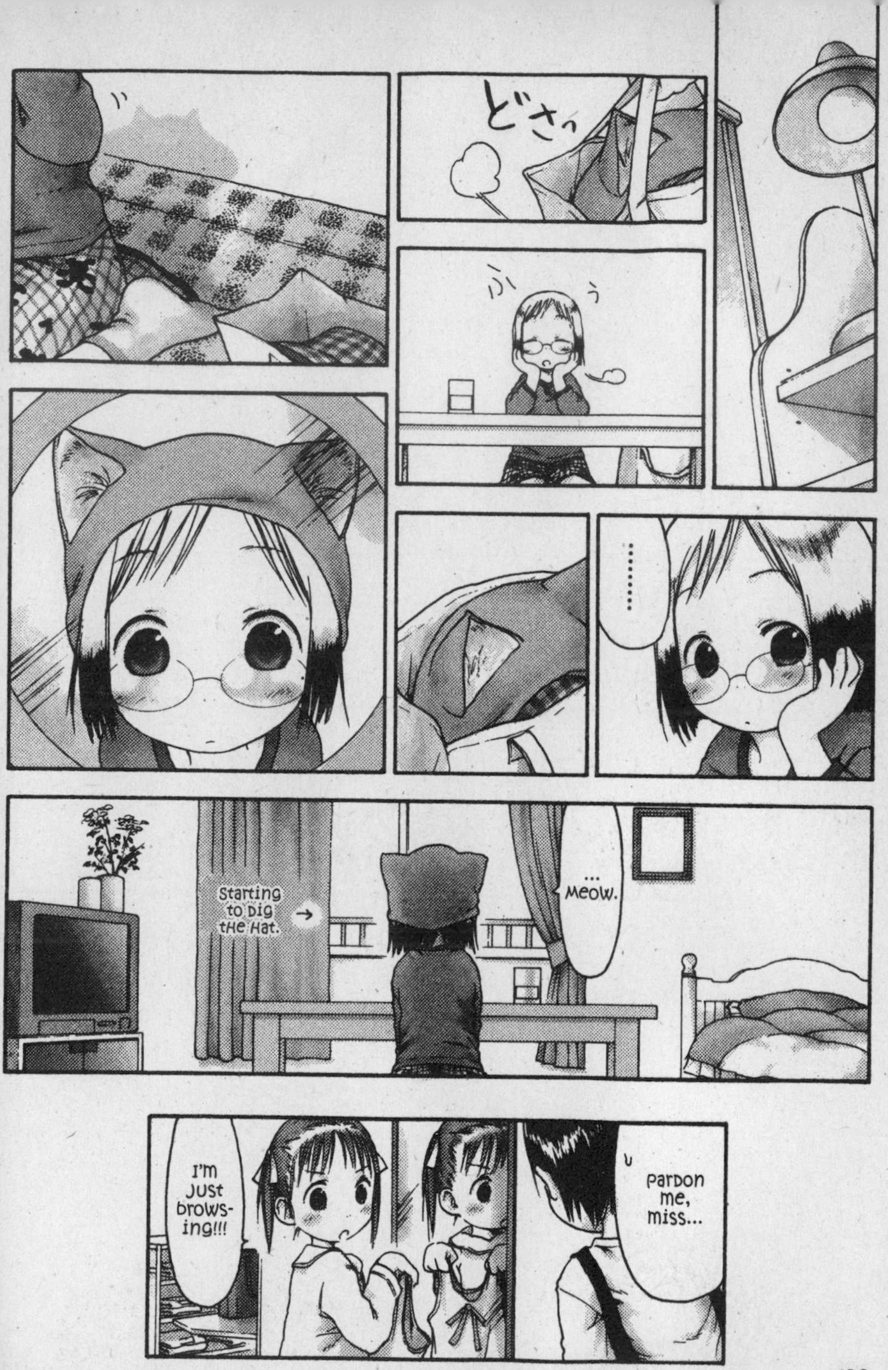

どさっ
ふぅ
......
...Meow.
Starting to dig the hat. →
Pardon me, miss...
I'm just browsing!!!

PAGE 137

name	*season*
☐NOBUE	☐SPRING
☐CHIKA	☐SUMMER
MIU	☐AUTUMN
☐MATSURI	WINTER

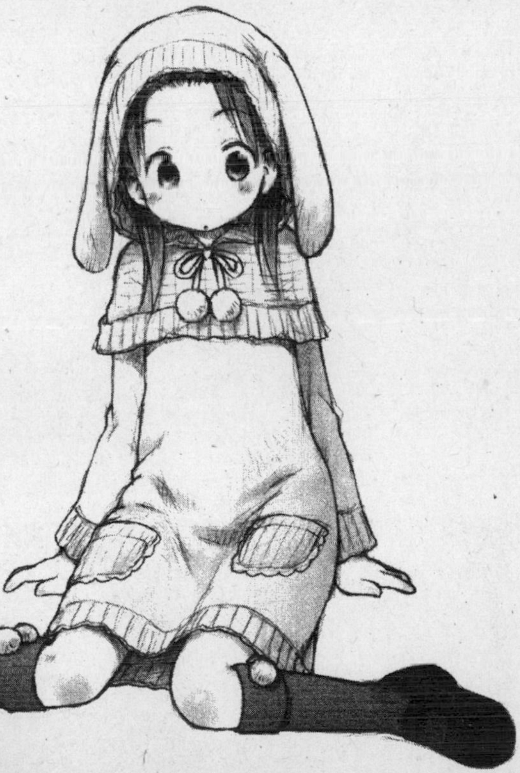

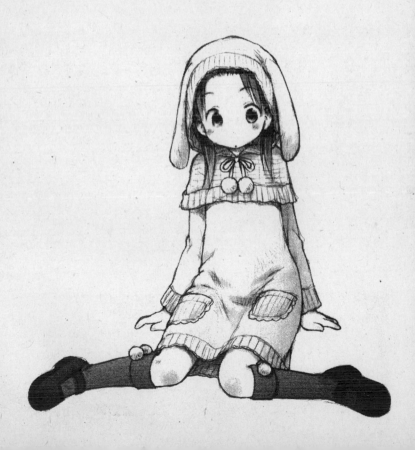

PAGE 138

name	*season*
☐NOBUE	☐SPRING
☐CHIKA	☐SUMMER
☐MIU	☐AUTUMN
■MATSURI	■WINTER

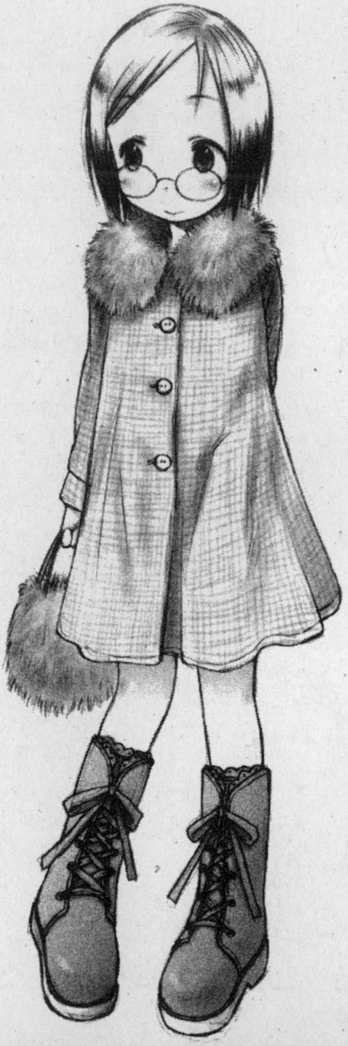

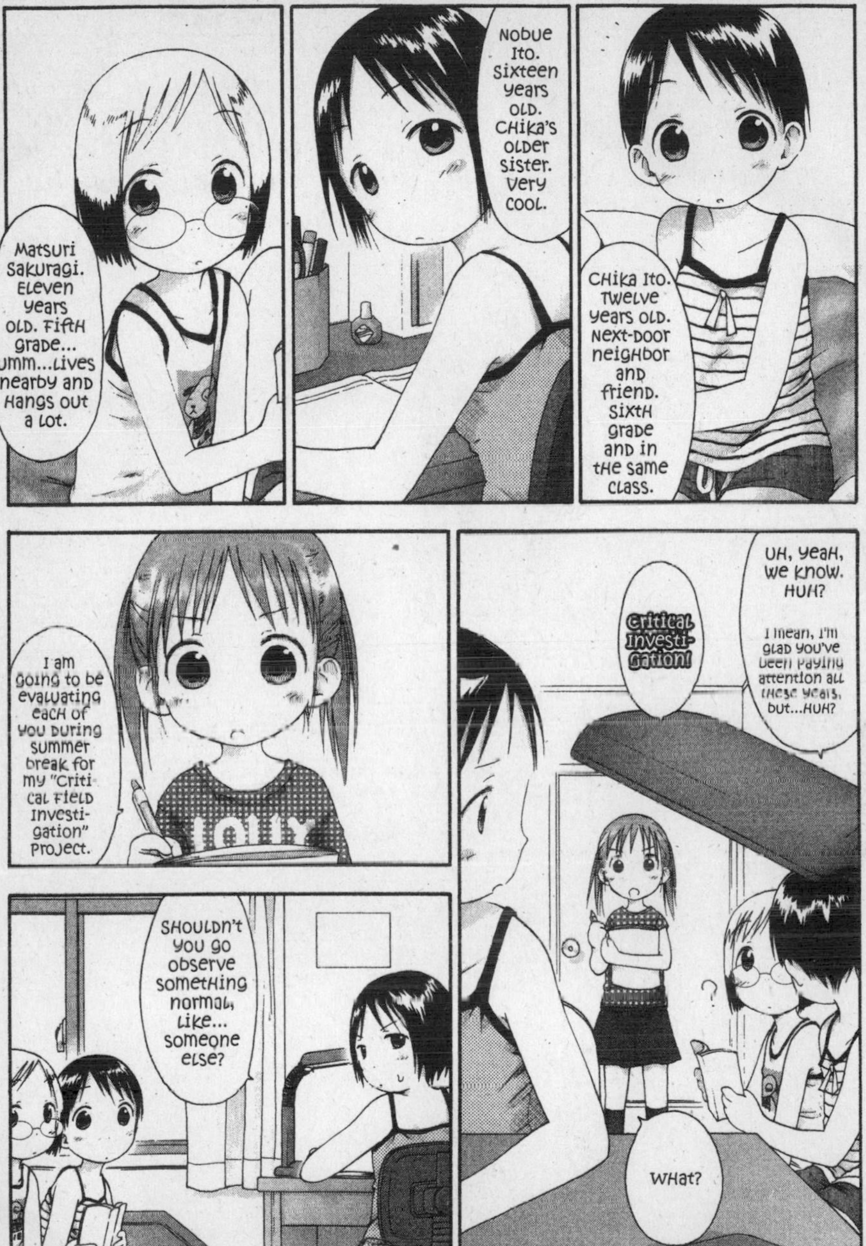
Chika Ito. Twelve years old. Next-door neighbor and friend. Sixth grade and in the same class.
Nobue Ito. Sixteen years old. Chika's older sister. Very cool.
Matsuri Sakuragi. Eleven years old. Fifth grade... umm...lives nearby and hangs out a lot.
UH, yeah, we know. HUH?
I mean, I'm glad you've been paying attention all these years, but...HUH?
Critical Investigation!
What?
I am going to be evaluating each of you during summer break for my "Critical Field Investigation" project.
Shouldn't you go observe something normal, like... someone else?

Objective Assessment of My Friends

Researcher:
Miu Matsuoka, Grade 6

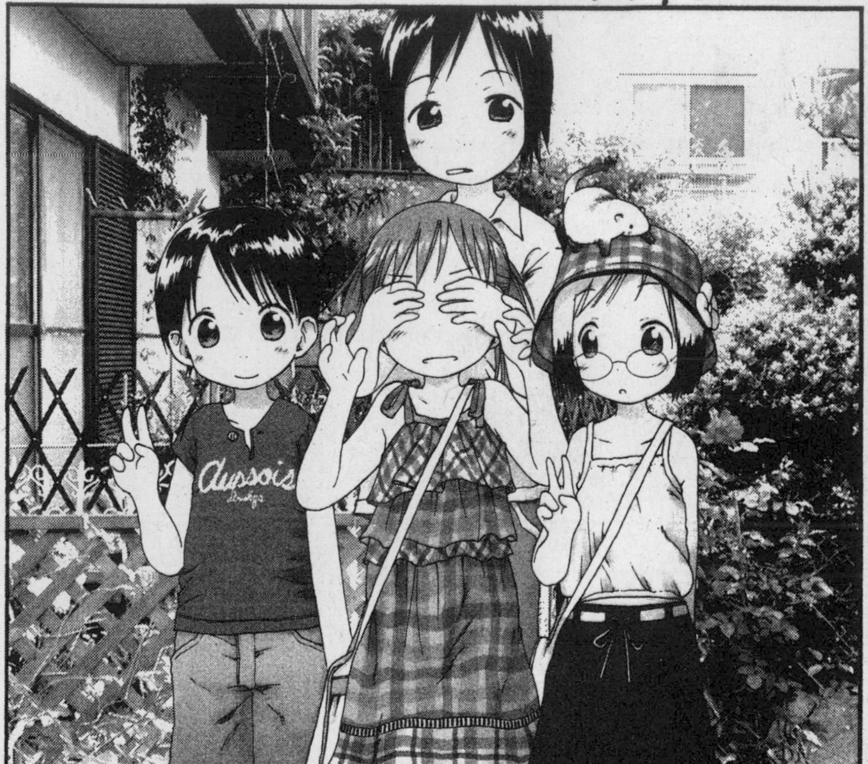
Aussois

(Nonfiction)

Episode.9

CRITICAL INVESTIGATION

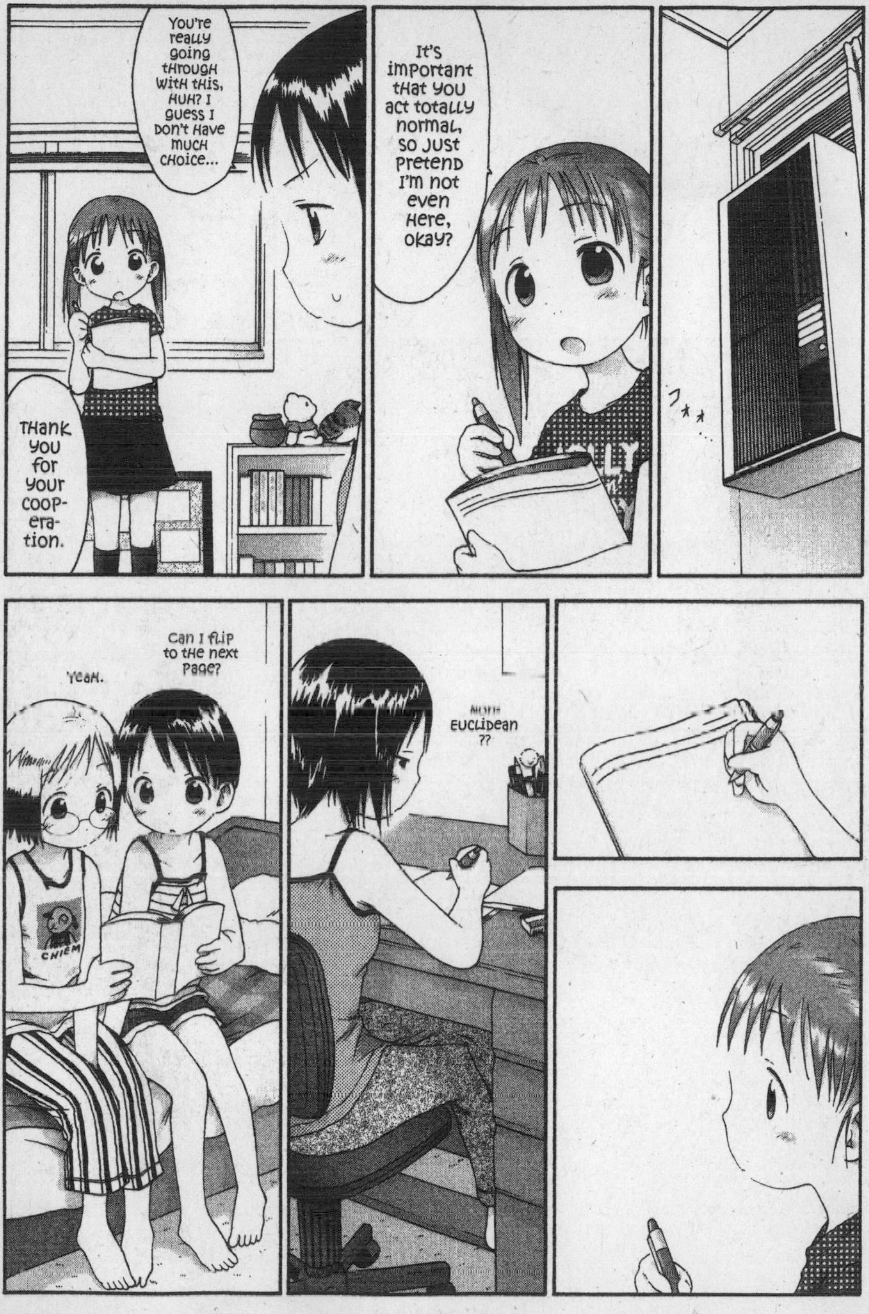
It's important that you act totally normal, so just pretend I'm not even here, okay?
You're really going through with this, huh? I guess I don't have much choice...
Thank you for your cooperation.
Euclidean ??
Can I flip to the next page?
Yeah.

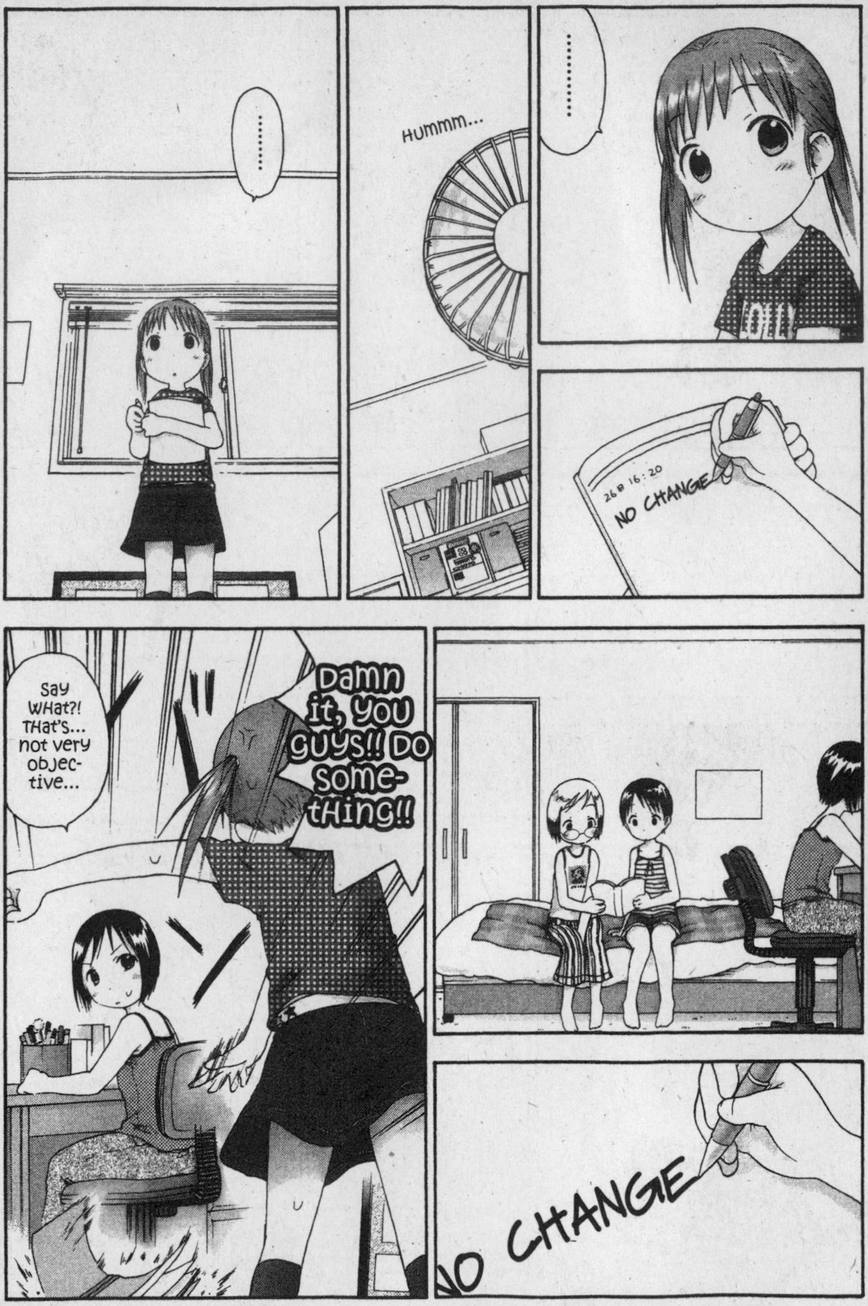
......
26日 16:20
NO CHANGE
HUMMM...
......
NO CHANGE
Damn it, you guys!! Do some-thing!!
Say what?! That's... not very objec-tive...

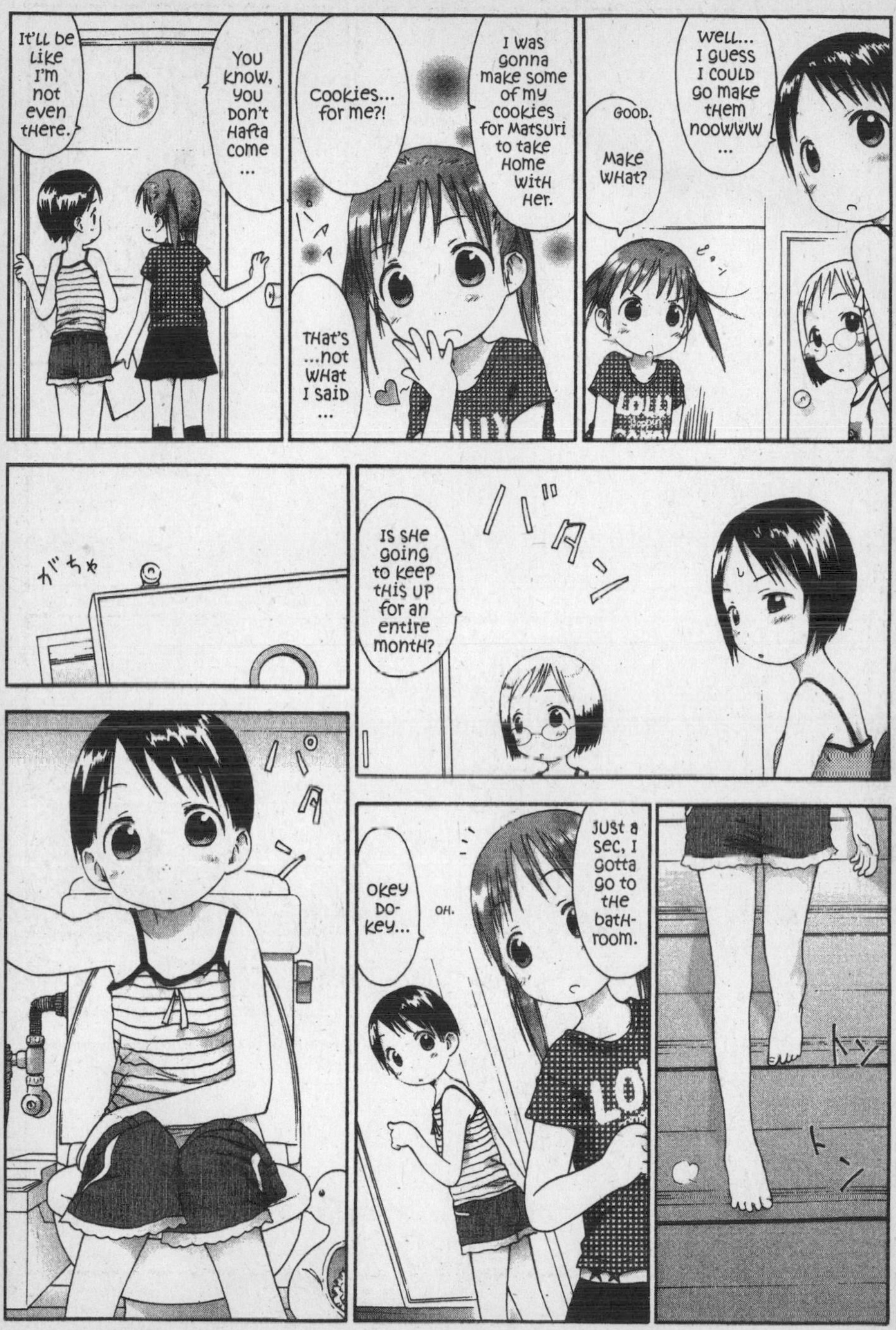
Well... I guess I could go make them nowwww...
Good.
Make what?
I was gonna make some of my cookies for Matsuri to take home with her.
Cookies... for me?!
That's ...not what I said...
You know, you don't hafta come...
It'll be like I'm not even there.
バタン
Is she going to keep this up for an entire month?
がちゃ
トン
トン
Just a sec, I gotta go to the bathroom.
Oh.
Okey dokey...

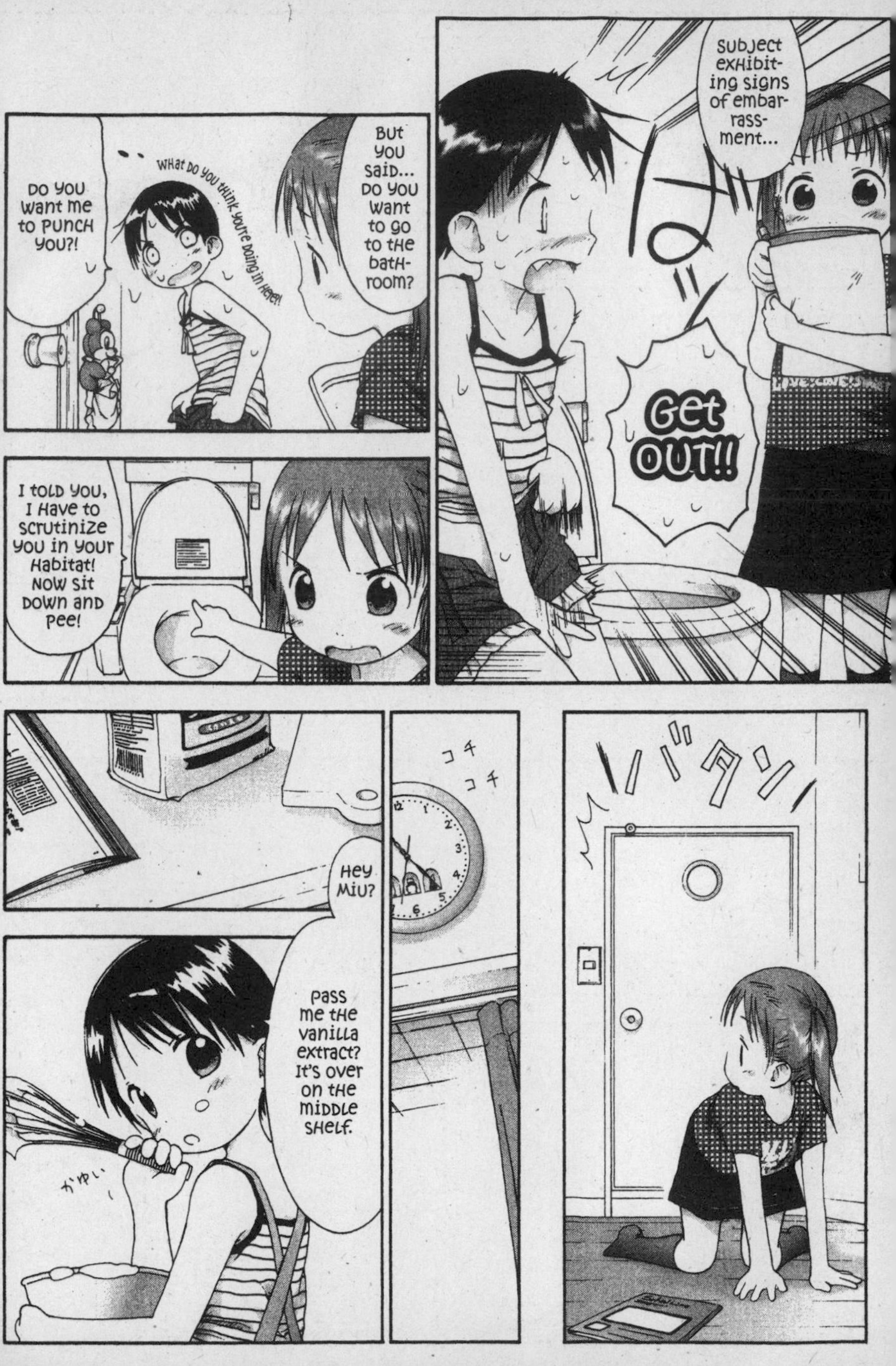
Subject exhibiting signs of embarrassment...
Get OUT!!
But you said... Do you want to go to the bathroom?
What do you think you're doing in here?!
Do you want me to punch you?!
I told you, I have to scrutinize you in your habitat! Now sit down and pee!
バタン
コチ コチ
Hey Miu?
Pass me the vanilla extract? It's over on the middle shelf.
かゆい

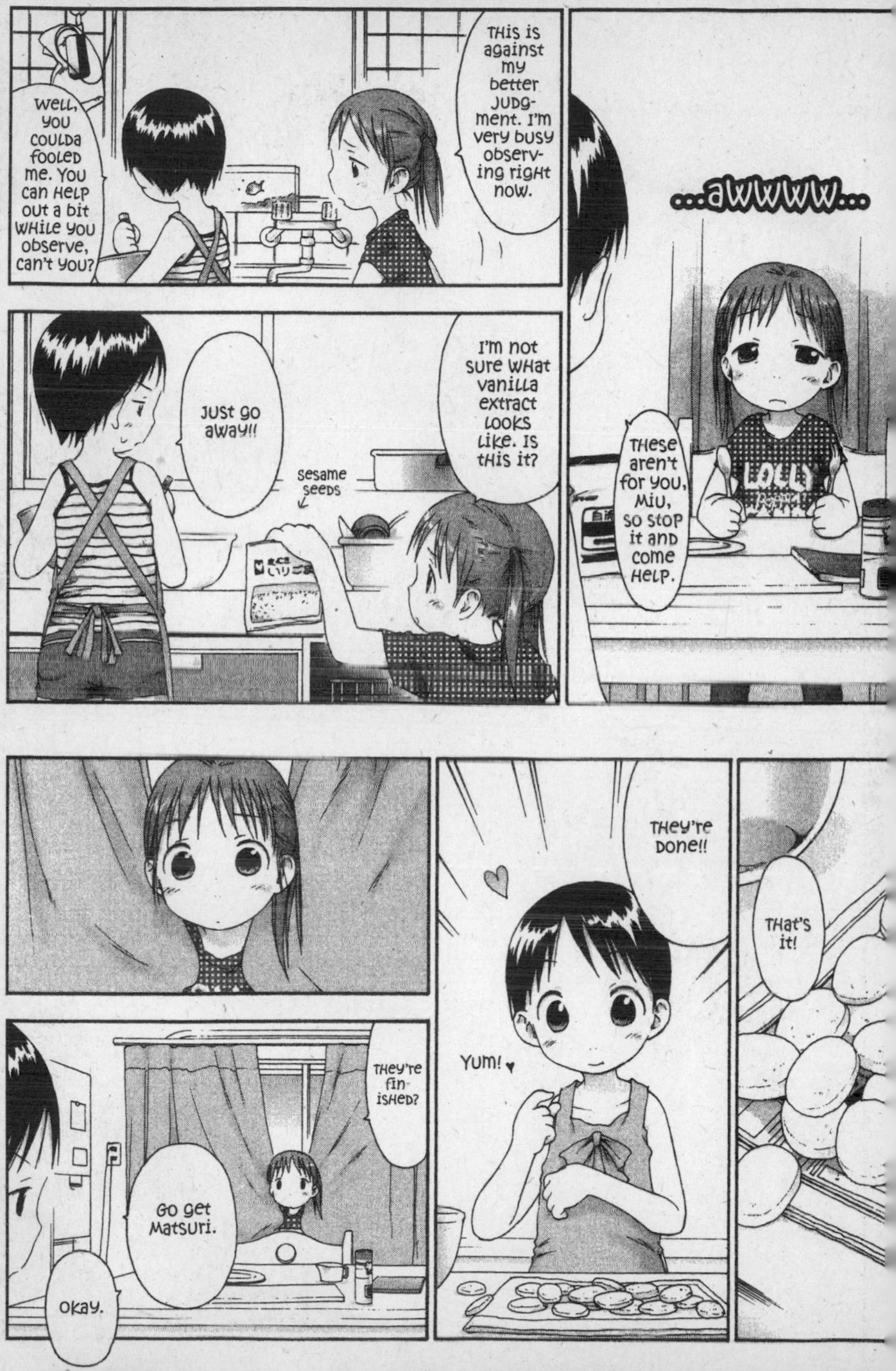
...awwww...
These aren't for you, Miu, so stop it and come help.
This is against my better judgment. I'm very busy observing right now.
Well, you coulda fooled me. You can help out a bit while you observe, can't you?
I'm not sure what vanilla extract looks like. Is this it?
sesame seeds
Just go away!!
That's it!
They're done!!
Yum!
They're fin-ished?
Go get Matsuri.
Okay.

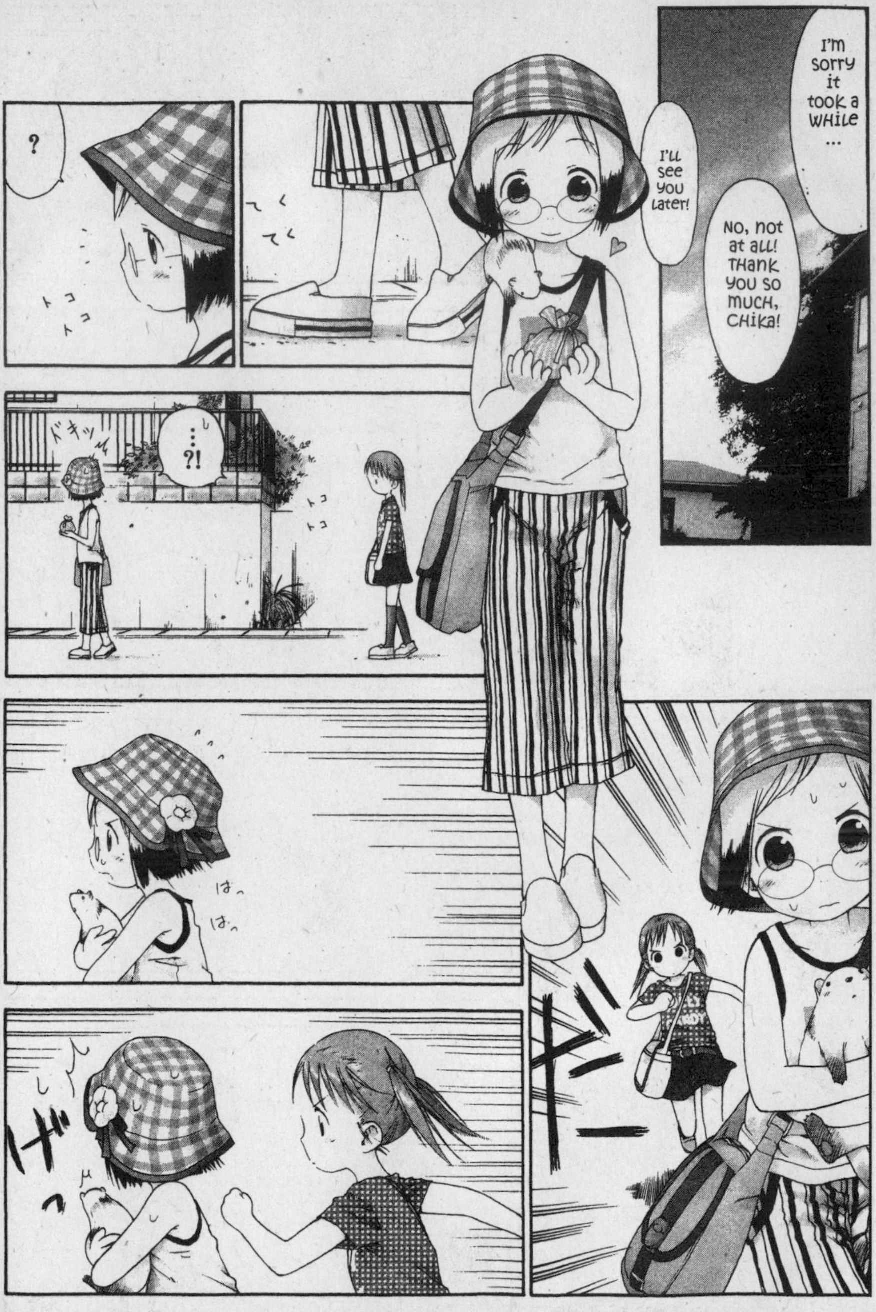
I'm sorry it took a while...
No, not at all! Thank you so much, Chika!
I'll see you later!
てく てく
?
トコ トコ
ドキッ
...?!
トコ トコ
はっ はっ

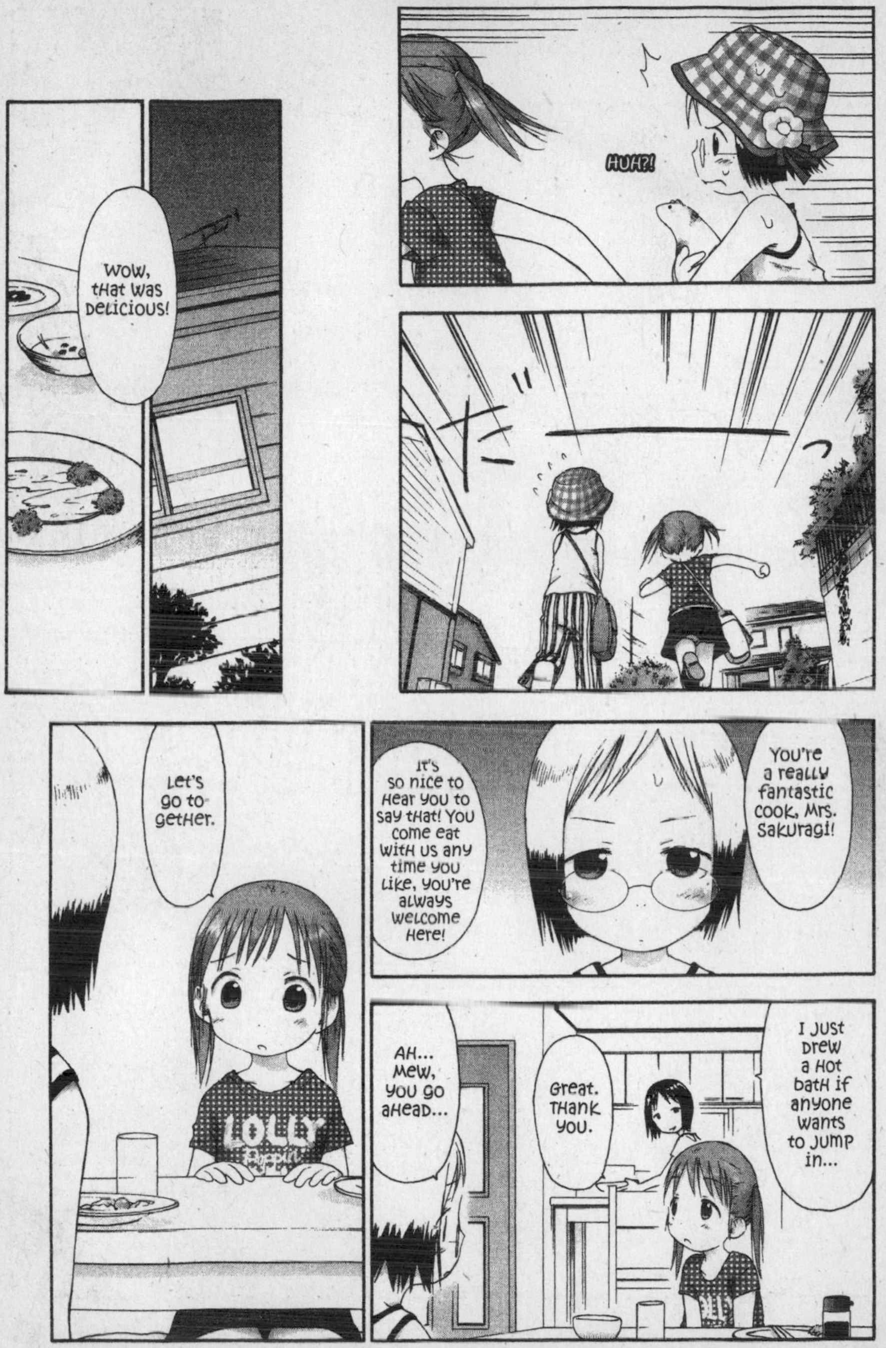
HUH?!
Wow, that was delicious!
You're a really fantastic cook, Mrs. Sakuragi!
It's so nice to hear you to say that! You come eat with us any time you like, you're always welcome here!
I just drew a hot bath if anyone wants to jump in...
Great. Thank you.
Ah... Mew, you go ahead...
Let's go together.

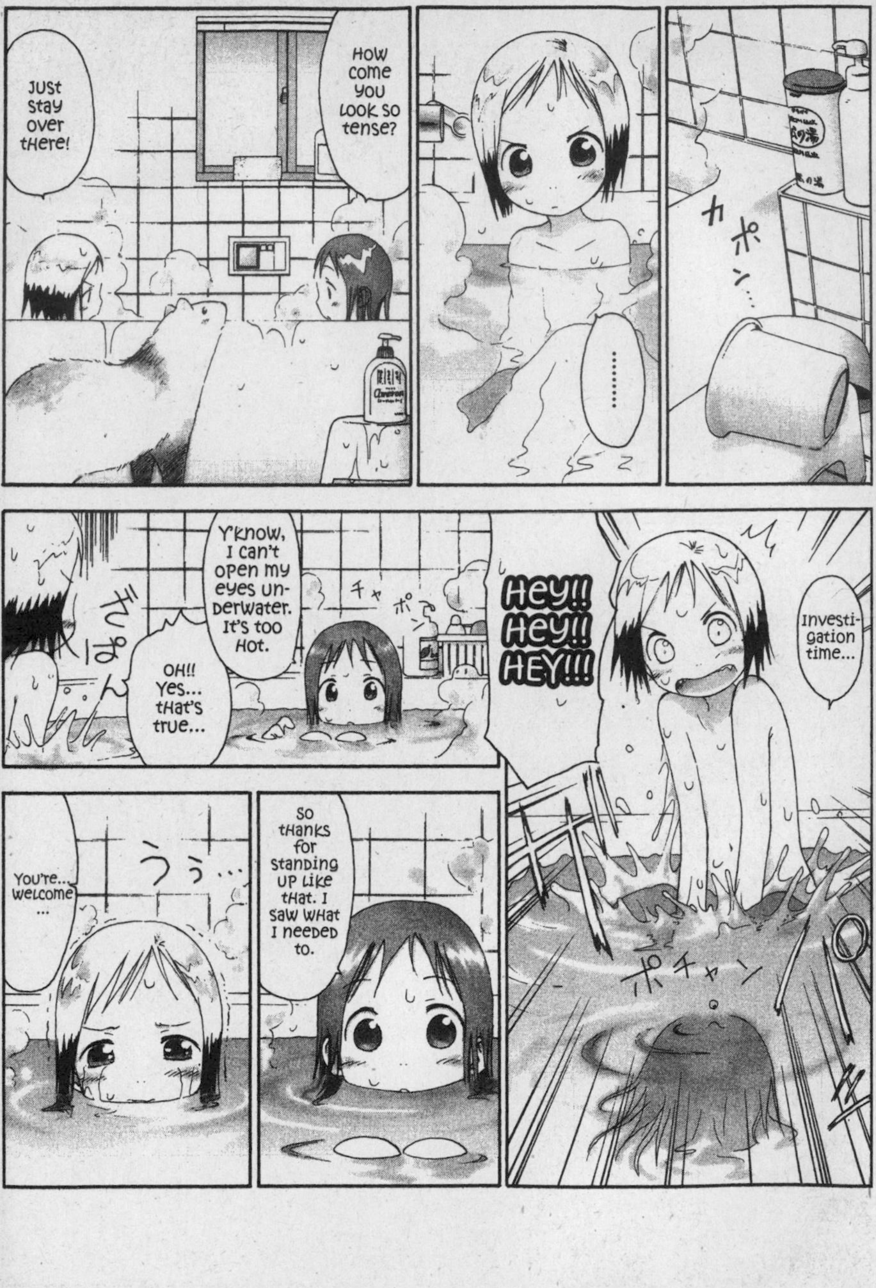
カポン…
……
How come you look so tense?
Just stay over there!
Investigation time...
HEY!! HEY!! HEY!!!
ポチャン
チャポン
Y'know, I can't open my eyes underwater. It's too hot.
OH!! Yes... that's true...
ざぱん
So thanks for standing up like that. I saw what I needed to.
You're... welcome...
うぅ…

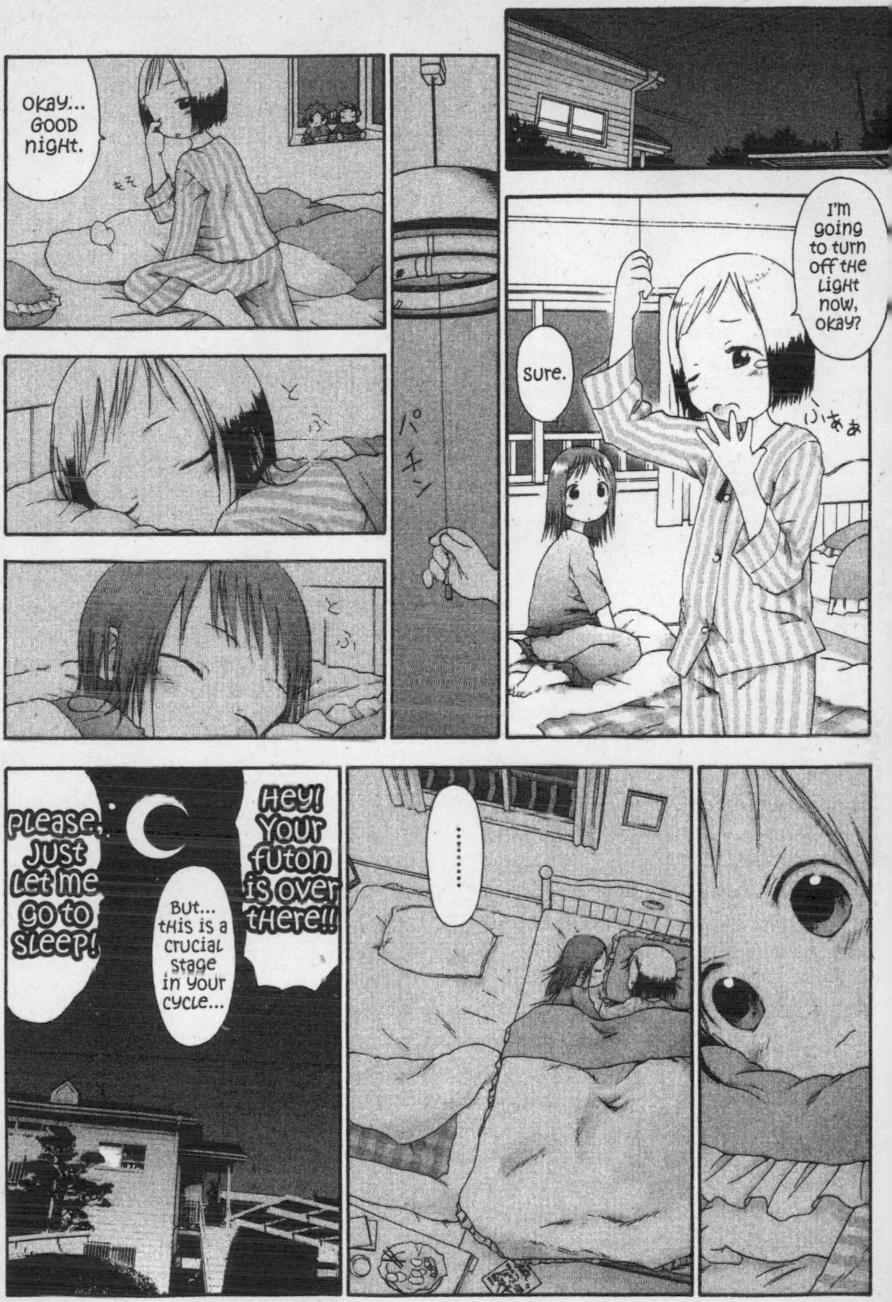
I'm going to turn off the light now, okay?
ふぁぁ
sure.
パチン
okay... GOOD night.
もそ
とふ
とふ
....
Hey! Your futon is over there!!
But... this is a crucial stage in your cycle...
please, just let me go to sleep!

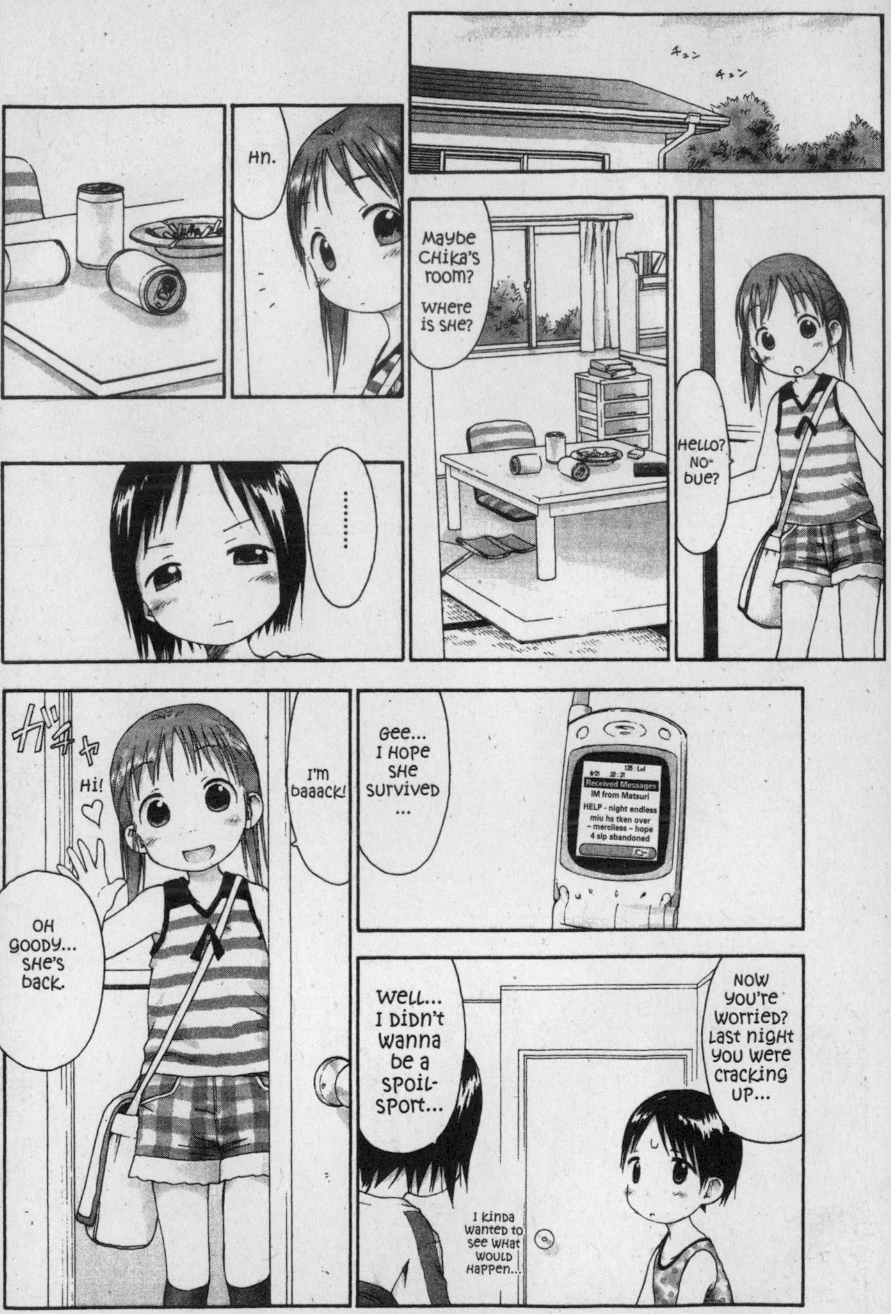
チュン
チュン
Hello? No-bue?
Maybe Chika's room?
Where is she?
Hn.
......
Gee... I hope she survived...
Received Messages
IM from Matsuri
HELP - night endless miu hs tken over - merciless - hope 4 slp abandoned
Now you're worried? Last night you were cracking up...
Well... I didn't wanna be a spoil-sport...
I kinda wanted to see what would happen...
I'm baaack!
ガチャ
Hi! ♡
Oh goody... she's back.

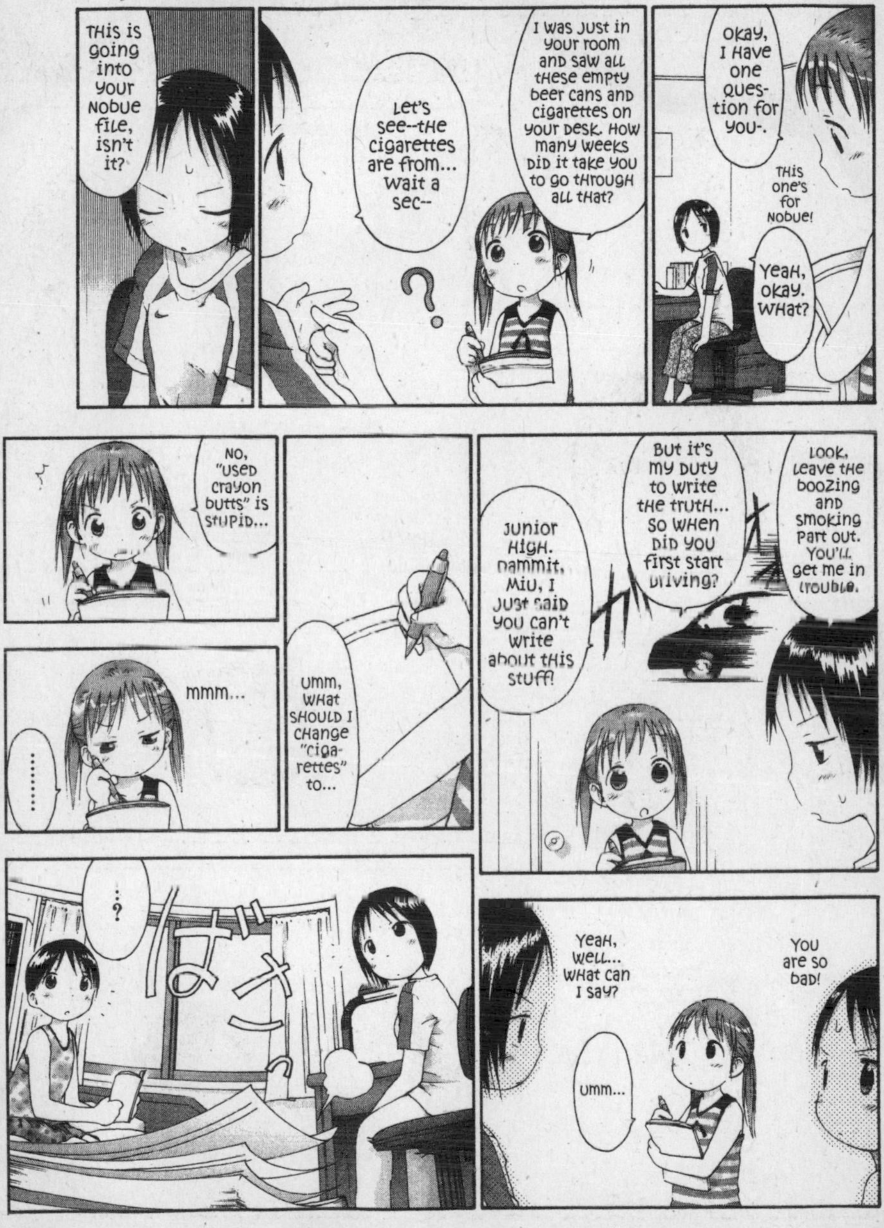
Okay, I have one ques-tion for you-.
This one's for Nobue!
Yeah, okay. What?
I was just in your room and saw all these empty beer cans and cigarettes on your desk. How many weeks did it take you to go through all that?
Let's see--the cigarettes are from... wait a sec--
This is going into your Nobue file, isn't it?
Look, leave the boozing and smoking part out. You'll get me in trouble.
But it's my duty to write the truth... so when did you first start driving?
Junior High. Dammit, Miu, I just said you can't write about this stuff!
Umm, what should I change "ciga-rettes" to...
No, "used crayon butts" is stupid...
mmm...
....
You are so bad!
Yeah, well... what can I say?
umm...
...?

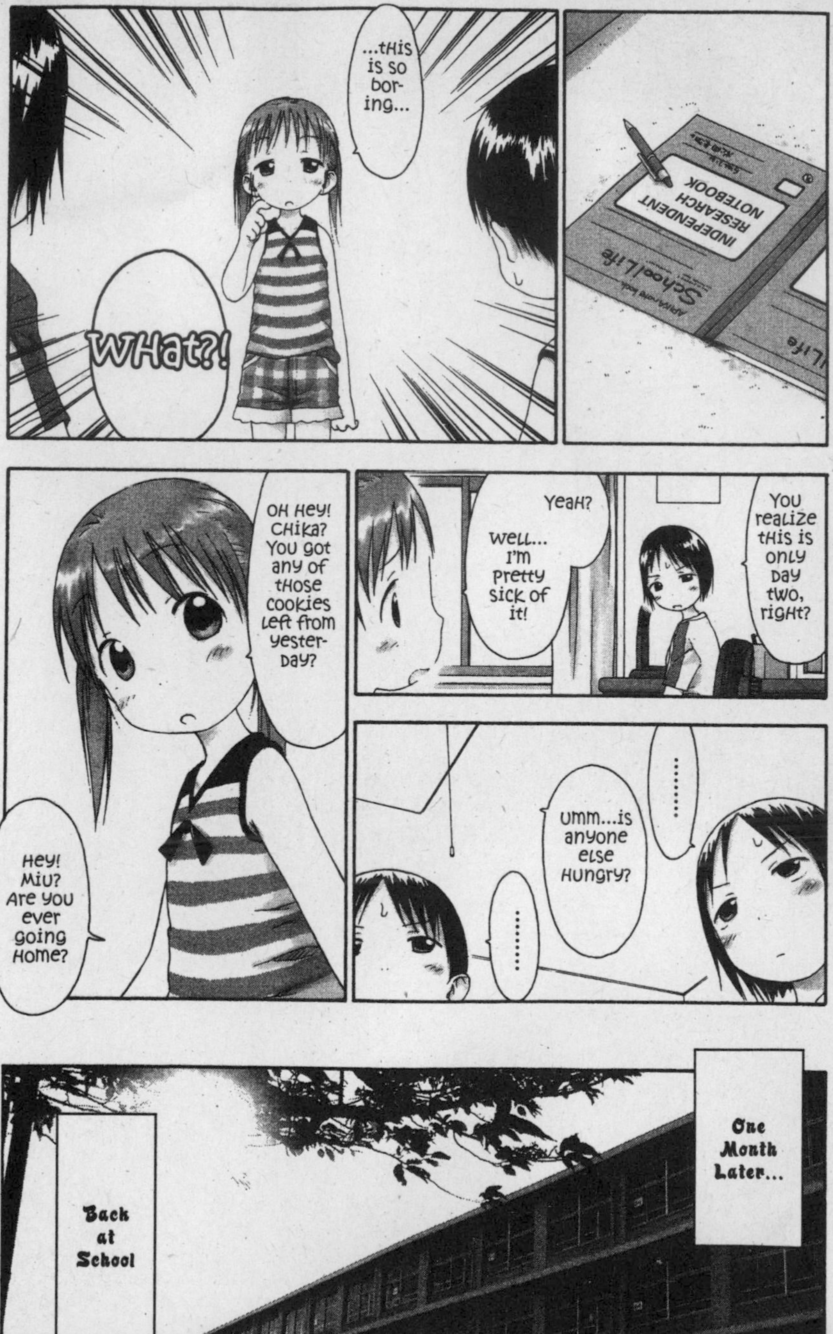

INDEPENDENT RESEARCH NOTEBOOK
School Life
...this is so boring...
WHAT?!
You realize this is only day two, right?
Yeah?
Well... I'm pretty sick of it!
......
Umm...is anyone else hungry?
......
Oh hey! Chika? You got any of those cookies left from yesterday?
Hey! Miu? Are you ever going home?
One Month Later...
Back at School

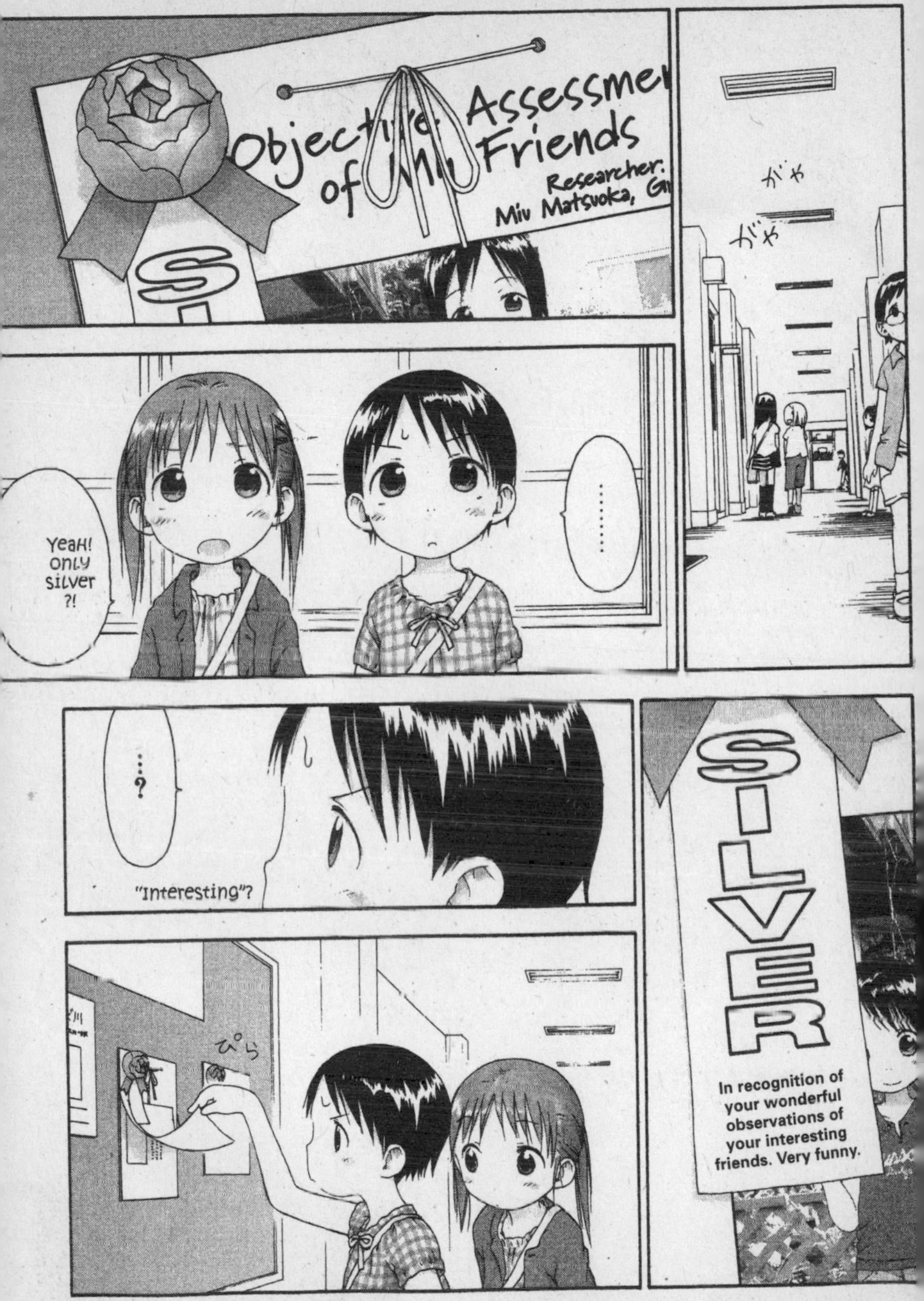
がや
がや
Objective Assessme
of My Friends
Researcher:
Miu Matsuoka, Gr
S
......
Yeah! Only silver?!
SILVER
In recognition of your wonderful observations of your interesting friends. Very funny.
...?
"Interesting"?
ぴら

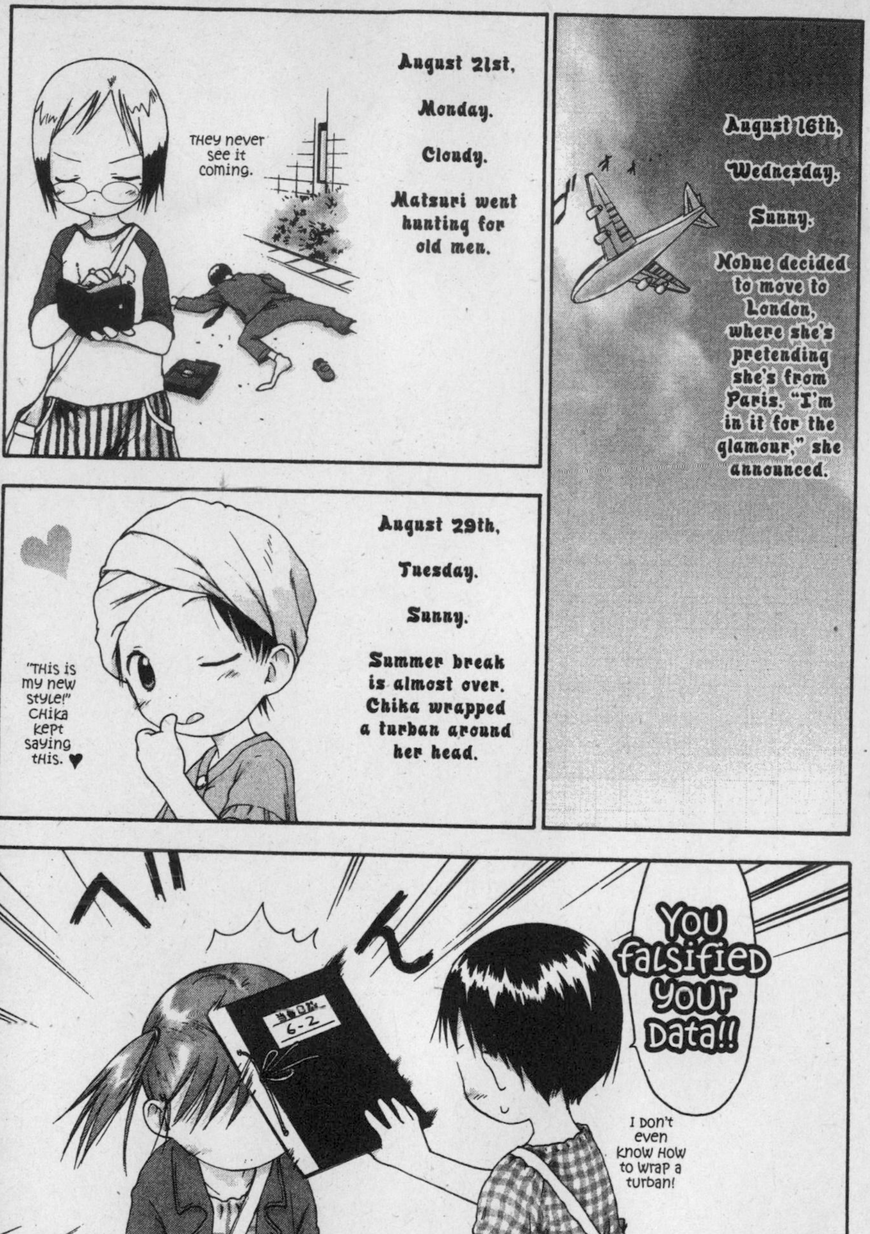
August 16th,
Wednesday.
Sunny.
Nobue decided to move to London, where she's pretending she's from Paris. "I'm in it for the glamour," she announced.
August 21st,
Monday.
Cloudy.
Matsuri went hunting for old men.
They never see it coming.
August 29th,
Tuesday.
Sunny.
Summer break is almost over. Chika wrapped a turban around her head.
"This is my new style!" Chika kept saying this. ♥
6-2
You falsified your data!!
I don't even know how to wrap a turban!

PAGE 155

name	*season*
☐NOBUE	☐SPRING
☐CHIKA	☐SUMMER
☐MIU	☐AUTUMN
☐MATSUDA	☐WINTER

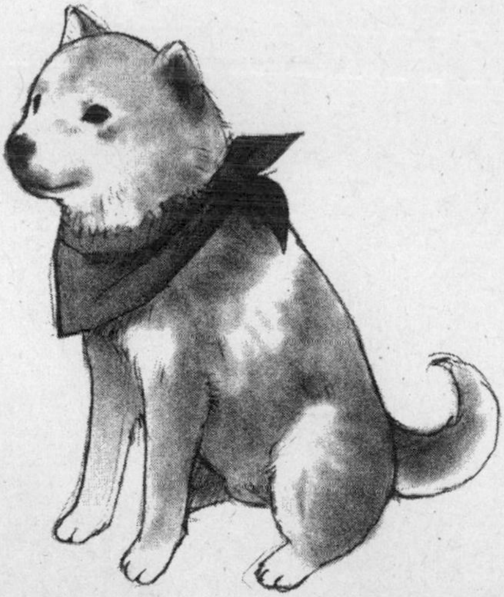

name	season
☐NONIE	☐SPRING
☐CHIKA	☐SUMMER
☐MIU	☐AUTUMN
☐MATSURI	☐WINTER

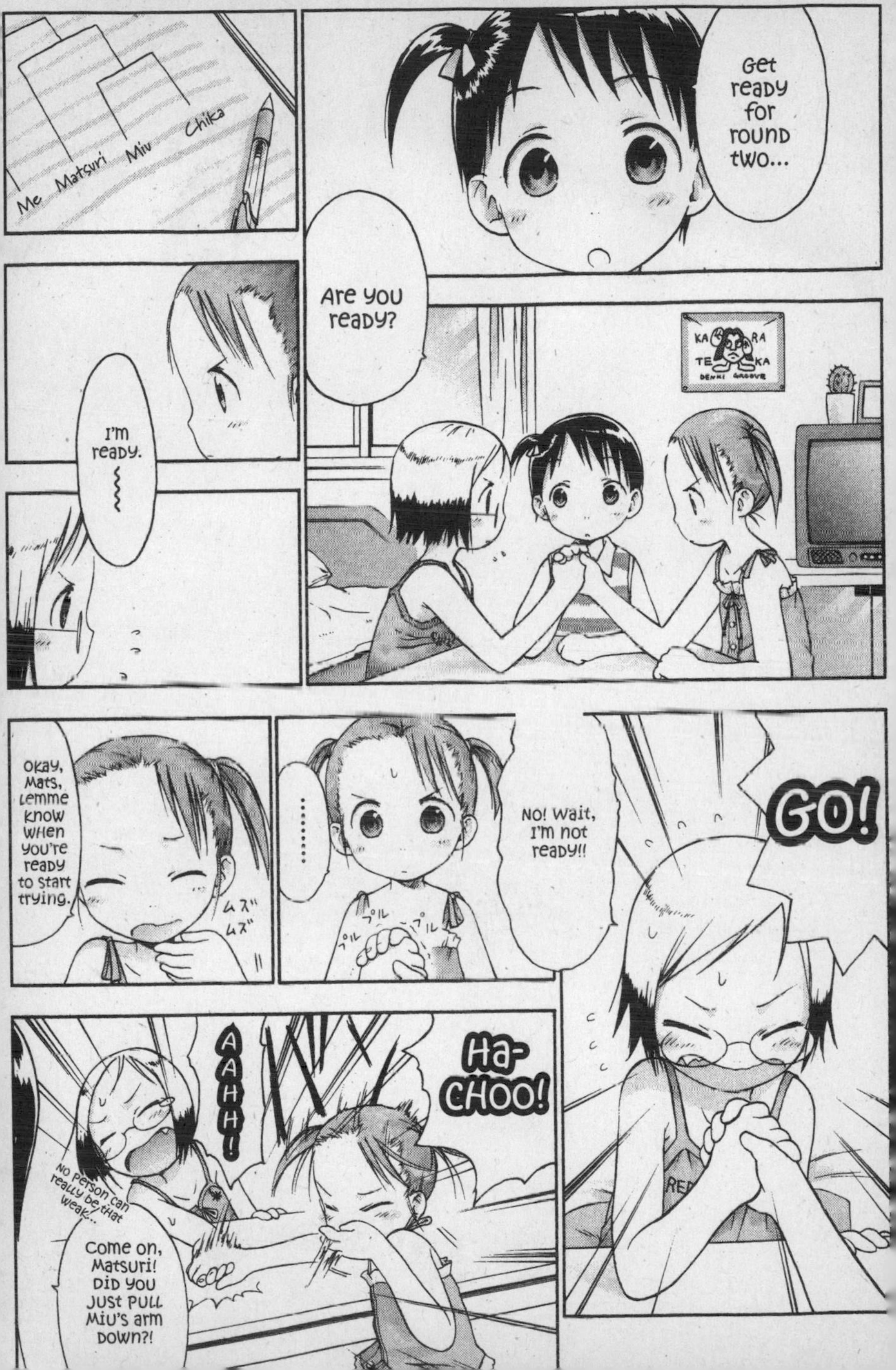

Get ready for round two...
Me
Matsuri
Miu
Chika
Are you ready?
KA RA TE KA
DENKI GROOVE
I'm ready.
GO!
No! Wait, I'm not ready!!
......
プルプル
プル
Okay, Mats, lemme know when you're ready to start trying.
ムズムズ
Ha-CHOO!
AAHH!
No person can really be that weak...
Come on, Matsuri! Did you just pull Miu's arm down?!

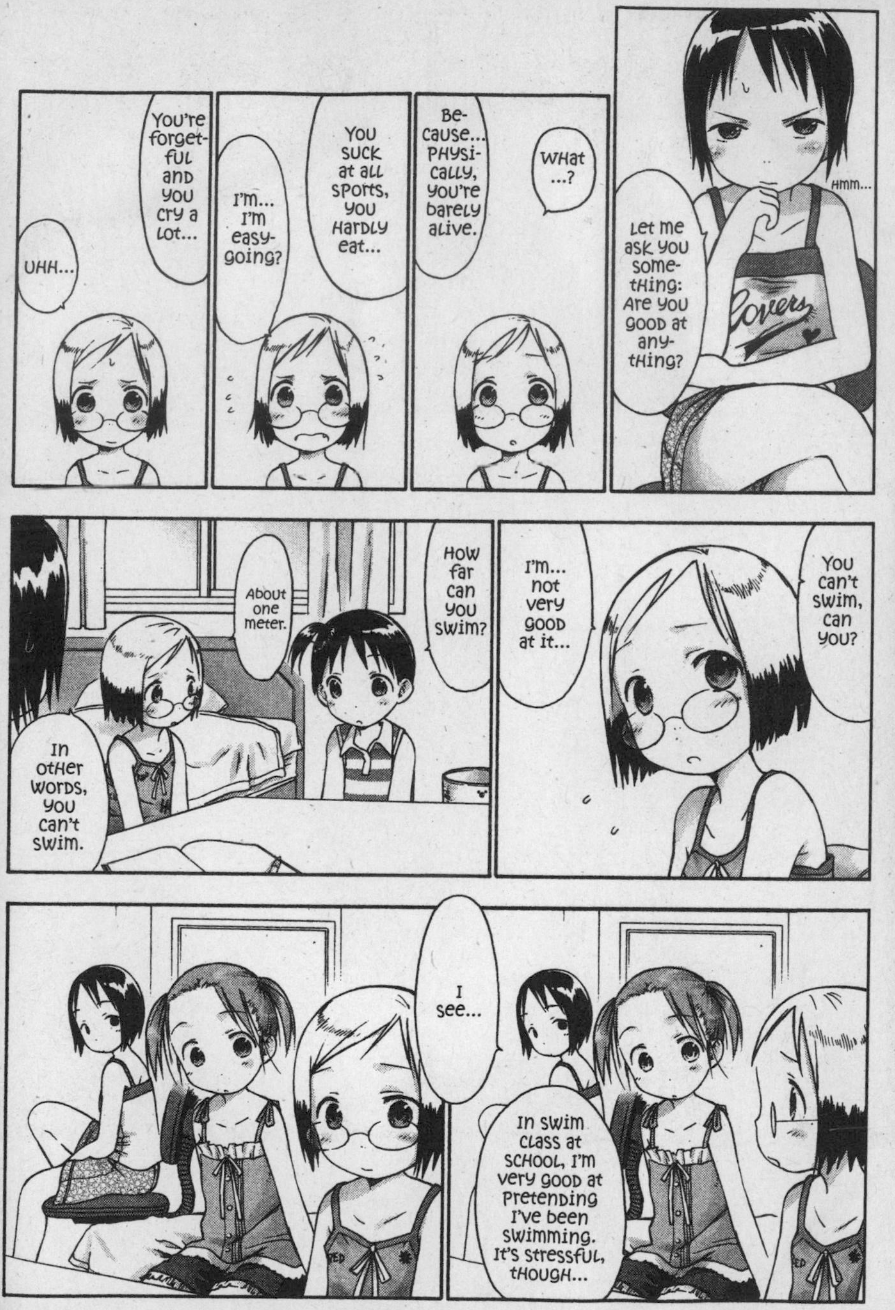
HMM...
Let me ask you something: Are you good at anything?
What ...?
Be-cause... physi-cally, you're barely alive.
You suck at all sports, you hardly eat...
I'm... I'm easy-going?
You're forget-ful and you cry a lot...
Uhh...
You can't swim, can you?
I'm... not very good at it...
How far can you swim?
About one meter.
In other words, you can't swim.
I see...
In swim class at school, I'm very good at pretending I've been swimming. It's stressful, though...

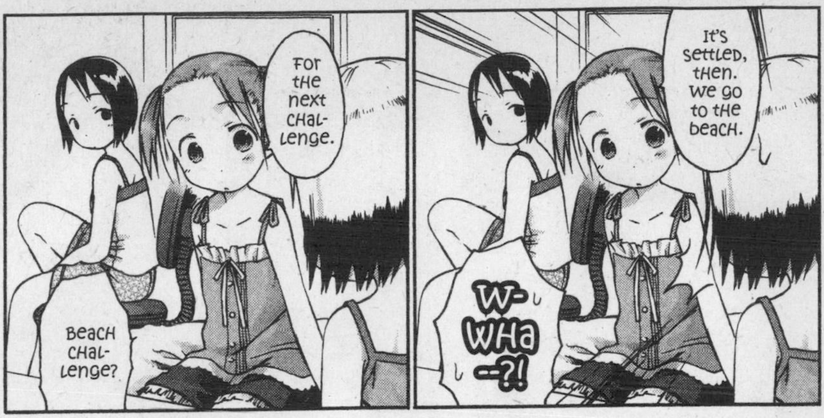
It's settled, then. We go to the beach.
W-WHA--?!
For the next chal-lenge.
Beach chal-lenge?

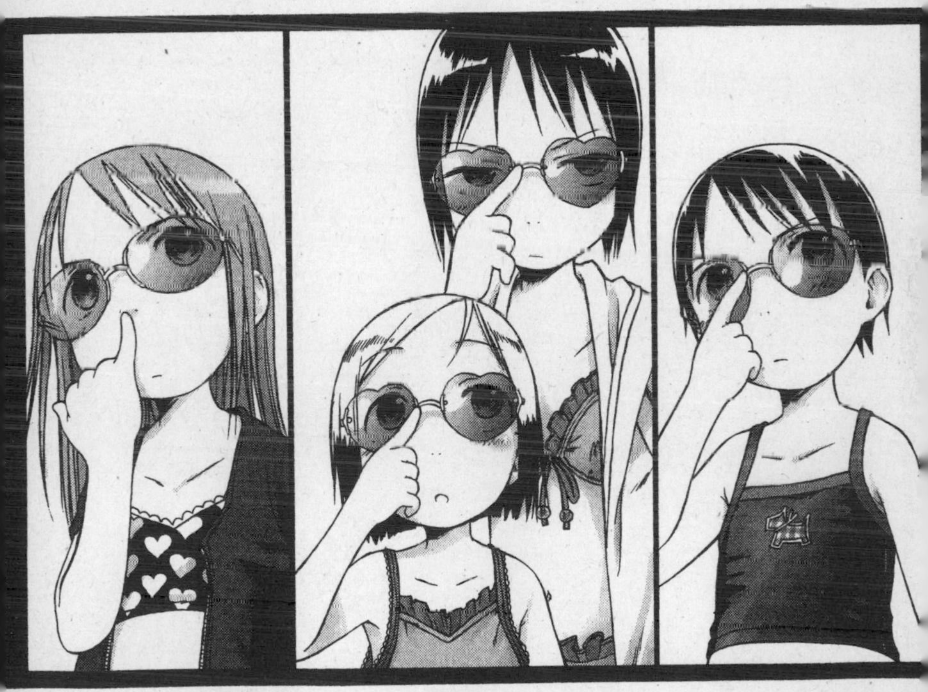

Episode. 10

BEACH CHALLENGE

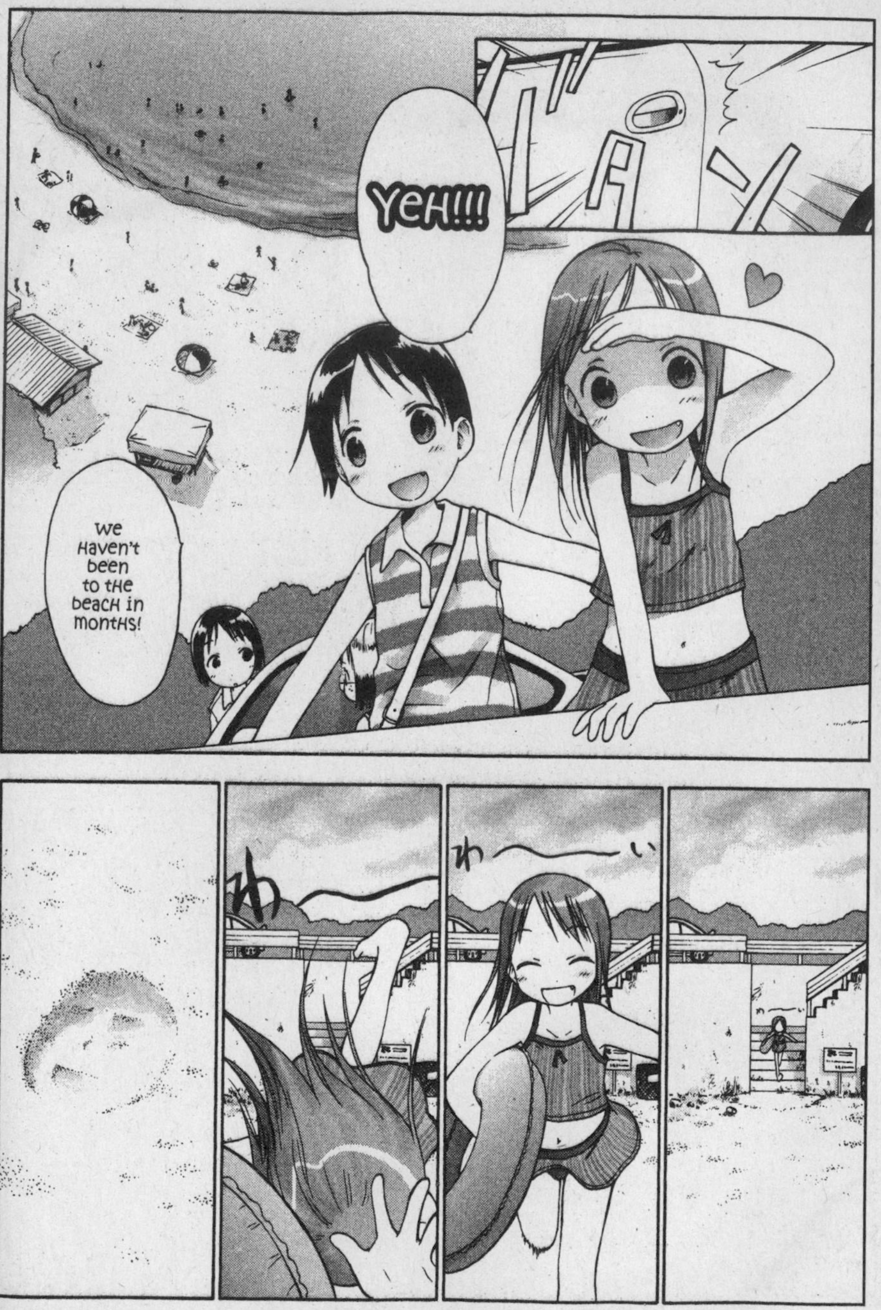
YEH!!!
We haven't been to the beach in months!
わ――――い

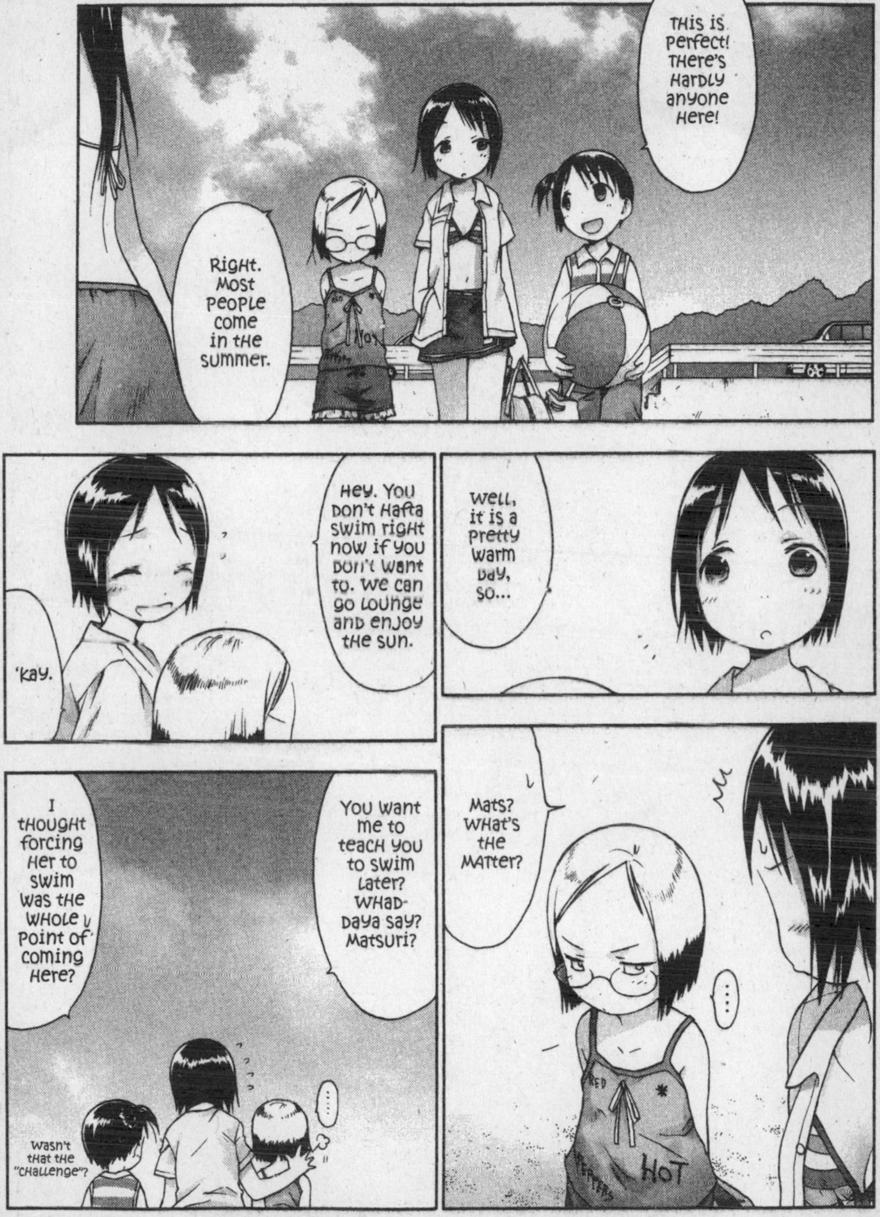
THIS IS PERFECT! THERE'S HARDLY ANYONE HERE!
RIGHT. MOST PEOPLE COME IN THE SUMMER.
WELL, IT IS A PRETTY WARM DAY, SO...
HEY. YOU DON'T HAFTA SWIM RIGHT NOW IF YOU DON'T WANT TO. WE CAN GO LOUNGE AND ENJOY THE SUN.
'KAY.
MATS? WHAT'S THE MATTER?
.....
YOU WANT ME TO TEACH YOU TO SWIM LATER? WHAD-DAYA SAY? MATSURI?
I THOUGHT FORCING HER TO SWIM WAS THE WHOLE POINT OF COMING HERE?
.....
WASN'T THAT THE "CHALLENGE"?

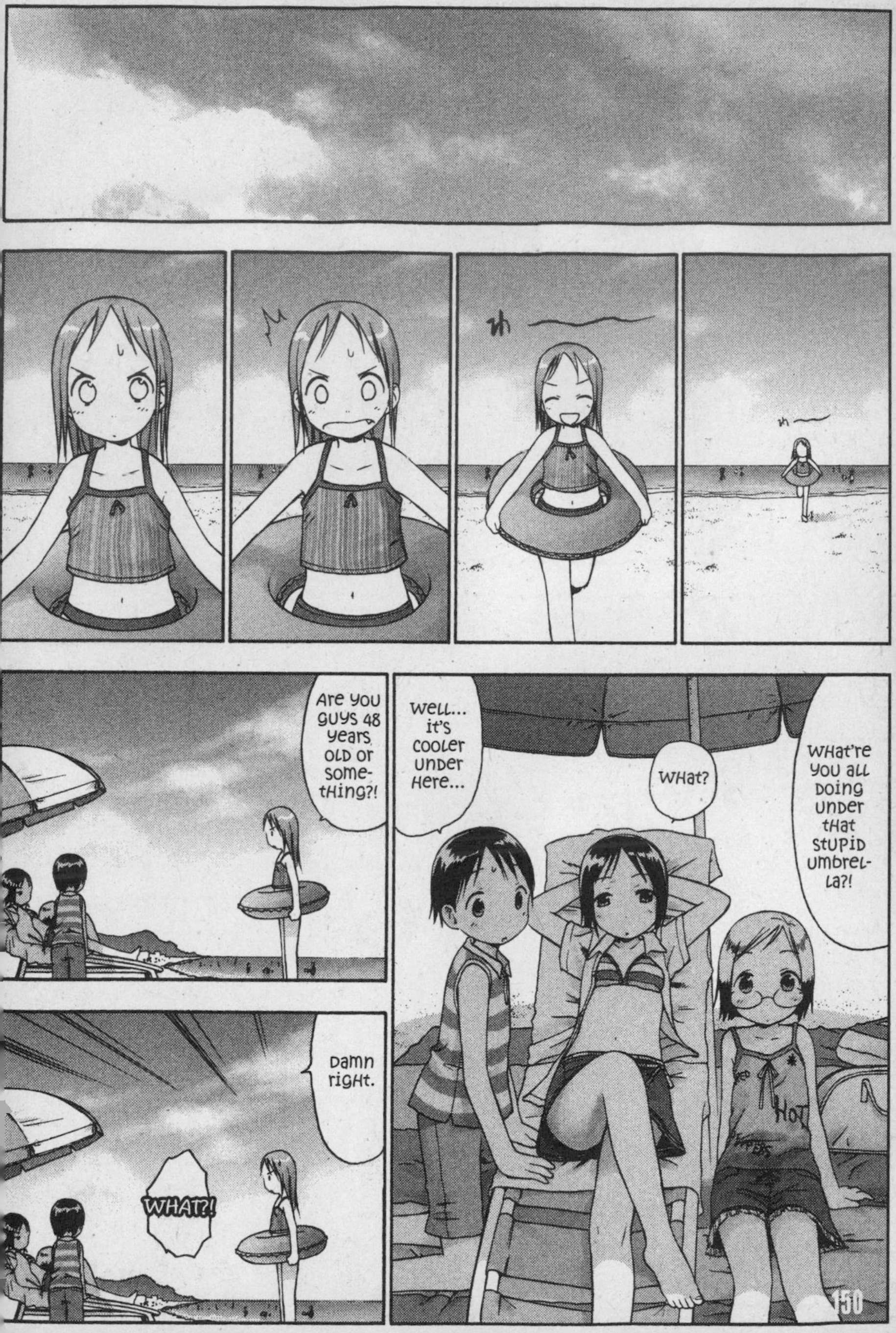
わー
わー
What're you all doing under that stupid umbrel-la?!
What?
Well... it's cooler under here...
Are you guys 48 years old or some-thing?!
Damn right.
WHAT?!

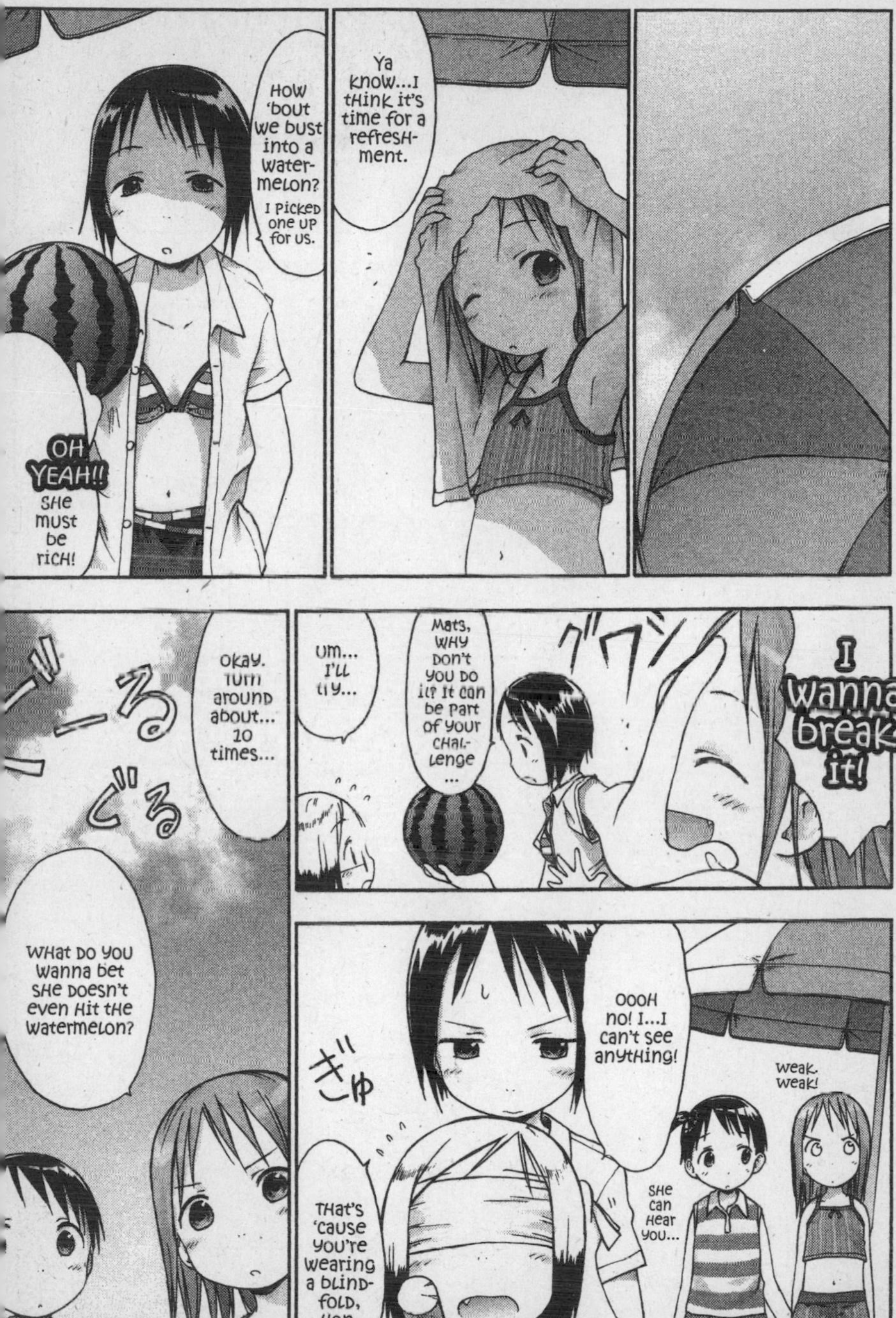
Ya know...I think it's time for a refreshment.
How 'bout we bust into a watermelon?
I picked one up for us.
OH YEAH!!
She must be rich!
I wanna break it!
グワン
Mats, why don't you do it? It can be part of your challenge...
Um... I'll try...
Oooh no! I...I can't see anything!
ぎゅ
Weak. Weak!
She can hear you...
That's 'cause you're wearing a blindfold, Hon.
Okay. Turn around about... 10 times...
What do you wanna bet she doesn't even hit the watermelon?

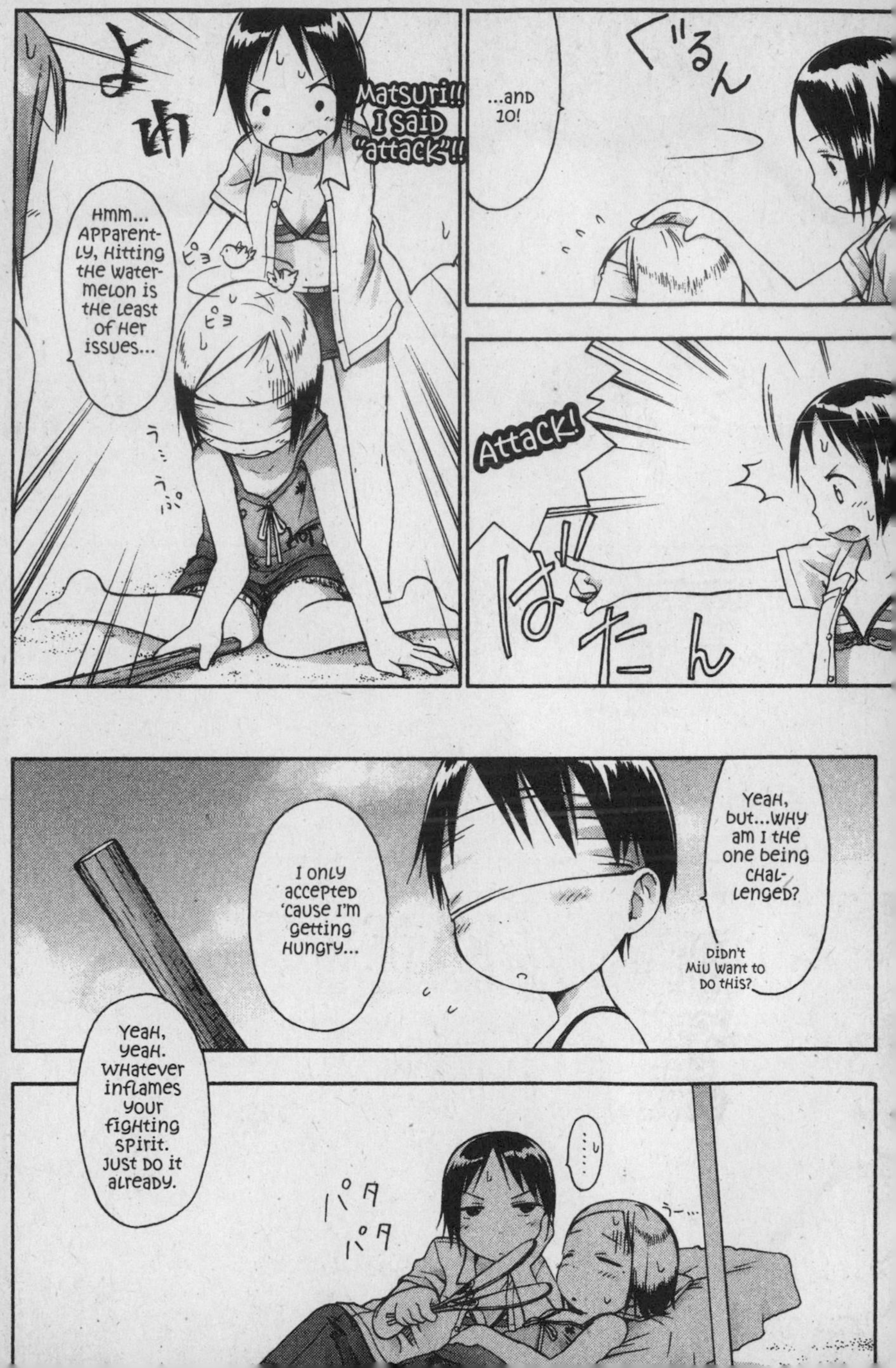
ぐるん
...and 10!
Attack!
ばたーん
よれ
Matsuri!! I said "attack"!!
Hmm... Apparently, hitting the watermelon is the least of her issues...
ピョ
ピョ
うぷ
Yeah, but...why am I the one being challenged?
Didn't Miu want to do this?
I only accepted 'cause I'm getting hungry...
Yeah, yeah. Whatever inflames your fighting spirit. Just do it already.
......
パタ パタ
うー...

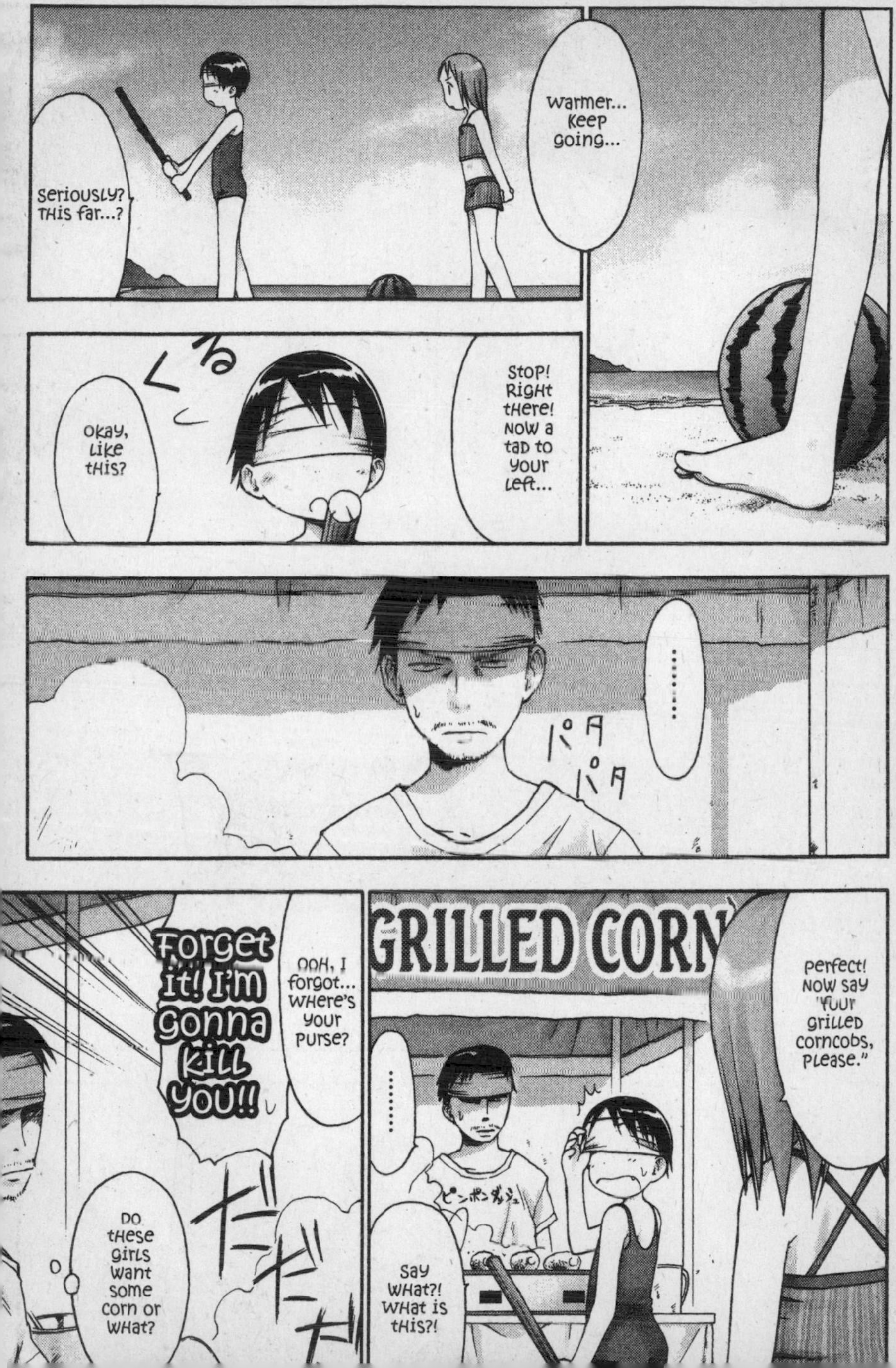
Warmer... keep going...
Seriously? This far...?
Stop! Right there! Now a tad to your left...
Okay, like this?
......
パタ パタ
Perfect! Now say "Four grilled corncobs, please."
GRILLED CORN
......
Say what?! What is this?!
Ooh, I forgot... where's your purse?
Forget it! I'm gonna kill you!!
Do these girls want some corn or what?

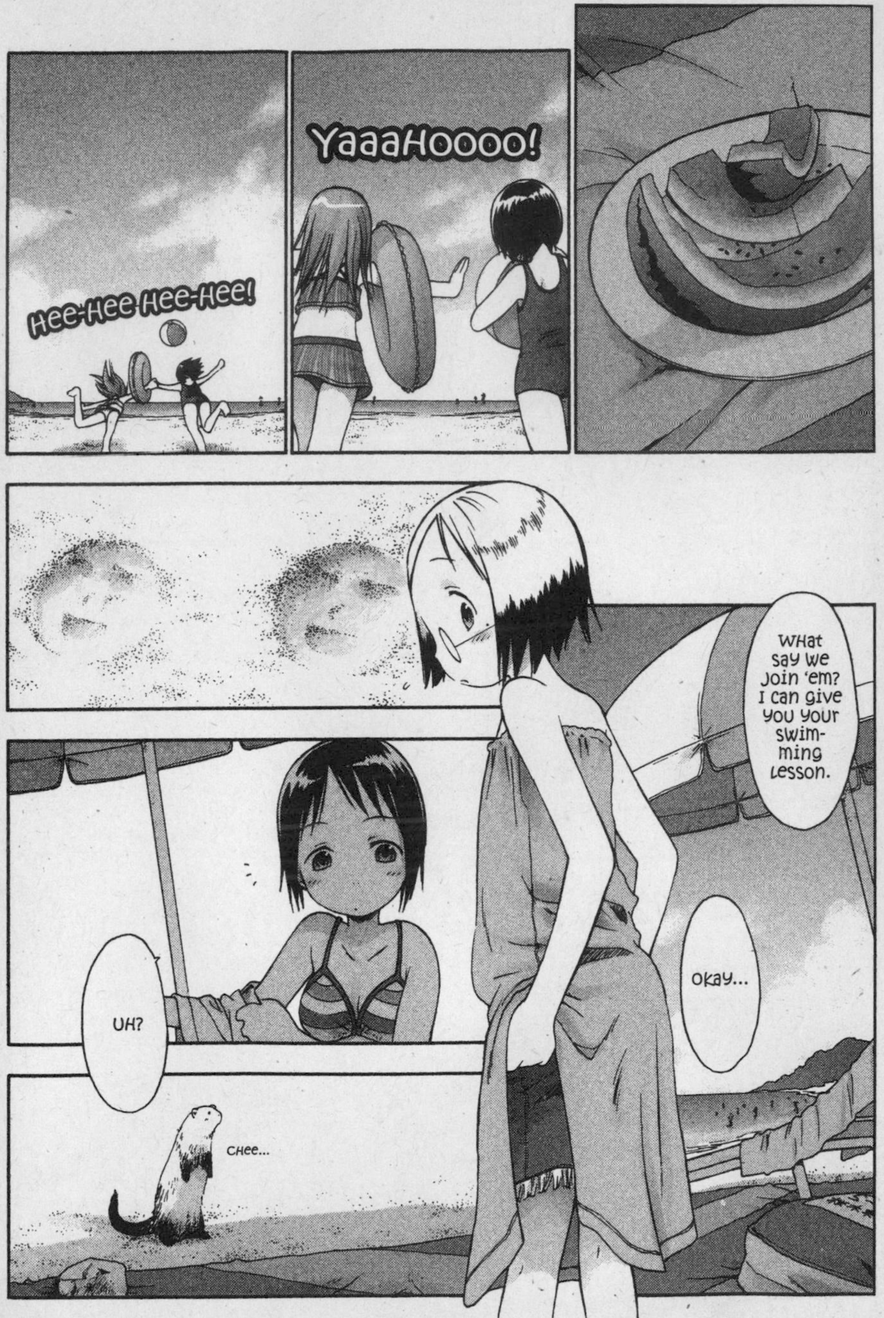
YaaaHoooo!
Hee-hee hee-hee!
What say we join 'em? I can give you your swimming lesson.
Uh?
Okay...
Chee...

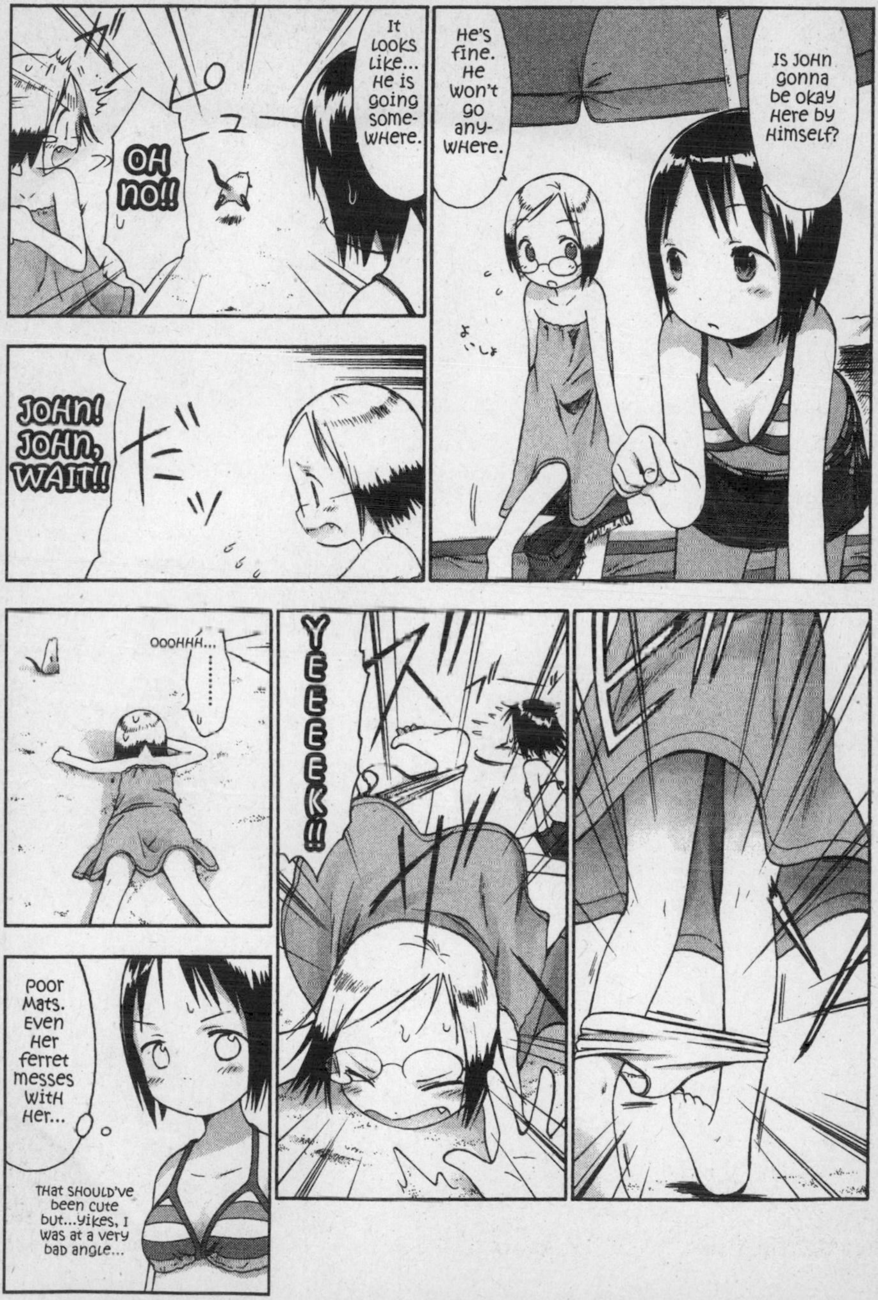
Is John gonna be okay here by himself?
He's fine. He won't go anywhere.
よいしょ
It looks like... he is going somewhere.
OH no!!
John! John, WAIT!!
YEEEEEK!!
OOOHHH... ....
Poor Mats. Even her ferret messes with her...
That should've been cute but...yikes, I was at a very bad angle...

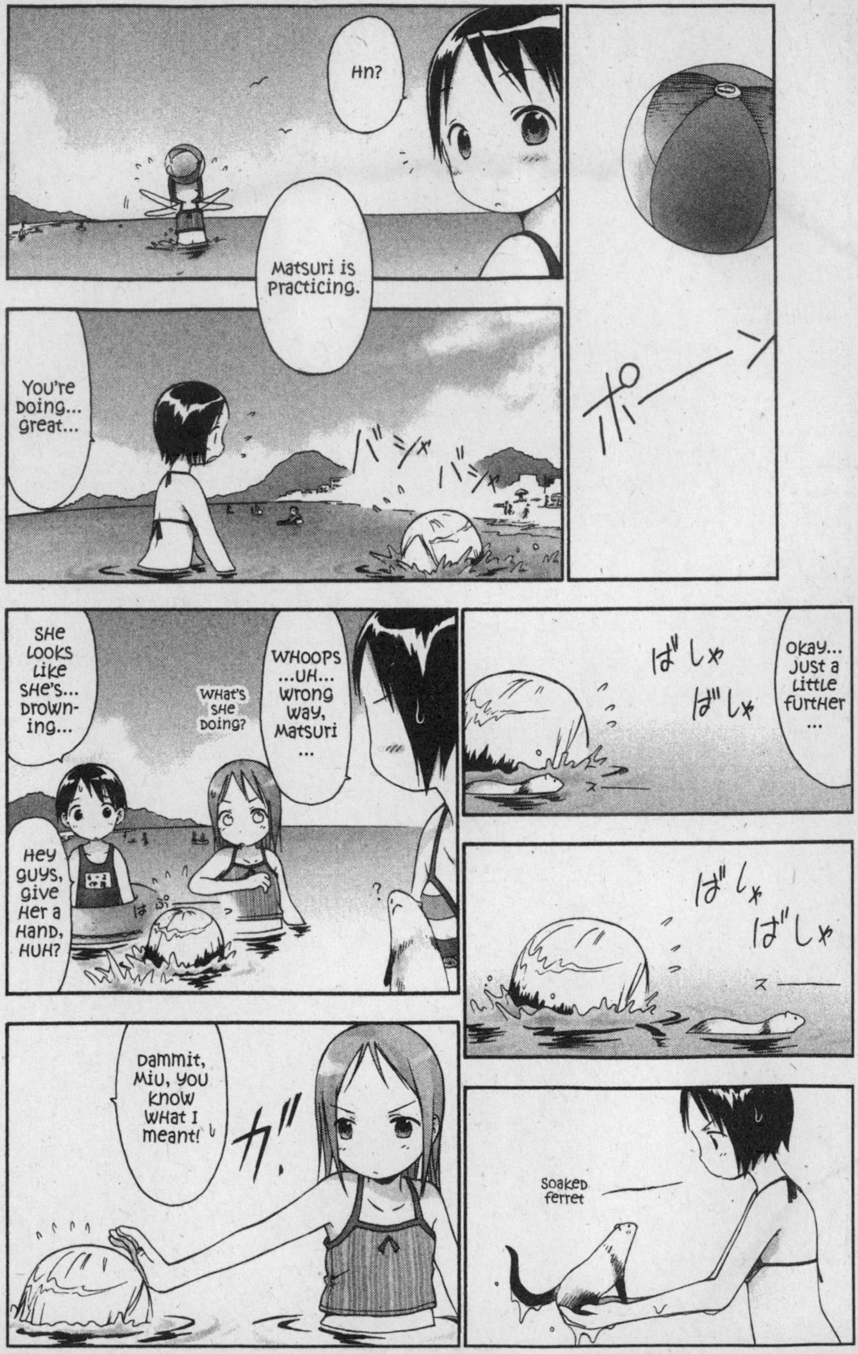
ポーーン
Hn?
Matsuri is practicing.
You're doing... great...
バシャ
バシャ
Okay... just a little further...
ばしゃ
ばしゃ
ばしゃ
ばしゃ
Soaked ferret
Whoops ...uh... wrong way, Matsuri ...
What's she doing?
She looks like she's... drowning...
Hey guys, give her a hand, huh?
ガ
Dammit, Miu, you know what I meant!

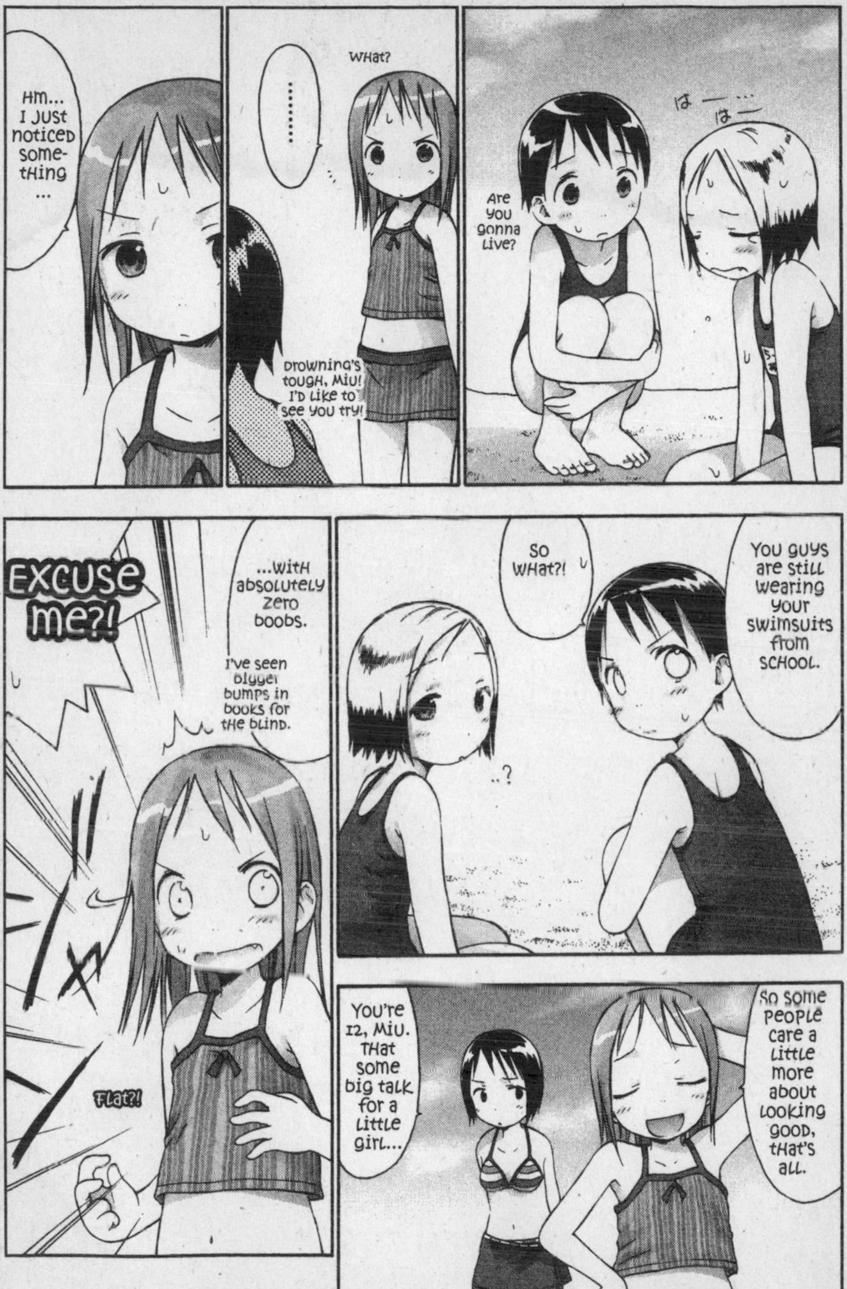

はー はー
Are you gonna live?
What?
......
Drowning's tough, Miu! I'd like to see you try!
Hm... I just noticed something...
You guys are still wearing your swimsuits from school.
So what?!
..?
So some people care a little more about looking good, that's all.
You're 12, Miu. That some big talk for a little girl...
...with absolutely zero boobs.
I've seen bigger bumps in books for the blind.
Excuse me?!
Flat?!

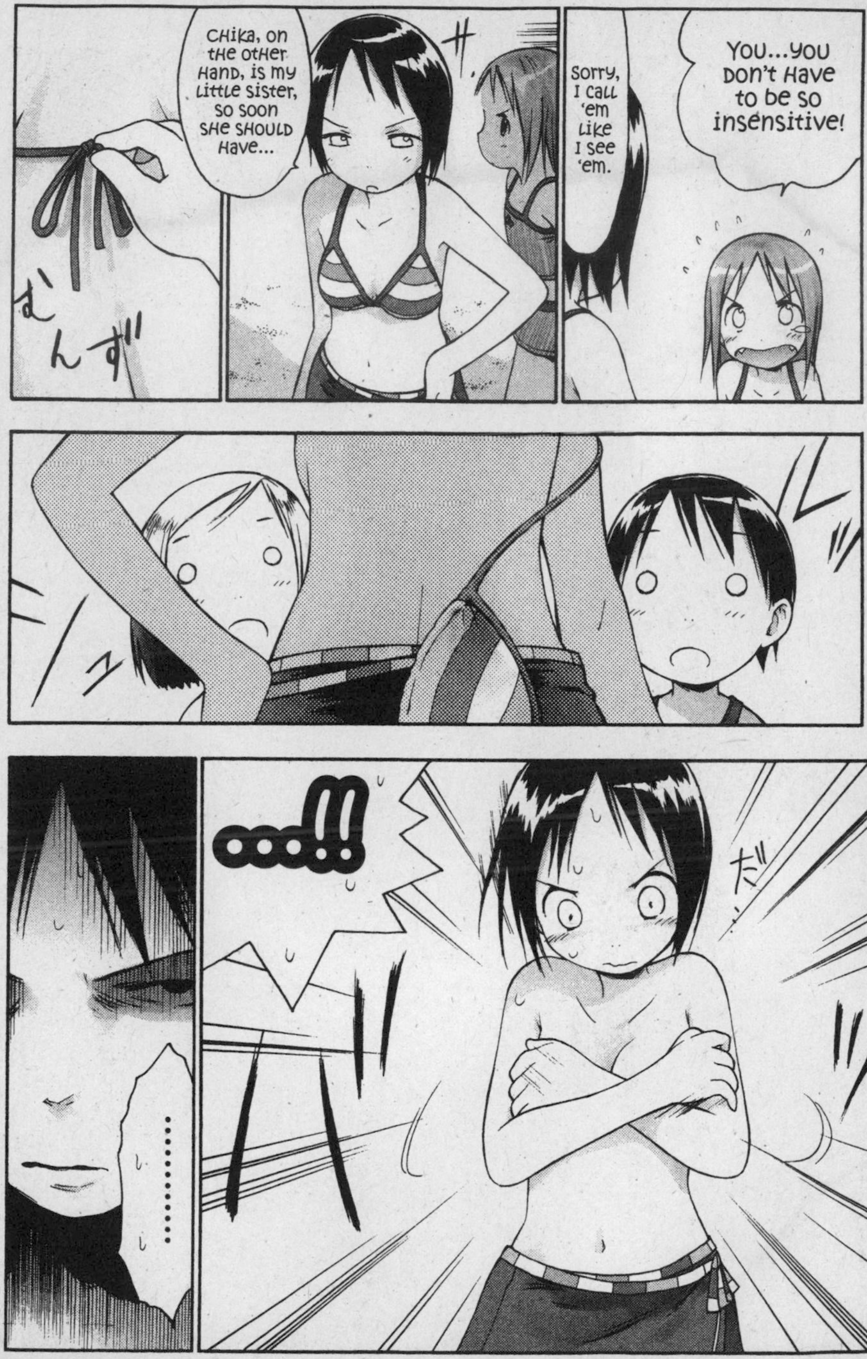
You...you don't have to be so insensitive!
Sorry, I call 'em like I see 'em.
Chika, on the other hand, is my little sister, so soon she should have...
むんず
...!!
だ
......

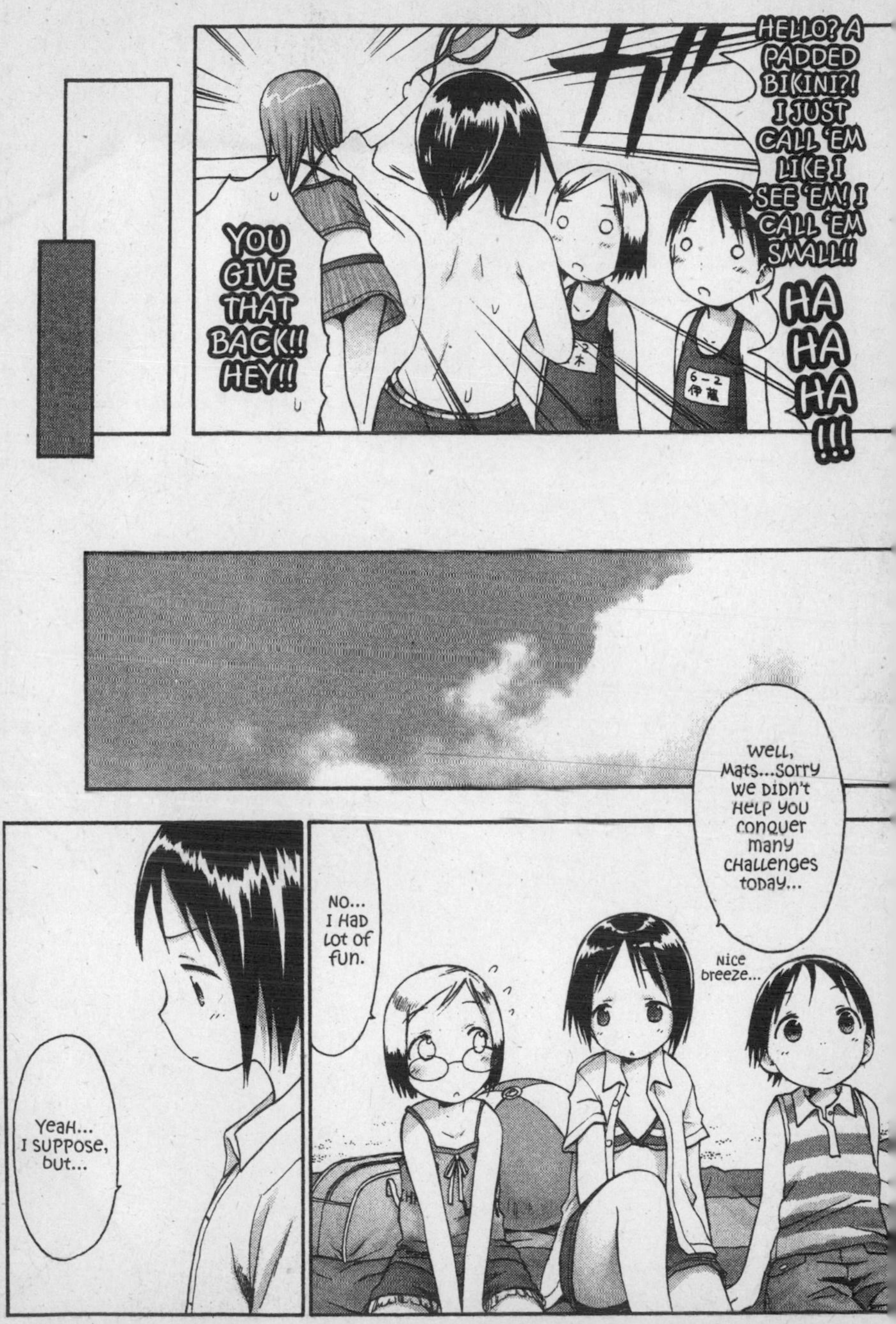
HELLO? A PADDED BIKINI?! I JUST CALL 'EM LIKE I SEE 'EM! I CALL 'EM SMALL!!
HA HA HA !!!
YOU GIVE THAT BACK!! HEY!!
Well, Mats...sorry we didn't help you conquer many challenges today...
Nice breeze...
No... I had lot of fun.
Yeah... I suppose, but...

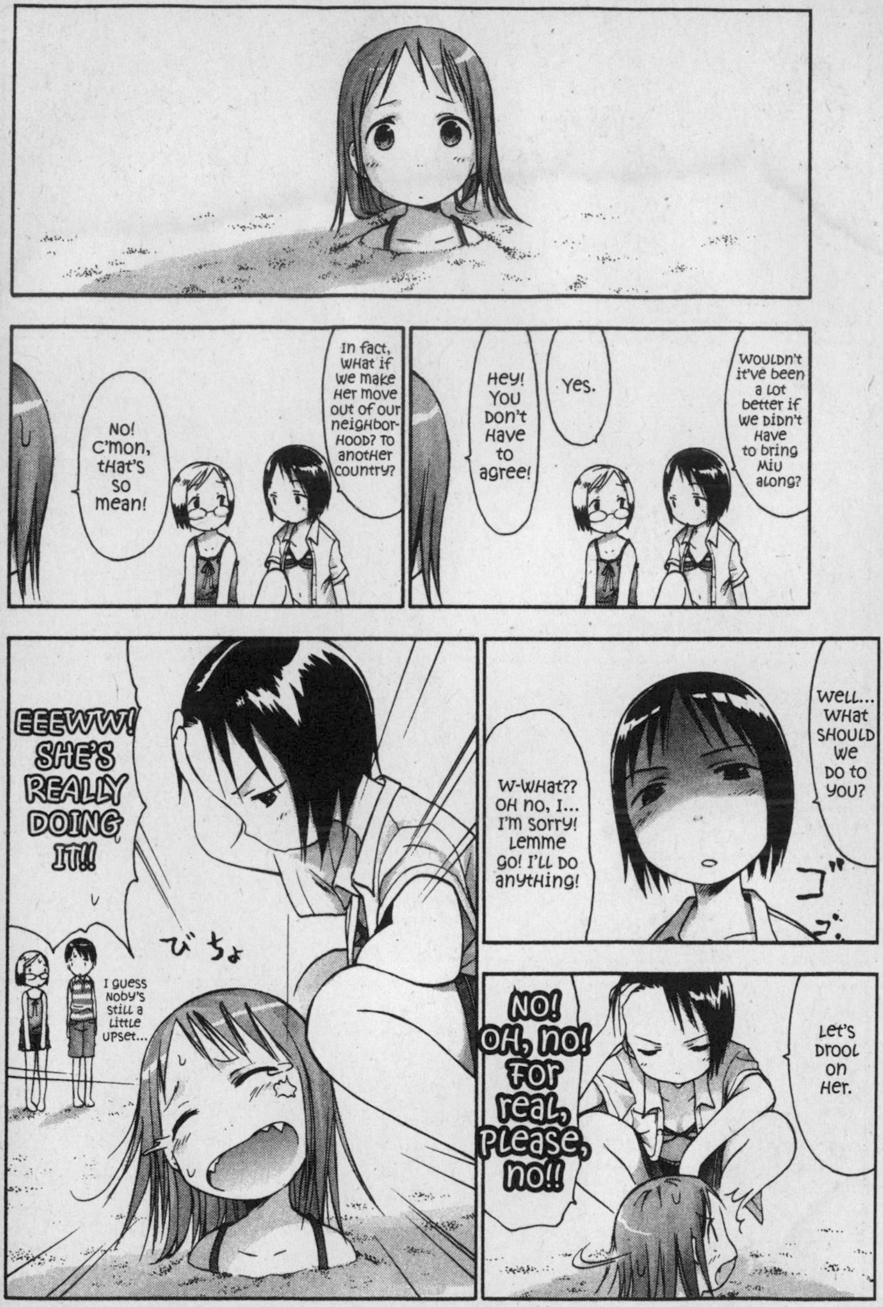
Wouldn't it've been a lot better if we didn't have to bring Miu along?
Yes.
Hey! You don't have to agree!
In fact, what if we make her move out of our neighbor-hood? To another country?
No! C'mon, that's so mean!
Well... what should we do to you?
W-what?? Oh no, I... I'm sorry! Lemme go! I'll do anything!
ゴゴ
Let's drool on her.
No! Oh, no! For real, please, no!!
EEEWW! SHE'S REALLY DOING IT!!
びちょ
I guess Noby's still a little upset...

END OF STRAWBERRY MARSHMELLOW 1

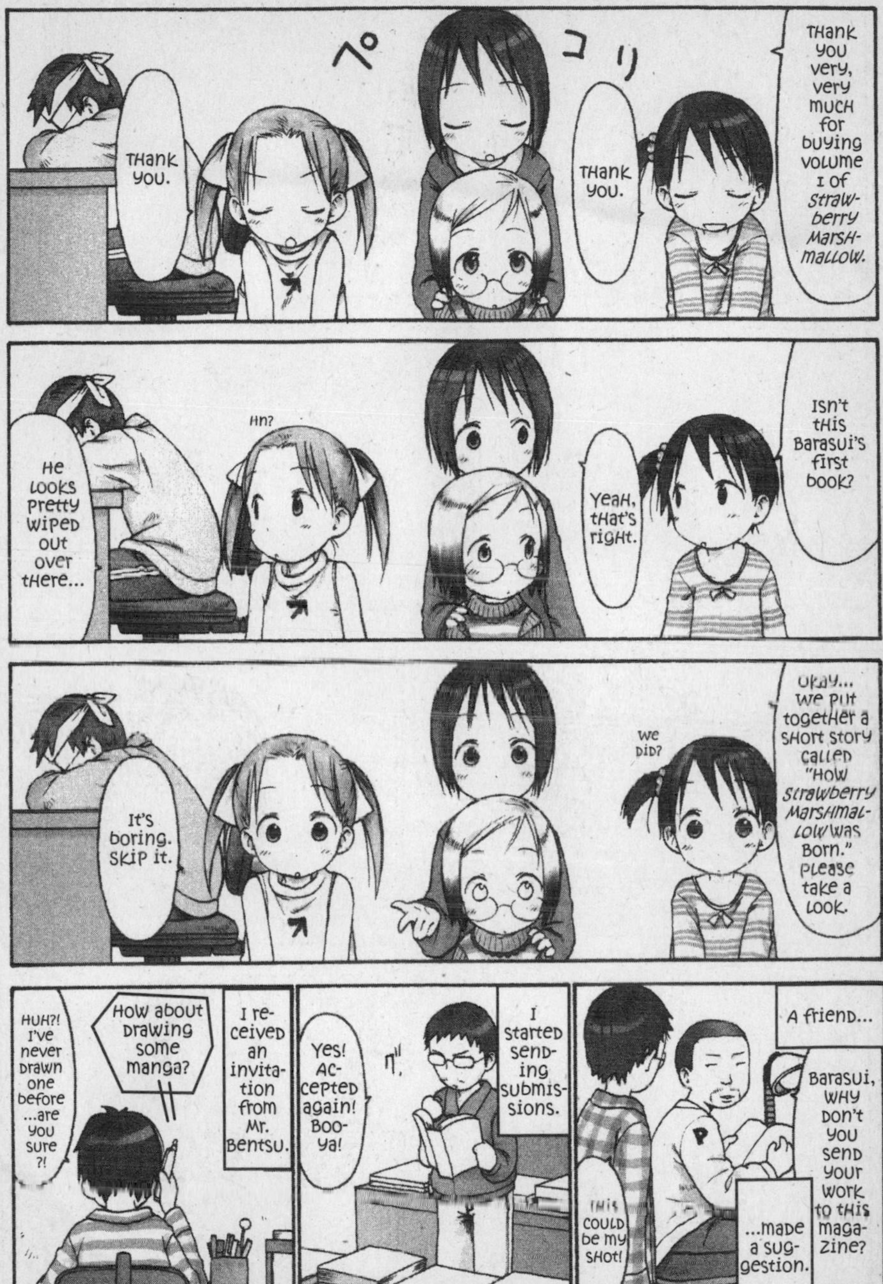
Thank you very, very much for buying volume 1 of Strawberry Marshmallow.
ペコリ
Thank you.
Thank you.
Isn't this Barasui's first book?
Yeah, that's right.
Hn?
He looks pretty wiped out over there...
Okay... we put together a short story called "How Strawberry Marshmallow Was Born." Please take a look.
We did?
It's boring. Skip it.
A friend...
Barasui, why don't you send your work to this magazine?
...made a suggestion.
This could be my shot!
I started sending submissions.
Yes! Accepted again! Boo-ya!
I received an invitation from Mr. Bentsu.
How about drawing some manga?
Huh?! I've never drawn one before ...are you sure?!

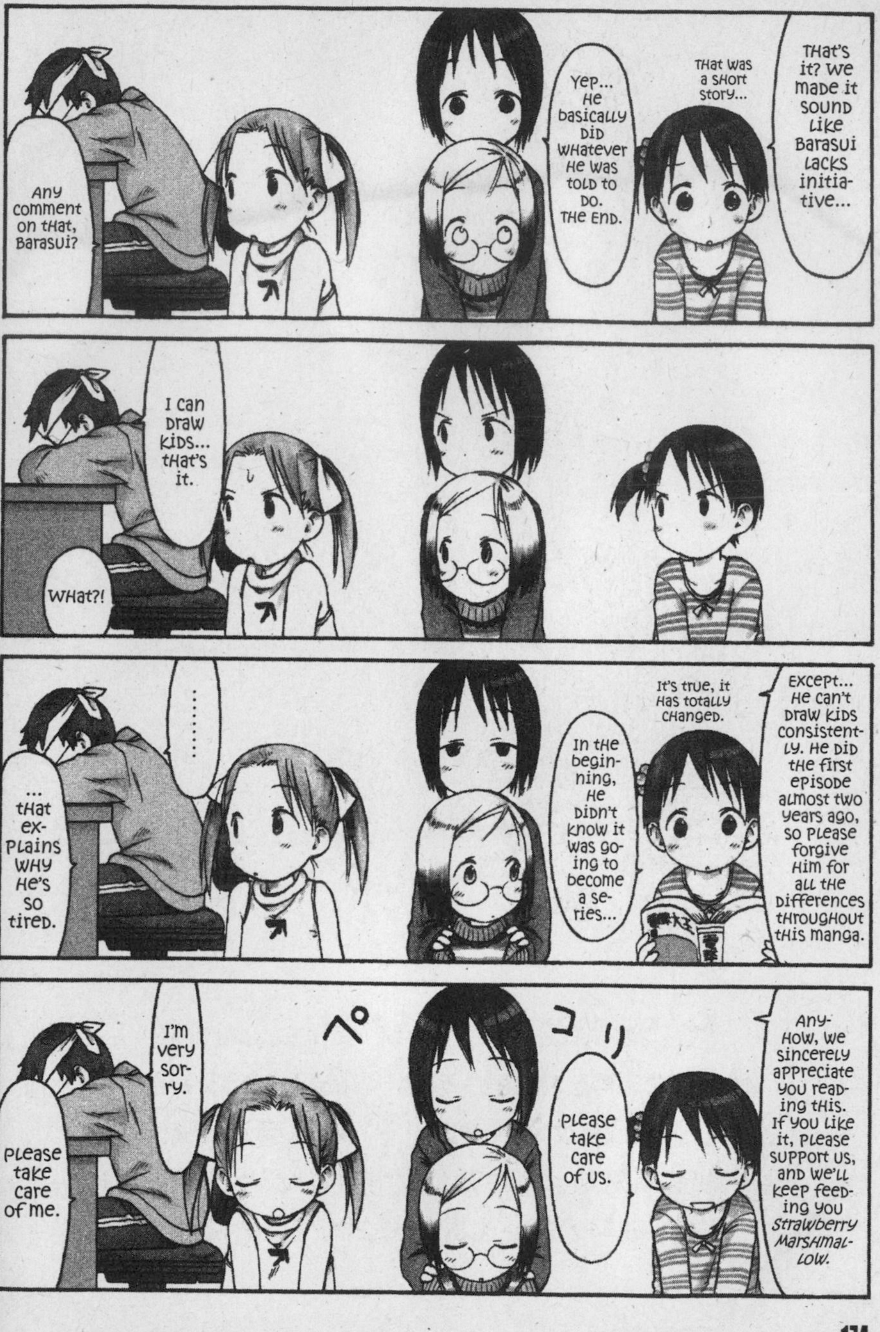

That's it? We made it sound like Barasui lacks initiative...
That was a short story...
Yep... He basically did whatever he was told to do. The end.
Any comment on that, Barasui?
I can draw kids... that's it.
What?!
Except... he can't draw kids consistently. He did the first episode almost two years ago, so please forgive him for all the differences throughout this manga.
It's true, it has totally changed.
In the beginning, he didn't know it was going to become a series...
....
...that explains why he's so tired.
Anyhow, we sincerely appreciate you reading this. If you like it, please support us, and we'll keep feeding you Strawberry Marshmallow.
ペコリ
Please take care of us.
I'm very sorry.
Please take care of me.

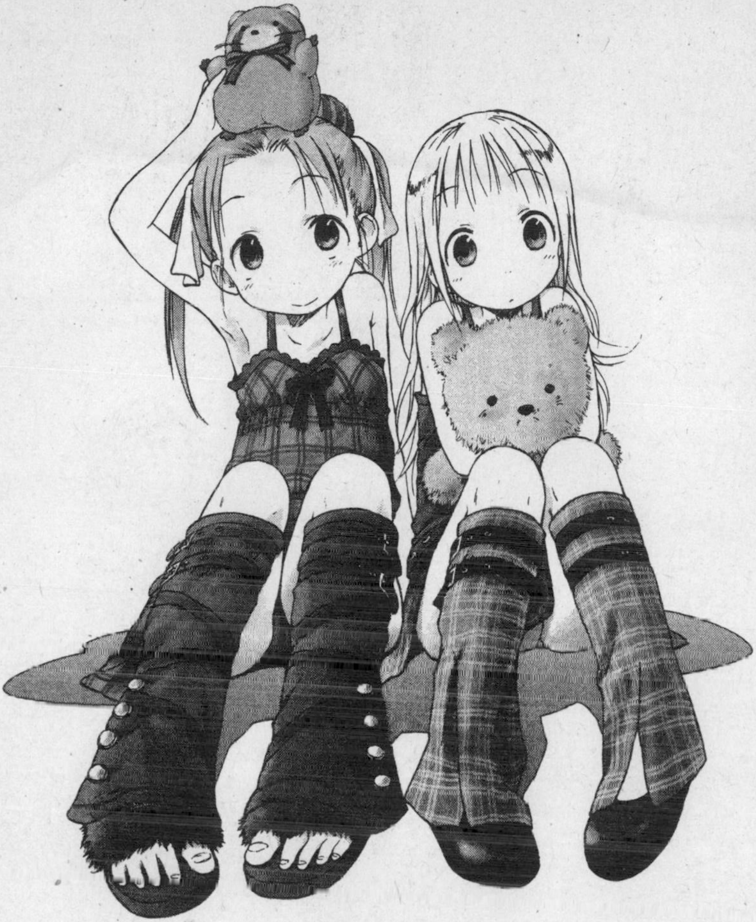

In the next volume of Strawberry Marshmallow, a new character joins Nobue, Chika, Miu and Matsuri! Meet Anna and join all the Strawberry Marshmallow girls on their continuing adventures!

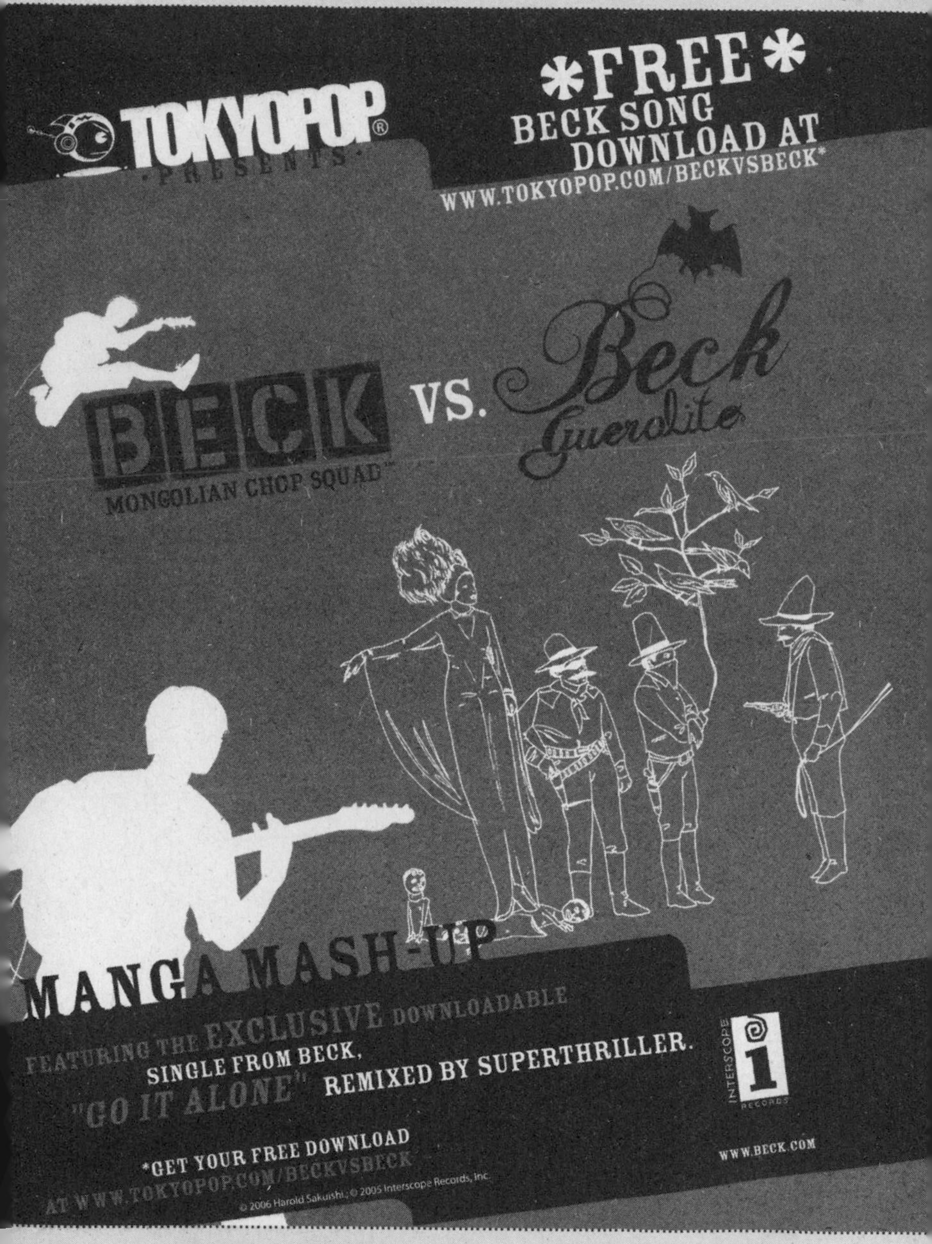

TOKYOPOP®
PRESENTS
FREE
BECK SONG
DOWNLOAD AT
WWW.TOKYOPOP.COM/BECKVSBECK*
BECK
MONGOLIAN CHOP SQUAD™
VS.
Beck
Guerolito
MANGA MASH-UP
FEATURING THE EXCLUSIVE DOWNLOADABLE
SINGLE FROM BECK,
"GO IT ALONE" REMIXED BY SUPERTHRILLER.
INTERSCOPE
RECORDS
*GET YOUR FREE DOWNLOAD
AT WWW.TOKYOPOP.COM/BECKVSBECK
WWW.BECK.COM
© 2006 Harold Sakuishi, © 2005 Interscope Records, Inc.

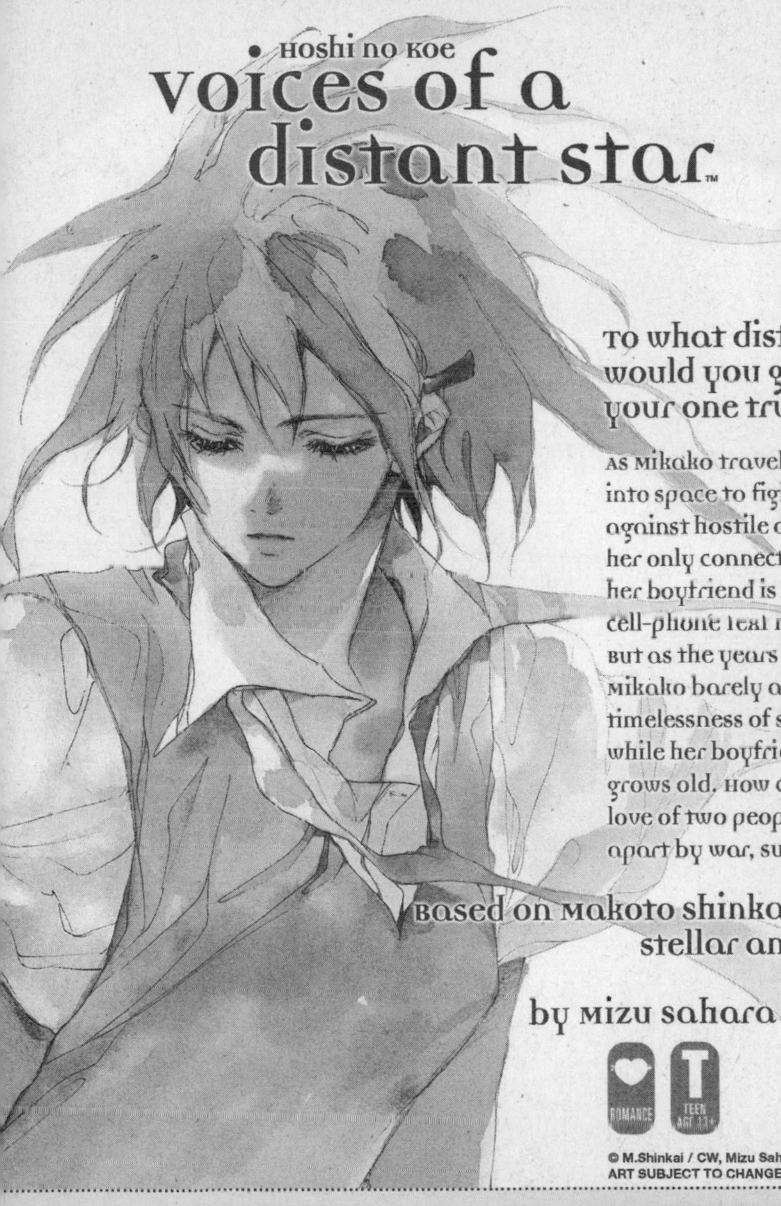

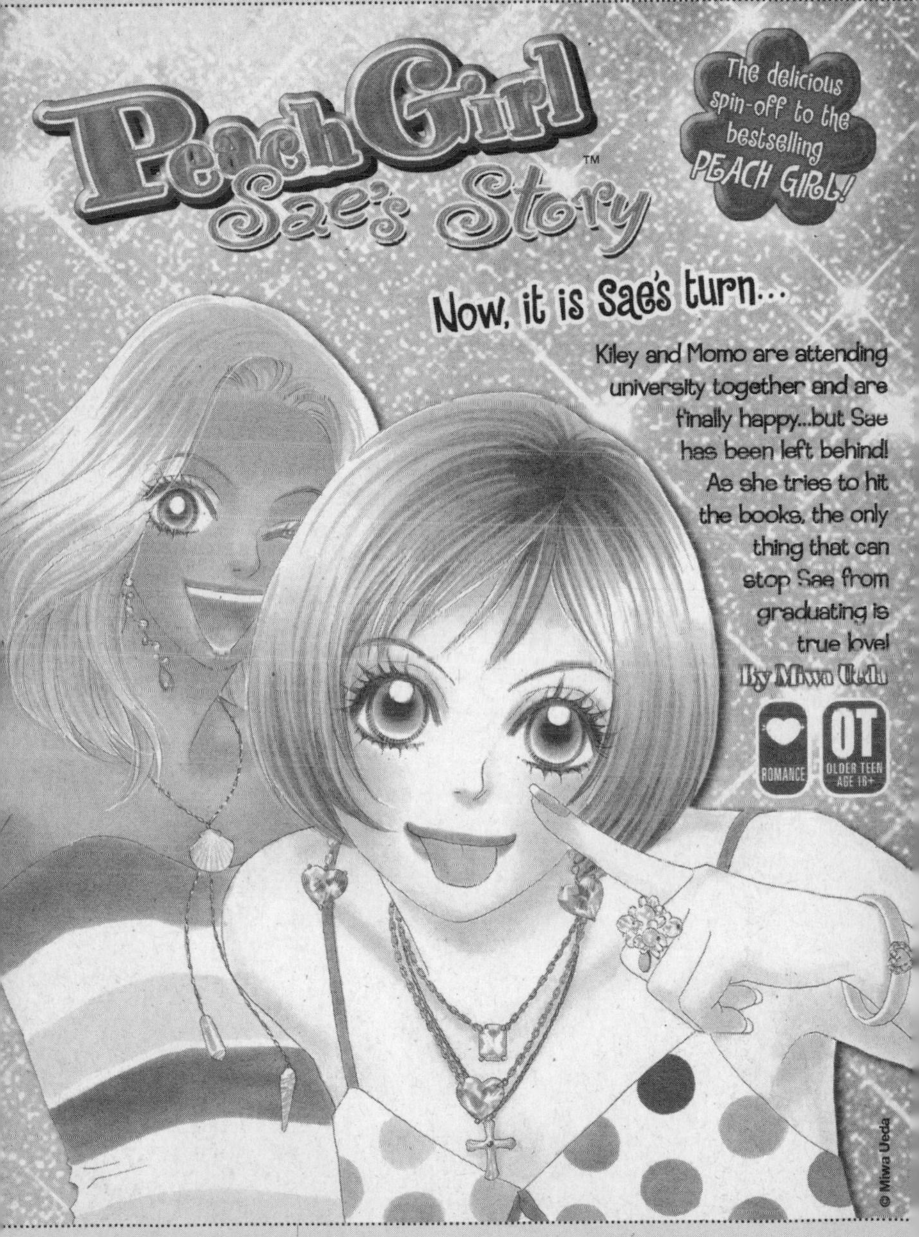
Peach Girl Sae's Story™
The delicious spin-off to the bestselling PEACH GIRL!
Now, it is Sae's turn...
Kiley and Momo are attending university together and are finally happy...but Sae has been left behind! As she tries to hit the books, the only thing that can stop Sae from graduating is true love!
By Miwa Ueda
ROMANCE
OT OLDER TEEN AGE 16+
© Miwa Ueda

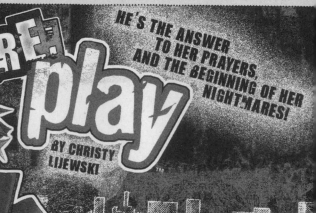

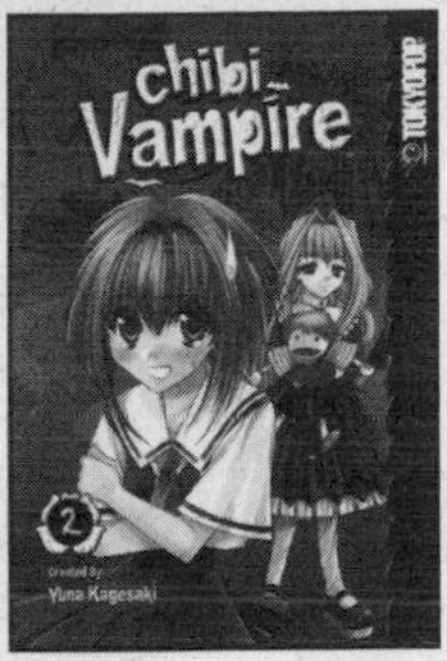
chibi Vampire
TOKYOPOP
2
Created By
Yuna Kagesaki

© YUNA KAGESAKI

CHIBI VAMPIRE VOLUME 2

BY YUNA KAGESAKI

This bloody-good vampire has a big crush on her prey!

COMEDY | OT OLDER TEEN AGE 16+

Inspired the hit anime!

DEVIL MAY CRY 3 VOLUME 2

BY SUGURO CHAYAMACHI

The secret of the seven seals will release the demon world unto the earth!

It's good against evil... and brother against brother!

ACTION | OT OLDER TEEN AGE 16+

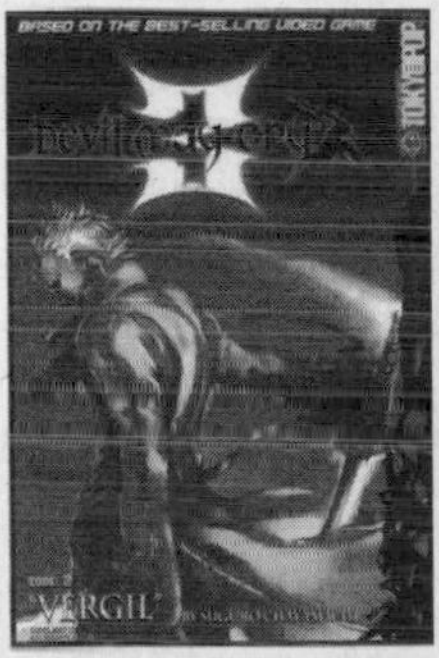
BASED ON THE BEST-SELLING VIDEO GAME
TOKYOPOP
VERGIL

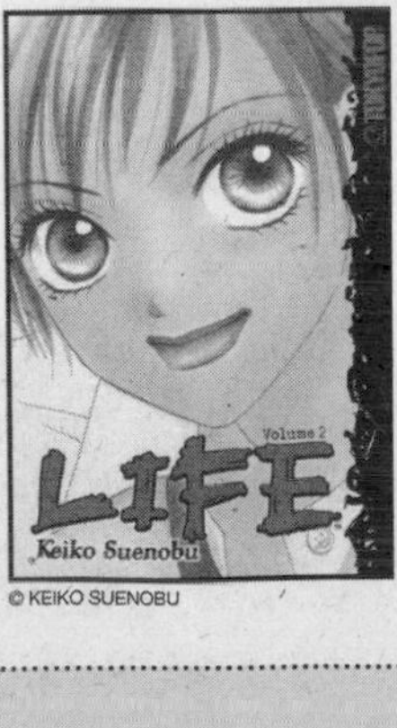
TOKYOPOP
Volume 2
LIFE
Keiko Suenobu

© KEIKO SUENOBU

LIFE VOLUME 2

BY KEIKO SUENOBU

It's about real teenagers...
real high school...
real life!

DRAMA | OT OLDER TEEN AGE 16+

**Every life has a story...
Every story has a life of its own.**

STOP!

This is the back of the book.
You wouldn't want to spoil a great ending!

This book is printed "manga-style," in the authentic Japanese right-to-left format. Since none of the artwork has been flipped or altered, readers get to experience the story just as the creator intended. You've been asking for it, so TOKYOPOP® delivered: authentic, hot-off-the-press, and far more fun!

DIRECTIONS

If this is your first time reading manga-style, here's a quick guide to help you understand how it works.

It's easy... just start in the top right panel and follow the numbers. Have fun, and look for more 100% authentic manga from TOKYOPOP®!